AF539055

W.M. Thackeray

VANITY FAIR

ANMOL PUBLICATIONS PVT. LTD.

H.O.: 4374/4B, Ansari Road, Darya Ganj,
New Delhi-110 002 (India)
Ph.: 23278000, 23261597

B.O.: No. 1015, Ist Main Road, BSK IIIrd Stage
IIIrd Phase, IIIrd Block
Bangalore - 560 085 (India)
Visit us at: www.anmolpublications.com

Vanity Fair

First Published, 2009

PRINTED IN INDIA

Printed at Mehra Offset Press, Delhi.

W.M. Thackeray

VANITY FAIR

[Edited with Introduction, Author's Background, Histotical Context, Summary, Study Questins and Critical Essays]

Misha Kandhari
M.A., M. Phil. English,
Delhi University

ANMOL PUBLICATIONS PVT. LTD.
NEW DELHI - 110 002 (INDIA)

Contents

Preface

Vanity Fair: A Novel without a Hero is a novel by William Makepeace Thackeray that satirizes society in early 19th-century England.

The term "*Vanity Fair*" originates from the allegorical story The Pilgrim's Progress, published in 1678 by John Bunyan where there is a town fair held in a village called Vanity. The novel has inspired several film adaptations.

Even before the last serial was published, critics hailed the work as a literary treasure. Although the critics were superlative in their praise, they expressed disappointment at the unremittingly dark portrayal of human nature, fearing he had taken his dismal metaphor too far. In response to his critics, Thackeray explained that he saw people for the most part "*Abominably Foolish and Selfish*". The unhappy ending was intended to inspire readers to look inward at their own shortcomings.

Author

Chapter 1

Introduction

Vanity Fair: A Novel without a Hero, the first major work published by William Thackeray under his own name, was published serially in London in 1847 and 1848. Previously, under various comic pseudonyms such as Michael Angelo Titmarsh and George Savage Fitzboodle Thackeray made clear, both in his role as the narrator of Vanity Fair and in his private correspondence about the book, that he meant it to be not just entertaining, but instructive. Like all satire, Vanity Fair has a mission and a moral. The first published installment had an illustration on its cover of a congregation listening to a preacher; both speaker and listeners were shown with donkey ears. In the pages, Thackeray explains the illustration thus: my kind reader will please to remember that these histories.... have "Vanity Fair" for a title and that Vanity Fair is a very vain, wicked, foolish place, full of all sorts of humbugs and falseness and pretentions. And while the moralist who is holding forth on the cover an accurate portrait of your humble servant professes to wear neither gown nor bands, but only the very same long-eared livery in which his congregation is arrayed: yet, look you, one is bound to speak the truth as far as one knows it.

That Becky is allowed to live, and to live well, is perfectly consistent with Thackeray's view of life and morality.... Losing is vanity, and winning is vanity.

By the halfway point in its serial publication, Thackeray's long, rambling tale of relentless and corrupt social climbing, told with biting humour and cynicism, was the talk of London. Readers eagerly awaited new episodes in the life of

Thackeray's deeply immoral, self-serving anti-heroine, Becky Sharp, who has since become one of the most well-known and most argued-about characters in literature. The novel secured Thackeray's place among the literary giants of his time; and the giants of his time, among them Charles Dickens, the Brontë sisters, Thomas Hardy, and Alfred Tennyson, have endured as giants to this day. Vanity Fair is considered a classic of English literature and one of the great works of satire in all history.

Vanity Fair was a turning point in Thackeray's life and career. A gentleman by birth and education, Thackeray was forced to earn his living by writing because most of his money had been lost in a financial crash. The articles, reviews, essays, and sketches he produced for magazines and newspapers did not provide sufficient income either to support a gentleman's status or to provide for the futures of his two daughters. In addition, writing for a living made his status as a gentleman somewhat tenuous. The serialization of Vanity Fair, which was a financial success, quickly established Thackeray's literary reputation. Thackeray was jubilant, "There is no use denying the matter or blinking it now. I am become a sort of great man in my way—all but at the top of the tree: indeed there if the truth were known and having a great fight up there with Dickens." Though Thackeray's novels never sold at the rate of Dickens's novels in the tens of thousands, he became financially secure with Vanity Fair. Also his social status as a gentleman was assured because of his acknowledged genius; he was no longer an amusing, talented hack writer, just one of a crowd of London journalists.

Contemporary Response to Vanity Fair

Contemporary reviewers and novelists appreciated the brilliance of the novel. John Forster wrote, "Vanity Fair is the work of a mind, at once accomplished and subtle, which has enjoyed opportunities of observing many and varied circles of society... his genteel characters... have a reality about them... They are drawn from actual life, not from books and fancy; and they are presented by means of brief, decisive yet always most discriminative touches". Charlotte Bronte, whose admiration for his genius was boundless, called him "the legitimate high priest of Truth":

The more I read Thackeray's works, the most certain I am that he stands alone—alone in his sagacity, alone in his truth, alone in his feeling his feeling, though he makes no noise about it, is about the most genuine that ever lived on a printed page, alone in his power, alone in his simplicity, alone in his self-control. Thackeray is a Titan, so strong that he can afford to perform with calm the most herculean feats; there is the charm and majesty of repose in his greatest efforts; he borrows nothing from fever, his is never the energy of delirium—his energy is sane energy, deliberate energy, thoughtful energy.

George Eliot's praise was more restrained, "I am not conscious of being in any way a disciple of his, unless it constitute discipleship to think him, as I suppose the majority of people with any intellect do, on the whole, the most powerful of living novelists".

Not all reviewers and readers agreed. Some were repelled by his realism and his focus on society's moral corruption. Robert Bell complained:

The people who fill up the motley scenes of Vanity Fair, with two or three exceptions, are as vicious and odious as a clever condensation of the vilest qualities can make them. The women are especially detestable. Cunning, low pride, selfishness, envy, malice, and all uncharitableness are scattered amongst them with impartial liberality. It does not enter into the design of Vanity Fair to qualify these bitter ingredients with a little sweetness now and then; to shew the close neighbourhood of the vices and the virtues as it lies on the map of the human heart, that mixture of good and evil, of weakness and strength, which in infinitely varied proportions, constitutes the compound individual.

An anonymous reviewer wondered, "is it advisable to raise so ruthlessly the veil which hides the rottenness pervading modern society?". Harriet Martineau could not finish the novel "from the moral disgust it occasions".

From Thackeray's day to the present, Vanity Fair has

generally been regarded as a masterpiece and as his best novel. What has changed is the flaw Thackeray, as well as Vanity Fair, is most commonly charged with. Critical readers of his day called him cynical and even depraved; comparable readers today call him sentimental and even cloying.

Humorist, Writer and Moralist

Until the publication of Vanity Fair, Thackeray was known as a humorous writer; he wrote regularly for Punch. Thackeray regarded humour as doing more than making readers laugh, "the best humour is that which contains most humanity, that which is flavoured throughout with tenderness and kindness." He was compelled to write the truth about what he saw and how he understood what he saw:

To describe it otherwise than it seems to me would be falsehood in that calling in which it has pleased heaven to place me; treason to that conscience which says that men are weak; that truth must be told; that faults must be owned; that pardon must be prayed for; and that love reigns supreme over all.

There may be wishful thinking in his statement that as the writer "finds, and speaks, and feels the truth best, we regard him, esteem him–sometimes love him." In order to tell the truth, the novelist must "convey as strongly as possible the sentiment of reality." Language should identify exactly, not elevate or exaggerate; for instance, a poker was just that—a poker, not a great red-hot instrument and a coat was only a coat, not an embroidered tunic. He disliked Dickens's highly emotional outbursts and vivid personification of objects; Thackeray protested that the very trees in Dickens's novels "squint, shiver, leer, grin and smoke pipes." A realist, Thackeray consistently deflated the heroic and the sentimental in life and in literature.

Thackeray saw the writer as serving a necessary function–to raise the consciousness of his readers. Concerned, he asked his mother in a letter, "Who is conscious?" He came to see himself as a Satirical-Moralist, with a responsibility both to amuse and to teach, "A few years ago I should have sneered at the idea of setting up as a teacher at all... but I have got to believe in the business, and in my other things since then. And our profession seems to me as serious as the Parson's own." He aimed not only to expose the false values and practices of society and its institutions and to portray the selfish, callous behaviour of individuals, but also to affirm the value of truth, justice, and kindness. This double aim is reflected in his description of himself as satiric and kind: "under the mask satirical there walks about a sentimental gentleman who means not unkindly to any mortal person."

Though Thackeray set his novel a generation earlier, Thackeray was really writing about his own society he even used contemporary clothing in his illustrations for the novel. Thackeray saw how capitalism and imperialism with their emphasis on wealth, material goods, and ostentation had corrupted society and how the inherited social order and institutions, including the aristocracy, the church, the military, and the foreign service, regarded only family, rank, power, and appearance. These values morally crippled and emotionally bankrupted every social class from servants through the middle classes to the aristocracy. High and low, individuals were selfish and incapable of loving.

Well aware of himself as flawed, he identified with the self-centered and foolish characters he portrayed in Vanity Fair; his object in writing the novel was

> to indicate, in cheerful terms, that we are for the most part an abominably foolish and selfish people "desperately wicked" and all eager after vanities....I want to leave everybody dissatisfied and unhappy at the end of the story–we ought all to be with our own and all other stories. Good God don't I see in that maybe cracked and warped looking glass in which I am always looking my own weaknesses wickednesses lusts follies shortcomings?.... We must lift up our voices about these and howl to a congregation of fools: so much as least has been my endeavour.

His identification with the fools and the sinners of Vanity Fair could not be stated more clearly. The image of the cracked-mirror provided the basis of the drawing for the frontispiece when the serialized novel came out in book form in 1848.

What were some of his flaws? By temperament, he inclined to be self-indulgent, liked to eat and drink well, and until he lost his money gambled enthusiastically; today, we would probably say he had a gambling problem. The Bohemian lifestyle and Bohemians had a strong attraction for Thackeray, as he acknowledged:

I like Becky in that book. Sometimes I think I have myself some of her tastes. I like what are called Bohemians and fellows of that sort. I have seen all sorts of society—dukes, duchesses, lords, and ladies, authors and actors and painters—and taken altogether I think I like painters the best, and Bohemians generally.

As you read the novel, think about whether Thackeray's identification with the characters and perhaps the life of Vanity Fair affects the novel. Does he show a compassion for the follies he describes and for the characters who commit those follies? Is there a sense of connection with them, or does Thackeray adopt a superior stance and look down on them, judging them harshly? Or is Thackeray ambivalent? Is Vanity Fair, as A.E. Dyson says, "one of the world's most devious novels, devious in its characterization, its irony, its explicit moralising, its exuberance, its tone. Few novels demand more continuing alertness from the reader, or offer more intellectual and moral stimulation in return"?

Chapter 2

Biography of W M Thackeray

William Makepeace Thackeray was born at Calcutta, India, on July 18, 1811, the son and grandson of officers of the East India Company. His father died when William was six, and the following year the future novelist was sent to England to be educated. After some years at private schools, he entered the Charterhouse in 1822, and remained till 1828. Neither there nor at Cambridge, where he was a member of Trinity College for a year and a half, did he distinguish himself as a scholar; and he finally left the university because he felt he was wasting his time, and determined to finish his education by travel. During a stay of several months at Weimar he met Goethe, and years afterwards used his reminiscences of the Grand Ducal Court there in his description of Pumpernickel in "Vanity Fair." On his return to England he took up the study of law, and though he was later called to the bar he never practised.

Thackeray's father had left him a considerable fortune, most of which had disappeared by the time he was twenty-three, part lost in an unsuccessful newspaper, part in unfortunate investments, and part through gambling. Finding that he had to earn his bread, he resolved to study art, and in 1834 went to Paris for this purpose. Two years later he was appointed Paris correspondent of a short-lived paper, "The Constitutionalist," and on the strength of this he married Isabella Shawe, the daughter of an Irish officer. After four years of happy married life, Mrs. Thackeray's mind gave way, and though she lived till 1894 she never recovered. For a number of years he had to struggle to keep his head above water, writing for newspaper and periodicals and doing a good deal of illustrating. Though he never acquired great technical skill as a draughtsman, he had a gift of turning out amusing sketches, and for ten years he was on the staff of "Punch" as both artist and author. It was in that publication, with "The Snobs of England," that he first achieved popularity, his earlier novels, "Catherine" and "Barry Lyndon," having failed to hit the popular taste. In January, 1847, "Vanity Fair" began to appear in monthly numbers, and by the time it was concluded in the July of the following year he was generally awarded a place in the first rank of English novelists. Dickens was then at the height of his fame, and, though the two men appreciated each other's work, their admirers were fond of debating their comparative merits—a form of criticism which, though futile enough in the case of talents so dissimilar, has not yet entirely gone out of fashion.

"Pendennis," the most autobiographical of Thackeray's novels, came out in 1848–50, and still farther strengthened his reputation. In 1851 he took up lecturing, beginning with the series on the English Humorists of the Eighteenth Century, which he delivered first in London. These were in a sense a by-product of "Esmond," published in 1852, in the autumn of which year he carried them across the Atlantic. He lectured at Boston, New York, Philadelphia, Baltimore, Richmond, Charleston, and Savannah, was received with great hospitality, made many friends, and went home the next spring the richer by some $10,000. A second tour in America, with "The Four Georges," followed in 1855, and was also successful. Meantime he had completed "The Newcomes," and while in Rome with his daughters for the Christmas season of 1853, he wrote and illustrated for some children the amusing burlesque of "The Rose and the Ring." Thackeray was now one of the notable figures of English society and was financially at ease. In 1857 he stood for Parliament for the city of Oxford, but missed election by a narrow margin. Apparently little downcast, he returned to his literary work and issued "The Virginians," 1857–59. It is commonly felt that with this book the quality of his work begins to fall off, and none of his subsequent novels achieved great success. In 1860 he undertook the editorship of the newly founded "Cornhill Magazine," and to it he contributed his delightful essays, "The Roundabout Papers." But his health, which for years had been far from good, unfitted him for the labour of editorship, and he resigned in 1862. On the morning of December 24, 1863, he was found dead.

The death of Thackeray was keenly felt through a wide circle both in England and abroad. His striking figure—he was six feet, three inches in height, with a massive head—had become familiar not only through his appearances on the platform but through the caricatures of himself that he had whimsically introduced into many of his drawings in "Punch" and elsewhere; and he was held in affectionate reverence by thousands who had never seen him. Though he first made his reputation as a satirist, he was a man without malice and of extraordinarily tender sensibilities. He had had to struggle hard to gain a footing in letters, and suffered more than his share of domestic sorrow; but he was generously helpful to others, even when he could little afford it, and found his greatest delight in brightening the lives of children. He used to be blamed for cynicism; but it has long been clear that it was the keenness of his appreciation of the loftier possibilities of human nature that lay at the root of his sadness that these possibilities are so seldom realized.

Though he achieved brilliant success in the fields of the burlesque and the essay, it is, of course, on his work as a novelist that his great reputation is chiefly based. But when the attempt is made to rank his novels among themselves, great diversity of opinion appears. Some specialists would give first place to the comparatively little read "Barry Lyndon"; more favour "The Newcomes." His style nowhere reaches greater perfection than in the astonishing reproduction of the diction of Queen Anne's reign in "Esmond." Yet, all in all, it is safe to say that he never surpassed his first great success, "Vanity Fair." Here we find at their height his distinguishing qualities: his power of conveying the spirit and atmosphere of an epoch, of delineating a throng of people and making them all living men and women, of conceiving great dramatic situations and presenting these so as to display character with the utmost vividness, of stripping away the veils that hide our motives not only from others but from ourselves. It is doubtful if any English novel possesses a heroine more completely vitalized than Becky Sharp, a creature so amazingly real that critics are occasionally to be found taking sides with her against her creator. And in his description of such figures, in his painting of their backgrounds, and in his characteristically intimate discussion with his readers of their faults and follies, he wields an English style unsurpassed for clarity, ease, and grace, capable of lofty eloquence, extreme tenderness, and fiery scorn, but always appropriate and always sincere.

Chapter 3

Background

AMONG THE professional Victorian writers who made a living, or even a fortune, from writing without the aid of outside sources of income, there were a fair number who were incompetent businessmen. Of those who made a fortune, Thackeray probably has the reputation of being the least businesslike. He is known as a lucky, careless genius, a lazy giant with great powers and equal weaknesses. Although he squandered a considerable part of his £17,000 inheritance through a weakness for gambling and in two ill-fated investments in periodicals, the Constitutional and the National Standard, the loss that threw him absolutely upon the resources of his pen appears to have been a bank failure in India-no fault of his own. Having struggled back to fiscal competence from his initial ruin, he invested £500 in the railroad mania in which he lost again in the general collapse of 1845. The success of Vanity Fair made his life easier but did not restore his lost fortunes. His lecture tours in America netted approximately £5,000, which Thackeray invested in American railroads and sold out during the Civil War for only £3,895 Letters 3: 275. Nevertheless, he left his daughters an estate nearly equaling the £ 10,000 apiece that he repeatedly said was his goal.

Explaining the differences between Thackeray and Dickens as professional writers, Anthony Trollope-certainly one of the most business-manlike of authors-wrote:

The one was steadfast, industrious, full of purpose, never doubting of himself always putting his best foot foremost and standing firmly on it when he got there; with no inward trepidation, with no moments in which he was half inclined to think that this race was not for his winning, this goal not to be reached by his struggles. The sympathy of friends was good to him, but he could have done without it. The good opinion which he had of himself was never shaken by adverse criticism; and the criticism on the other side, by which it was exalted, came from the enumeration of the number of copies sold. He was a firm reliant man, very little prone to change, who, when he had discovered the nature of his own talent, knew how to do the very best with it. It may almost be said that Thackeray was the very opposite of this.

Unsteadfast, idle, changeable of purpose, aware of his intellect but not trusting it, no man ever failed more generally than he to put his best.foot foremost. Full as his works are of pathos, full of humour, full of love and charity, tending, as they always do, to truth and honour and manly worth and womanly modesty, excelling, as they seem to me to do, most other written precepts that I know, they always seem to lack something that might have been there. There is a touch of vagueness which indicates that his pen was not firm while he was using it. He seems to me to have been dreaming ever of some high flight, and then to have told himself, with a half-broken heart, that it was beyond his power to soar up into those bright regions. I can fancy as the sheets went from him every day he told himself, in regard to every sheet, that it was a failure. Dickens was quite sure of his sheets.

It is not quite clear if Trollope was aware of the potential double meaning of that last assertion, but Thackeray was. In any case, this passage is the sort of realistic fiction for which Trollope is justly famous. But though it is misleading, if not an outright falsehood, Trollope's Thackeray has stuck in the popular mind. The image Trollope evoked corresponds generally with the one promoted by Thackeray himself in such things as his vignette drawing of a printer's devil waiting at the door to carry his manuscripts to a presumably impatient printer and by stories like the one James T. Fields told of Thackeray coming to one of his own dinner parties well over an hour late with ink on his fingers announcing the completion of the last sheet of The Virginians. Fields, pp. 17-18 It is indisputable that Thackeray produced much of his work under the pressure of deadlines. That need not mean he was lazy. John Sutherland has argued that Thackeray may even have written better under pressure than at leisure. Thackeray spoke often in his letters of living, eating, drinking his novels to the exclusion almost of his own daily life. He relished the creative pressure induced by deadlines, though he also knew the pace would wear him out. It has been altogether too easy to overplay Thackeray in the role of procrastinator, the would-be gentleman of leisure, and to lose sight of the facts concerning Thackeray the businessman and professional writer, This part of the picture can be filled out from two other sources: his comments in his fiction on the craft of writing and the facts of his relations with his publishers revealed in letters, contracts and publishers' account books.

A key episode in establishing the image of Thackeray's view of his profession, its rank, rights, and responsibilities, took place in 1850. Thackeray brought the wrath of John Forster upon his head when, in Pendennis, he had George Warrington remark to Pen on their way home from a dreary publisher's party, "And now that you have seen the men of letters, tell me, was I far wrong in saying there are thousands of people in this town, who don't write books, who are, to the full, as clever and intellectual as people who do?" Thackeray went on in the voice of his narrator, "And it may be whispered to those uninitiated people who are anxious to know the habits and make the acquaintance of men of letters, that there are no race of people who talk about books, or perhaps, who read books, so little as literary men".

Forster's objection, printed in the Examiner for 5 January 1850, was directed against Thackeray for disparaging literary men as a whole by presenting the Shandons, Waggs, and Bunions of the party as representative of all literary men and women. Forster attributed Thackeray's "attack" to a desire to curry favour with the nonliterary classes. In defending himself, Thackeray gave one view of the professional writer. He claimed never to have "been ashamed of his profession, or except for its dulness of any single line from his pen." He considered the charge that he was currying favour among the nonliterary classes absurd, since in his experience people honored writers, and he would gain nothing through the supposed stratagem of which he was accused. Finally, he defended his portrait of the literary world on the grounds that it was true. Why, he asked, "are these things not to be described... it such exist, or have existed, they are as good subjects for comedy as men of other callings".Forster would not let the subject alone, showing himself totally unmoved by Thackeray's explanations, He distinguished between identifying humbug in a profession and identifying humbug with a profession. Here the public debate lapsed into silence without a winner. It is quite likely that Forster was predisposed to pick a fight with Thackeray over this issue because of a long-standing and fundamental difference between them, friends though they had been, concerning the status of professional writers and their role and in society. Forster and Dickens, as has been suggested by Craig Howes, represented the author in a romantic light, as a dignified, inspired artist. The author's role, according to this view, was that of inspirer and castigator-as social conscience for the betterment of society. Michael Lund has cited various nineteenth-century versions of this view suggesting that authorship is not work like other trades or professions but rather a gift or inspired avocation. Thackeray, on the other hand, had long been speaking and writing from a different perspective, emphasizing the trade relations, admitting the work involved, and making fun of pretentious writing and pretentious writers. Thus, the controversy over the dignity of literature boils down to one side trying to uphold an ideal and a social responsibility which they see as doing good and the other side trying to be honest and unpretentious which they see as being true. The object of fiction for the one is to change society; for the other, to understand it. There is no resolution for such a controversy.

Privately, in a letter to his friend Abraham Heyward, Thackeray admitted, however: "The words in Pendennis are untenable be hanged to them: but they were meant to apply to a particular class of literary men, my class who are the most ignorant men under the Sun, myself included I mean. But I wrote so carelessly that it appears as if I would speak of all, and even if it were true I ought never to have written what I did". Yet this apology expresses regret for having written carelessly, not for having thought the thought. Thackeray did not change his mind about writers; rather, he was sorry to have stirred up this particularly fruitless controversy.

In the novel Pendennis goes on to become a successful novelist, serving first a sort of apprenticeship writing reviews. He later becomes the author of Thackeray's The Newcomes, in which he gives the following description of the profession of authorship:

The drawbacks and penalties attendant upon our profession are taken into full account, as we well know, by literary men, and their friends. Our poverty, hardships, and disappointments are set forth with great emphasis, and often with too great truth by those who speak of us; but there are advantages belonging to our trade which are passed over, I think by some of those who exercise it, and for which, in striking the balance of our accounts, we are not always duly thankful. We have no patron, so to speak-we sit in ante-chamber no more, waiting the present of a few guineas from my lord; in return for a fulsome dedication. We sell our wares to the book purveyor, between whom and us there is no greater obligation than between him and his paper-maker or printer. In the great towns in our country, immense stores of books are provided for us, with librarians to class them, kind attendants to wait upon us, and comfortable appliances to study. We require scarce any capital wherewith to exercise our trade. "at other so called learned profession is equally fortunate? A doctor, for example, after carefully and expensively educating himself, must invest in house and furniture, horses, carriage, and men-servants, before the public patient will think of calling him in. I am told that such gentlemen have to coax and wheedle dowagers, to humour hypochondriacs, to practise a score of little subsidiary arts in order to make that of healing profitable. How many many hundreds of pounds has a barrister to sink upon his stock in trade before his returns are available? There are the costly charges of university education-the costly chambers in the Inn of court -certain expenses all to be defrayed before the possible client makes his appearance, and the chance of fame or competency arrives. The prizes are great, to be sure, in the law, but what a prodigious sum the lottery ticket costs! If a man of letters cannot win, neither does he risk so much. Let us speak of our trade as we find it, and not be too eager in calling out for public compassion.

This description of the author's life and work emphasizes one aspect at the expense of others. Pendennis, as the narrator of The Newcomes, has constantly to remind himself not to think in inflated terms about authorship. This litany of the trade relations and modest requirements reveals that authorship is open to one and all who care to risk the chance of publication. Elsewhere, Thackeray emphasized other requirements, most notably the need to develop, through extensive reading, a sense of history. The comparison with the professions of medicine and law both elevate and deflate the picture being presented. It is not so difficult nor so lucrative as those relatively bourgeois professions; but if it is like a trade involving paper sellers, printers, and booksellers, it yet also has freedoms and responsibilities unlike those trades which made it nonetheless a profession. Among those responsibilities Thackeray included the moral one of avoiding inflated language and slipshod moral implications-the two main butts of his humorous attacks in Novels by Eminent Hands7.

Like Thackeray's celebrated redefinitions of snob and gentleman, his view of the professional writer as tradesman is a double one reconciling in itself traditionally opposing views. just as a middle-class or poor gentleman seemed a contradiction in Regency terms, so too the poet as tradesman seemed contradictory in romantic terms. Both Dickens and Forster remonstrated with Thackeray for his failure to hold high enough the dignity of the profession-their arguments smacking of conventional notions of the smudge of trade. There is a tawdry irony in the notion of Dickens and Forster, both with tradesman connections in their backgrounds, and particularly Forster, who besides writing was a paid employee of a publisher, objecting to Thackeray's portraits of writers as tradesmen. But Thackeray's view cuts through the pomposity and cant about the dignity of literature to the heart of the ideals of his profession-to love and truth, upholding the ideals without losing sight of the mundane business facts of authors writing for money, relying on and being relied upon in turn by publishers in much the same way that the printers and the paper sellers rely on one another in the business transactions that make books and periodicals. To admit that the author is one in a line of necessary manufacturers and purveyors of literature that includes the publisher, printer, stationer, and bookstall vendor is to pursue truth where there seems to be nothing to gain except the miserable satisfaction of knowing it. In fact, however, that view is subversive to establishment conventions-a fact that goes a long way toward explaining the disagreement between Forster and Thackeray. Of course, this truth is not the whole truth any more than is that other much better known image Thackeray created of the novelist as the preacher in cap and bells That is to say, Thackeray was not just an exposer of sham, nor was he just a satirist.

Thackeray's double view of the word trade as it applied, without shame, to his own profession, is reminiscent of his similar treatment of trade in Vanity Fair where poor Dobbin in school is the butt of all the jokes because his father, a grocer, pays his bill in goods. Dobbin gains respect by beating Cuff in a fight, but the narrator notes that the lordly little George Osborne's grandfather was a tradesman too. Dobbin's father becomes a respected alderman albeit none too refined a man, and Dobbin is unquestionably the real gentleman of the book. If authorship and publishing have the taint of trade, they also can have the honour of trade. And where there is honour, there is the risk of dishonor. The ideals of the profession could be traduced not only by inflated rhetoric but by dishonest shows of learning or of sentiment. In an early review Thackeray complained of writers who sugared their instructions in manners and morals and academic subjects by putting them into fiction, but at the same time he firmly believed in the novelist's responsibility, even in the guise of a clown's cap and bells, to instruct-not with moral platitudes, of course, but with the lessons inherent in what he thought was unvarnished truth. To the editor of Punch, Mark Lemon, he wrote on concluding the "Snobs of England": "A few years ago I should have sneered at the idea of setting up as a teacher at all, and perhaps at this pompous and pious way of talking about a few papers of jokes in Punch-but I have got to believe in the business, and in many other things since then. And our Profession seems to me to be as serious as the Parson's own"

One need not agree with Trollope that the vagueness or ambivalence in Thackeray's work reveals lack of commitment or conviction or strength. What some of his contemporaries thought of as a feigned "want of earnestness," an "undervaluing of his art," a carelessness about details, plain ineptitude, or tired repetitions in narrative structures may better be understood as the deliberate manifestations of a cast of mind that rejected, or at least suspected, the values represented by earnestness and narrative order. Thackeray's narrative technique undermines surface realism and the sense of certitude and stable values implied by authorial omniscience.

I think it likely that Thackeray deliberately undermined such values because he did not believe in them, because he thought the danger lay in overvaluing art. Thackeray saw more clearly than most of his contemporaries the problems of trying to create or capture "reality" in "fiction," and he knew more clearly than many a historian of his day that the coherence created by the orderly arrangement of historical data, commonly taken for "truth" in "history," is an illusion.

Jack Rawlins has recognized and described in some detail Thackeray's habit of undercutting the fictional realities he had created, but Rawlins seems not to have understood the implication of the narrative strategy, deploring Thackeray's refusal to adopt the novelist's responsibility to impose a moral order beneficial to society." In this regard Rawlins agreed with Forster.

From time to time scholars, noting the "lapses" in Thackeray's "artistic values," explain them as carelessness or as the inevitable, though lamentable, results of a hectic mode of production-John Sutherland, in Victorian Authors and Publishers, and N. N. Feltes, in Modes of Production of Victorian Novels, have turned this argument on its head as a means of praising Henry Esmond, which was produced under circumstances different from those attending any other Thackeray work; it is the only novel Thackeray finished before it was published. However, the very same kinds of disruptions of realism occur throughout that book, as a multitude of readers have noted, particularly Elaine Scarry.

John Sutherland has remarked that "the mode of production confirmed in Thackeray a kind of narrative opportunism. One always feels that he has reserved the right to switch the course of his narrative whenever and however it suits him. He allusdes jokingly to the arbitrariness of his power over plot in the preface: 'Perhaps the lovers of "excitement" may care to know that this book began with a very precise plan, which was entirely put aside. Ladies and gentlemen, you were to have been treated and the writer's and publisher's pocket benefited, by the recital of the most active horrors.... Nay, up to nine o'clock this very morning, my poor friend, Colonel Altamont, was doomed to execution, and the author only relented when his victim was actually at the window."

Sutherland opined that this was "high-spirited nonsense" and the "element of truth" about Thackeray's work was the lamentable one of "narrative opportunism." That particular interpretation is apparent only to persons committed to the tradition of English fiction adhering to Jamesian inevitability, to Trollope's insistence on the novelist's right to be able to adjust the beginning to the end, to a Joycean refining of the author out of existence. But it is not "nonsense," high-spirited or otherwise, to anyone willing to face the possibility that these "lapses" they seem rather too frequent and to come in too strategic locations to be lapses are, if not deliberate, at least characteristic gestures reflecting a point of view about history, fiction, and reality that is controlled by a value system rejecting the Jamesian striving for realism precisely because realism is a contrived illusion. The particular example of "opportunism" in question is from Pendennis. It illustrates the carefully planned contrivance of this illusion, for the "communicating leads" and window box that make Altamont's escape possible were first planted, so to speak, 330 pages earlier and had already been used by Colonel Strong to escape a bailiff.

No reader finding Altamont cornered in the same apartments could be surprised by the escape. To accuse Thackeray of opportunism-that is, to take seriously his remark about relenting at the last moment-is both to underestimate the control he had over his materials and to misunderstand his deliberate exposure of the illusion of reality in order to make his point.

For Thackeray, fiction was fun, and the illusion of reality was fascinating. All his sympathies were on Dobbin's side, for example, when on a school half-holiday the boy sits under a tree, carried away by a book into the world of the Arabian Nights. But he continually insisted that that world was not real; reality obtrudes for the reader of Thackeray's fiction in the form of his "lapses" just as surely as it did for Dobbin when the altercation between Cuff and George Osborne broke in on his fictive Arabian world. Thackeray addresses the reader, laughs in his sleeve, imagines Jones yawning over the number, and "reserves the right to switch the course of his narrative whenever and however it suits him" because, much as he likes creating the illusion of reality, he likes more reminding his readers that in actuality he, Thackeray, is telling the reader, sitting in a chair, a story.

That is realism with a significant philosophical point: that the author, like the reader, is subject to human limitations of knowledge and judgment. Authors may have a keen view of human foibles but are no better at prescribing for the world than any other reader, Thackeray refused to set himself up to be the hero as man of letters. And for all that, paradoxically, there is more of truth in his sheets than in the pages of many a self-proclaimed regenerator of the age.

Thackeray's realism is one that his contemporaries and,

it seems, many later generations of Thackeray's readers have been unprepared to see or accept. Thackeray must have known that, for he introduced his disruptions of fictive realism gently; they can be dismissed as "lapses" or the eccentricities of genius. Perhaps it has been too easy for readers to miss the implications. Thackeray's sardonic view of aristocratic airs, his tracing of meanness and snobbery from top to bottom of the social scale, his "failure" to produce a moral framework within which the indeterminacies can come to moral closure have variously been explained as gentlemanly detachment, as declining to be the moral enthusiast, or as a weakness of spirit or lack of moral fibre.

Among Thackeray's most enthusiastic fans, these matters have been, at worst, irritations to be ignored. Thackeray was, to my mind, deliberate and committed in this fundamental point from his early writings throughout his life. But he was not prepared to make the point at the expense of his livelihood or the fortune he intended to make and leave for his daughters. He was very much aware of the commercial exigencies of novel writing, and it was not his aim to disrupt profits by focusing attention on his private beliefs and values.

But there was good and ample reason for him to introduce into his fiction those elements that so irritated John Forster and Charles Dickens and that apparently disappointed Trollope and John Sutherland. In such passages as the one in Philip where Thackeray discussed the amount of money the paragraph he was writing would earn him or the closing of Vanity Fair where the emphasis falls so heavily on the show and contrivance that his puppets "really are," he reminded his readers that the illusion of realism is created in the reality of storytelling. The neat wrapping up of loose ends where villains are punished and heroes vindicated and rewarded, Thackeray knew, is an illusion.

Reality is ambiguous and indeterminate. The true realist does not know enough to pass out poetic justice justly. So Thackeray reminds his readers constantly and truthfully that the puppet show is not real. He forces an ultimate realism upon his readers by denying the possibility of honest satisfaction in fictive endings. To him, the truth about the world included the truth about writing fiction for a living, Thackeray's methods expose the sham realism in which the author pretends to know not only what his characters think and do but by what moral standards characters should he measured. Thackeray's tentativeness, his apparently cynical view of good, and his supposedly infirm or sentimental stance on evil resulted, I believe, from honesty, humility, and simple acknowledgment of the true limits of authorial knowledge.

Henry Dodd Worthington's description of his father in James Gould Cozzens's Morning Noon and Night suggests something of what I am trying to identify in Thackeray's character. Then there was that manner of his. You could not say it was shy, but you felt some lack of self-assertion, by most people associated with weakness, infirmity of purpose....What these were plain signs of I can now see. They were signs of deep and thorough skepticism, That I then didn't see it wasn't, I think, just boyish imperceptiveness, I would guess that few people saw it, that few people ever thought of him as skeptical. What people expect from a skeptic is skepticism in its commoner loud, assertive form of scorning, challenging, contemptuously rejecting.

This kind of skepticism will often be superficial, professings of men who basically are cynics, men of shallow thinking and loose feeling. My father's kind of skepticism made no show. It worked as a sort of silent patient withholding of judgment, almost as though his mild steady distrust of all appearances or supposed certainties went so far that when he felt serious doubts about anything those very doubts had to he held open to doubt. To many of his contemporaries, Trollope and Carlyle particularly, Thackeray was a weak man, indecisive, lacking positive force. I believe they mistook his distrust of certainty.

The other extreme response to Thackeray, typified by Charlotte Brontë's remarks in the dedication of the second edition of Jane Eyre, calling Thackeray "the first regenerator of the day" who resembled Henry Fielding "as an eagle doth a vulture," is a corrective that goes too far. Reacting to

Thackeray's bold cutting through the cant and hypocrisy of the upper middle class, Brontë and other admirers tended to see in him a prophet whose attack on conventional values established art alternative foundation of values enshrining duty, loyalty, humility, and social responsibility. When upon meeting him Brontë discovered that Thackeray was no Carlyle, her disappointment arose from a misunderstanding not far removed from Trollope's. Alike, they failed to recognize and admire the profound honesty of Thackeray's aversion to overconfident assertions of values. Intense assertion of values was a common Victorian stance, but it was not Thackeray's.

Thackeray's respect for the "uncertainty principle," the humility with which he declined to be sure, is, of course, not peculiar to him, though it was a rare enough position in Victorian England. The position has had its influential manifestations, notably following periods of rigid or excessive authoritarianism. It played roles in the decline of the Spanish Inquisition and the rejection of Puritan rigidity following the excess of the Salem witch trials. But it can be seen also in the tremendous variety of human foibles tolerated without authorial condemnation in Shakespeare and in the attitudes revealed in Fielding's Tom Jones, Sterne's Tristram Shandy, and Keats's Odes — all hesitating to judge too finely or too finally and, consequently, all creating problems for earnest moralists. In Thackeray's case it is particularly necessary to distinguish, also, between a mere dislike of rigidity or discipline which he indeed had and a deeply felt suspicion of certitude which I think he also had. The former results from an irritable or sensitive personality, the latter from a philosophical position.

In his own day Thackeray's satiric view of the romantic ideals of his profession made him appear weak, ambivalent, his own worst enemy. And that view, with a hefty boost from Trollope, has carried over into the image of Thackeray as an undisciplined craftsman, leading more than one critic to characterize him as a "careless putter forth" or hasty or even lazy improviser the phrase comes from George Saintsbury's Introduction to Pendennis, in which he also calls Thackeray a shrewd reviser. And this unflattering view extends to the image of Thackeray the businessman or, as he implied with characteristic deflation, tradesman.

The word tradesman in Victorian England denoted, as it still to some extent does, an outlook and a rank in life that were incompatible with imagination and beauty, which were central to the concept of artist, poet, or even novelist. One equates tradesman in Victorian England with Mr. Pumblechook in Great Expectations and Mr. Polly in H. G. Wells's History of Mr. Polly or, on a higher economic — though not sensibility — scale, Mr. Freeman in John Fowles's French Lieutenant's Woman, whose industrial and commercial sensibilities are impervious to art. But Thackeray was a practical man who had learned, from more than one penniless crisis, the reality of writing for money. That reality was a fact to be honestly acknowledged. If authorship had certain high ideals, it included, on the other hand, the mundane practical details of the trade of writing. By using the loaded word trade for the artist, Thackeray undercut both the social snobbery and the mystical trappings of artist, which some writers cultivated.

The social snobbery probably was an unconscious outgrowth, rather than a desired aim, of earlier proponents of the mystical view. The Victorian version of that view derived at least in part from the notions of poet or artist promulgated by Wordsworth in the preface to Lyrical Ballads, where the poet's sensibilities above the common run of men is claimed, and by Shelley's "Defence of Poesie," where the poet's position as an unacknowledged legislator of the world is proclaimed. But perhaps the strongest impetus to view the writer's calling in a special light with special capabilities and privileges was Thomas Carlyle's portrayal of the "Man of Letters" in On Heroes, Hero Worship, and the Heroic in History.

Thackeray's early send-ups of Dr. Lardner and Sir Edward Bulwer Lytton as pompous snobs playing off their roles as artists in social settings is an indication of his suspicion of the role. As a practicing writer, he turned to the trade rather than the calling in order to deflate the aggrandized view. Thackeray became, in fact, an able and a reliable businessman who expected publishers and illustrators to fulfill their commitments with equal promptness. To his publishers, Bradbury and Evans, Thackeray wrote in May 1854 to complain of Richard Doyle, the illustrator Thackeray himself had chosen for The Newcomes: "However much I may regard Doyle as a friend it is clear that as men of business we cannot allow our property to suffer by his continual procrastination.

The original agreement with Doyle, made between Bradbury myself & him was that the blocks & plates for the ensuing month should always be supplied by Doyle on the 15th of the month current. I have now written to him, to say that I shall hold him to his agreement & that if by the 15 June the plates & blocks of No 10 of the Newcomes are not in your hands I shall employ another designer". It would have been the height of arrogance and insensitivity for Trollope's Thackeray to require promptness and commitment from another man — holding Doyle to standards too rigid for himself. But Trollope's Thackeray was a fiction. The real Thackeray was a reliable professional masked by a public image. The popular concept of a harried Thackeray dashing off the last lines of the monthly number for the printer just in the nick of time is a romantic misunderstanding of serial publication.

In thirty years of professional writing, Thackeray failed to meet only three deadlines that seriously affected a publisher. Only one of these commitments lay within his power to fulfill. The October 1844 installment of Barry Lyndon was delayed one month for lack of copy, and even then there were mitigating circumstances. He mailed off the October installment on 23 September from Smyrna while on his Eastern tour recounted in From Cornhill to Grand Cairo, and it arrived too late in London for the October number of the magazine. He finished the book on 3 November Ray, Adversity, p. 343; Letters 2: 154-54, 156. In September 1848 he become so ill he had to suspend the writing and publishing of the monthly numbers of Pendennis for three months, and in August 1859 he was too ill to write a complete final double number for The Virginians, providing instead a one-part number 23 and a one-part final number in September. Thackeray's sense of the business requirements of authorship was hard won. Though he had earned his livelihood by journalism for ten years when he began Vanity Fair, he was in 1846 still very much a petitioner appealing to the largess of the proprietors of Punch and other publishers, and he was dependent on their valuation of the goods he brought for sale.

But by 1854 the author of The Newcomes saw himself as coproprietor with the publisher, The change is dramatic, and the composition, production, and financial success of Vanity Fair mark the watershed of Thackeray's career as a businessman, transforming him from the investor/ gambler, the writer waiting upon publishers with his goods, into the propertied tradesman who built himself a debt-free mansion at 2 Palace Green, Kensington.

Five chapters of Vanity Fair were written by early spring 1846. Thackeray announced to his mother that serial publication would begin on 1 May, and in March or April the first five chapters were set in type18. Production problems immediately became apparent: when the corrected galleys were paged, it was discovered that the fourth chapter reached page 28 and the fifth chapter extended to the middle of Page 35 Serial publication, however, required exactly thirty-two pages, no more and no less. The first of May passed with no publication. The type for chapters 1-5 was knocked down and redistributed to the typecases, while Thackeray eked out his living with "The Snobs of England" and "Novels by Eminent Hands" — contributions to Punch lasting beyond the publication of the revised initial number of Vanity Fair in January 1847.

What Thackeray learned during the eight-month delay in the publication of Vanity Fair can only be surmised from the regularity of his serial numbers from 1 January 1847 to the end of his life except in the fall of 1848 and August 1859 when illness, not lassitude, prevented the professional fulfillment of his commitments to the public. The process he worked out was fairly simple but has only recently been understood by scholars. Except when he wrote The Newcomes, a few numbers of Philip, and Denis Duval, Thackeray never completed a monthly installment before the month it was due at the print shop. Hs contract for Vanity Fair — written and signed, curiously enough, on 25 January 1847 as the second installment was being printed — specifies that he was to submit copy by the fifteenth of each month. According to his letters, however, often on about the twenty-fifth of the month he would write that he had "just ended his number." Such statements, along with his frequent self-accusations of procrastination and the picture of the sleeping printer's devil waiting at the door, combine to give the superficial and false impression of a writer who could not meet his contracted deadlines. In fact, the process was a smooth, if hectic, coordination of writing, typesetting, proofreading, correcting, and printing responsibilities.

The reason Thackeray "ended" his numbers on the twenty-fifth or so is that serial publication does not lend itself to the submission of a finished manuscript on the fifteenth. The first time Thackeray tried that, his installment would have occupied either twenty-eight or thirty-five pages had it been published. Instead, he would submit about three-quarters of an installment to the printer — probably by the twentieth or earlier — to be set in type. With as many as five compositors working on a single installment their names are an the manuscripts, typesetting twenty to thirty pages could be completed in a day or less.

The printer's devil would then carry proofs to Thackeray, who corrected them and measured them with a string corresponding in length to a page of the printed book. Arriving at a fairly accurate estimate of the amount of text still required to fill the number, he would revise and augment or cut as necessary. A printer's boy or the mails would then return the corrected and augmented proof to the printshop. Second proofs with page headings and page numbers embedded would be ready in another day or so, making it possible for Thackeray to read proofs and make final adjustments in length by the twenty-fifth or twenty-sixth of the month. The printers and binders then usually had about five days to get an installment ready for distribution by the last day of the month. This coordination of production effort lends itself to the concept of writing as a trade. The artist's fancy is not free; the grinding schedule of production curtailed the craftsman's time and forced his energies in ways which Thackeray is on record as both appreciating and lamenting.

The conditions of serial novel writing were not very different from newspaper journalism or the scheduled inches of letterpress Thackeray was responsible for in Punch. Novel writers of Thackeray's standing today may have a fellowship or an advance front the publisher and a full year or eighteen months to write the novel. Not so Thackeray. Yet the pressure was invigorating; he lived, talked, ate, slept his fiction up until deadline time. Thackeray's enthusiasm for the invigorating aspect of the engines of journalism shows in George Warrington's praises of it in Pendennis:

There she is — the great engine-she never sleeps. She has her ambassadors in every quarter of the world-her couriers upon every road. Her officers march along with armies, and her envoys walk into statesmen's cabinets. They are ubiquitous. Yonder journal has an agent, at this minute, giving bribes at Madrid; and another inspecting the price of potatoes in Covent Garden. Look! here comes the Foreign Express galloping ire. They will be able to give news to Downing Street tomorrow: funds will rise or fall, fortunes be made or lost; Lord B. will get up, and, holding the paper in his hand, and seeing the noble marquis in his place, will make a great speech; and-and Mr. Doolan will be called away from his supper at the Back Kitchen; for he is foreign sub-editor, and sees the mail on the newspaper sheet before he goes to his own.

The mock-heroic tone of the adjective "ubiquitous, " of the exclamation "Look!", and of the juxtaposition of bribes in Madrid with the price of potatoes in Covent Garden introduces a faint distrust of the enthusiasm but does not belie the excitement Warrington feels for the press. The positive part of the passage echoes the spirit of historic significance that prompted the 1832 pressmen's parades in London, complete with a working press carried in a cart producing ink-wet pamphlets on freedom of the press for the crowd. But Warrington's detachment, echoing Thackeray's own balances the sentiment with the dash and the pun on Mr. Doolan's mundane diurnal oscillation between the printed sheets and his bed sheets. The double view suggests that the situation is too complex to be captured by one feeling or one attitude. That same sleepless engine is also the inexorable, insatiable engine which fed on the writer and caused the haste and the drain of energy which sapped the health of more men than just Thackeray.

Thackeray's sense of the economic realities of publishing was acute-won at the price of two failed literary magazines and years of journalistic hand-to-mouth work. His image of Pegasus drawing a wagon and his unaristocratic equation of the literary profession with the trades are of a piece with his mockery of inflated self-importance in any calling in life. These self-deprecatory remarks cannot be taken to mean more than they do-that literary men must work hard, must meet their deadlines, must accept the consequences of the responses of publishers as merchandisers and readers as the market for art: they must write what will be published and purchased. Thackeray's remarks on his profession do not mean that he held it in low regard or that he had no sense of the dignity of literature. For Thackeray the dignity of the profession lay in the integrity of presenting the world he knew as he saw it-including the business of authorship.

In a letter to John Forster he indicated what humbug he thought lay at the root of attempts to assert the dignity of literature by any other means: "I don't believe in the Guild of Literature I dont believe to the Theatrical Scheme; I think i s against the dignity of our profession, — but you are honest and clever men and free to your opinion thank you for nothing say you well, believe that mine's loyally entertained too. " Thackeray was saying that the artist cannot with honesty or true dignity hide behind cant about a high calling.

Thackeray's position is neither starry-eyed or simpleminded. He knew the plight of many literary men who could be said to want the dignity of a bare living; his purse was frequently open to them. With similar honesty he acknowledged the ambiguity of good and evil, a view which more positive men took to reveal weakness. Nor is his position uncomplicatedly open and without subtlety of its own. A chapter of Thackeray's life remains to be written by someone who can see beyond or beneath the surface and untangle the remark in John Chapman's diary for 14 June 1851: "I find that his religious views are perfectly free, but he does not mean to lessen his popularity by fully avowing them, he said he had debated the question with himself whether he was called upon to martyrise himself for the sake of his views and concluded in the negative.

His chief object seems to be the making of money. He will go to America for that purpose. He impresses me as much abler than the lecture I heard, but I fear his success is spoiling him." Thackeray's net worth when he died unexpectedly on 23 December 1863, at age fifty-three, attests for our material age his business success. His house was sold for £10,000. His furniture and personal effects sold for £2,000; his wine for £400. His copyrights brought his daughters £5,000.

A total of about £18,000-one thousand more than his father had left him. It is difficult to understand in modern terms the meaning of £18,000 or of an annual income O £2,000 to £4,000, which Thackeray was making in the last six or seven years of his life, An exchange rate does not help much because buying power changes as goods and services go up or come down. According to an article on the Royal Literary Fund in the Smithsonian Magazine, London postmen made £50 a year in 1839 Strebigh, p. 126. Of Anthony Trollope, John Sutherland has said, "With a bit of scrimping £250 was a tolerable annual salary23." Sutherland, p. 16 Another source claims that £250 was the minimum required to be a gentleman. By such meaningless standards the man who wrote a chapter of Vanity Fair called "How to Live on Nothing a Year" was twelve times a gentleman.

How Thackeray became a writer has been the subject of many books and articles, but recounting the story with some new material emphasizes the connections between his experiences as writer and the point of view about the writer's trade presented in the preceding chapter. It illustrates how a romantic youth developed into a young dilettante; how, without a "useful" education, Thackeray was thrown rather summarily upon the resources of his pen to survive and to support a young and trouble-ridden family; how years of hackwork and dogged determination won for him a combination of pride in his journalistic achievements and a humility or at least unpretentiousness about art; and how, when the laurels of fame and fortune finally became his, he found the dignity of literature in the economic and social rewards for hard labour rather than in the mantle of the hero as man of letters.

His contributions as a schoolboy at the Charterhouse to the Carthusian, as a teenager in 1828-29 to the Western Luminary, and as a college student in 1829-30 to the Snob and Gownsman literary newspapers conducted by students at Cambridge have been described in detail by Harold Strong Gulliver, an account still worth reading, though corrections as well as new material can be found in Gordon Ray's Thackeray: The Uses of Adversity2. In some ways, the best account of these activities and of Thackeray's attitude toward the Muse and literary work at this time is his own fictional account of young Pendennis.

As important as these ventures were in whetting Thackeray's appetite for literary work, they cannot be seen as the beginnings of his professional career. These literary endeavors, on a par with his contributions in 1831 to Ottilie von Goethe's Weimar literary paper, Chaos, were works of amateur enthusiasm. They were not undertaken for pay, nor were they part of any endeavor to forge a literary career, whether "for a living" or as the work of a gentleman of the world, which Thackeray could have been but for his weakness for gambling and, more importantly, the bank failures in India in late 1833 that virtually wiped out his considerable inheritance.

On his return from Weimar in March 1831, having chosen to forgo the rest of his education at college, where he had lost

11, 500 at play, he sampled with distaste the rigors of reading for the law, turned twenty-one on 18 July 1832, dissipated in Paris for three or four months, and tried his hand for three months as a bill discounter. By May 1833 he was ready to invest his money in something more congenial to his tastes and talents. He purchased a periodical, the National Standard, thereby making himself a publisher. He was also the editor and chief contributor. His motive was only partially economic, as is perhaps clear from the oft-quoted self-satire he printed thirty years later in Lovel the Widower where Mr. Batchelor gave himself "airs as editor of that confounded Museum, and proposed to educate the public taste... and made a gabby of" himself Lovel the Widower. London: Smith, Elder, 1861, chap. 1 The National Standard lasted till February 1834, by which time Thackeray had learned of the Indian bank failures and knew himself to be a poor man, the bulk of his remaining inheritance having evaporated, for though the estate may still have amounted to £7000, it was encumbered by annuities which left Thackeray financially hobbled.

Even before this misfortune, while still Paris correspondent for the National Standard, Thackeray had undertaken the formal study of art in Paris as "an independent man who is not obliged to look to his brush for his livelihood." But by the end of 1833 all that changed. Thackeray first thought to repair his condition by pursuing with serious intent the calling he had chosen from inclination at a better time; however, he knew by the summer of 1835 that he could not succeed as a painter. From need he sought out literary assignments, selling at least one article to Fraser's Magazine, working for Galignani's Messenger in Paris, projecting and abandoning a "Picturesque Annual" for which he would both write and draw, producing Flore et Zéphyr, a book of lithographs from which he apparently made nothing, and perhaps starting, editing, or at least working for a Paris rival to Galignani's.

Like painting, writing was a high-risk speculative venture without guaranteed returns. Flore et Zéphyr, Thackeray's first book, has no text beyond captions to the lithographs. It was published in April 1836 in London by John Mitchell while Thackeray was in France. Thackeray's letters to Mitchell betray the confusion characterizing this effort: "I cannot understand from yr. notes what is the drawing wanted," and the next day, "I do not know whether you propose to publish any letterpress with the drawing, will you allow me to see it, before its appearance". The publication of Flore et Zéphyr was financed by Thackeray's wealthy friend John Bowes Bowes, who held an interest in Galignani's Messenger in Paris and who later wrote Thackeray that he thought Mitchell had fudged on the accounts "and put a lot of money in his pocket." Whether Mitchell made any money is not known, but Thackeray and Bowes did not, though it may not have mattered much to the later. Time heals all wounds, it seems, for in 1851, Mitchell reappears in Thackeray's affairs as the manager of the London lectures on eighteenth-century humorists.

Thackeray's depression over blasted hopes as a painter was alleviated somewhat by his meeting and falling in love with Isabella Shawe, an event with financial implications requiring an even more assiduous pursuit of literary work. Thackeray found that writing for a living, which he could do with some success, was far more demanding than writing occasional pieces for fun and glory. So when in early 1836 the opportunity arose to become involved with a politically radical literary paper, the Constitutional and Public Ledger, which was supposed to have a broadly subscribed economic base, Thackeray persuaded his stepfather, Major Carmichael-Smyth, to help him by subscribing the venture and serving as chairman of the company.

Thackeray's salary was set at eight guineas a week. In the flurry of setting up the company and gathering a staff, Thackeray wrote to Isabella that he was to have £450 per year, and serious courtship and plans for marriage became possible in spite of the obstacles provided by his future mother-in-law, Mrs. Shawe. Thackeray's writings for the Constitutional began appearing in September, one month after his marriage. The account given by Ray of those next months suggests that Thackeray thought himself arrived at stability and contentedness, with the leisure to secure and execute additional jobs as illustrator Ray, Adversity, pp. 188-89. But the whole project collapsed by July of the next year, crippling Major Carmichael-Smyth financially and throwing Thackeray once again upon the resources of his free-lance pen, this time with a wife and child to support. Thackeray would not again enjoy the leisure and stability of those few months as Paris correspondent for many years to come, but he had broken into print, he knew how to do it, he had developed some confidence in his abilities, and he set about his work with vigour.

When in 1833 Thackeray had commented to his mother that the National Standard was "very rapidly improving, & will form I have no doubt a property", he was still the investor seeking to acquire and improve a property ready made; now he was to discover that he had "no other saleable property" than his writings.

Chapter 4

Chronology

1811	Born July 18 in Calcutta.
1815	Death of father.
1817	Sent to school in England.
1822-28	Attends Charterhouse School, London.
1829	Enters Trinity College, Cambridge.
1830-31	Leaves Cambridge and travels in Germany.
1831-32	Studies law in London.
1833	Loss of inheritance.
1834-35	Studies art in Paris.
1836	Marries Isabella Shawe in Paris; first article appears in The Constitutional.
1837	Moves to London where begins to write for Fraser's Magazine and where daughter, Anne, is born.
1837-38	The Yellowplush Correspondence in Fraser's.
1839-40	Catherine in Fraser's.
1840	First book published in England, The Paris Sketch Book; A Shabby Genteel Story appears in Fraser's. Daughter, Harriet Marian born; Isabella Thackeray suffers the nervous collapse that leads to permanent insanity.
1841	The Great Hoggarty Diamond in Fraser's; 2-volume collection of Comic Tales and Sketches.
1842	First contribution to Punch.
1843	The Irish Sketch Book.
1844	The Luck of Barry Lyndon in Fraser's. Tour of Mediterranean and Mideast.
1846	Notes of a Journey from Cornhill to Grand Cairo. Daughters join Thackeray in London.

1846-47	The Snobs of England, retitled The Book of Snobs in book form.
1847	Punch's Prize Novelists retitled Novels by Eminent Hands in book form, 1856.
1847-48	Vanity Fair January 1847—July 1848.
1848	Friendship with Jane Brookfield, wife of the Reverend William Brookfield, deepens.
1848-50	The History of Pendennis November 1848—December 1850.
1850	Rebecca and Rowena.
1851	Lectures on humorists of eighteenth century in London ublished as The English Humourists of the Eighteenth Century in 1853. Break with Jane Brookfield.
1852	The History of Henry Esmond.
1852-53	First American tour.
1855	The Rose and the Ring.
1855-56	Second American tour, lectures on the Hanoverian kings ublished as The Four Georges in 1860.
1857	Runs unsuccessfully for the Oxford seat in Parliament.
1857-59	The Virginians November 1857—October 1859.
1859-62	Editor of Cornhill Magazine.
1860	Lovel the Widower in Cornhill.
1860-63	Roundabout Papers in Cornhill.
1863	Begins Denis Duval unfinished, published posthumously in Cornhill in 1864.
1863	Dies December 24 in London.

Chapter 5

Major Works

William Makepeace Thackeray -Pseudonyms Charles James Yellowplush, Michael Angelo Titmarsh, George Savage FitzBoodle

English journalist, novelist, famous for his novel VANITY FAIR, a tale of two middle-class London families. Most of Thackeray's major novels were published as monthly serials. Thackeray studied in a satirical and moralistic light upper- and middle-class English life-he was once seen as the equal of his contemporary Dickens, or even as his superior.

"This I set as a positive truth. A woman with fair opportunities, and without a positive hump, may marry whom she likes." from Vanity Fair William Makepeace Thackeray was born in Calcutta, India, as the only son of Richmond Thackeray, a Collector in the East Indian Company's service. After his father died he was sent to home to England. He was educated at Charterhouse and at Trinity College, Cambridge. Thackeray abandoned his studies without taking a degree, having lost some of his inheritance of twenty thousand pounds through gambling. In the beginning of the 1830s he visited Germany, where he met Goethe.

During 1831-33 Thackeray studied law at the Middle Temple, London, but had little enthusiasm to continue his studies. In 1833 he brought with a large heritage the National Standard, but lost his fortune a year later in the Indian bank failures and other bad investments. According to an anecdote, Thackeray offered to undertake the task of illustrating Dickens's Pickwick Papers in 1836, but the author himself found Thackeray's drawings unsuitable.

After art studies in Paris, Thackeray returned in 1837 to London and started his career as a hard working journalist. Often he used absurd pen names such as George Savage Fitz-Boodle, Michael Angelo Titmarsh, Théophile Wagstaff, and C.J. Yellowplush, Esq. In 1836 he married a poor Irish girl, Isabella Shawe; they had three daughters. Their first child, Anne Thackeray Ritchie, became a writer-her impressionistic texts impressed Virginia Woolf, who drew a portrait of her in Night and Day as 'Mrs Hilbery'. Ritchie published several novels, and contributed to an 1898-99 edition of her father's works. A prominent intellectual figure of her time and well-acquainted with a number of the great names of British literature, she also wrote memoirs of her contemporaries, including Tennyson and Ruskin.

Thackeray began to contribute regularly to Fraser's Magazine, Morning Chronicle, New Monthly Magazine and The Times. His writings attracted first attention in Punch, where he satirized English snobbery. These sketches reappeared in 1848 as THE BOOK OF SNOBS, in which he stated that "he who meanly admires mean things is a Snob."

In 1840 Isabella Thackeray suffered a mental breakdown, from which she never recovered, through she survived Thackeray by thirty years. The author was forced to send his children to France to his mother. The children returned to England in 1846 to live with him.

Already in his first novel, CATHERINE, originally written for Fraser's Magazine, Thackeray broke with the literary conventions of his day: "The characters of the tale ARE immoral, and no doubt of it; but the writer humbly hopes the end is not so. The public was, in our notion, dosed and poisoned by the prevailing style of literary practice, and it was necessary to administer some medicine that would produce a wholesome nausea, and afterwards bring about a more healthy habit." In THE LUCK OF BARRY LYNDON, Thackeray portrayed an adventurer, opportunist, and gambler, who serves in the Seven Years War, first under the English flag and then in the Prussian army, gains wealth, and eventually is punished for his imperfections. "Suppose in a game of life-

and it is but a twopenny game after all-you are equally eager of winning," Thackeray wrote much later in 'Autour de mon Chapeau'. "Shall you be ashamed of your ambition, or glory in it?"

In Vanity Fair, set at the time of the Napoleonic wars, Thackeray created one of the most fascinating immoral female characters, Becky Sharp, who manages to avoid the fate of Barry Lyndon: "I think I could be a good woman if I had five thousand a year." from Vanity Fair The book brought Thackeray prosperity and made him an established author and popular lecturer in Europe and in the United States.

Vanity Fair was sub-titled 'A Novel without a Hero'. "Everybody in Vanity Fair must have remarked how well those live who are comfortably and thoroughly in debt; how they deny themselves nothing; how jolly and easy they are in their minds." The vast satirical panorama of a materialistic society centers on Becky Sharp and Amelia Sedley, good-natured but 'silly'. They are two boarding-school friends, whose destinies are contrasted. Clever and ambitious Becky is born into poverty as the daughter of a penniless artist. Her plans to marry Amelia's brother Joseph fail. She marries Rowdon Crawley, but he is disinherited. Becky manages to live at the height of fashion through the patronage of Lord Steyne. When her husband discovers the truth, he departs to become the governor of Coventry Island. Becky is ostracized and she moves to the Continent. In the meantime Amelia's stockbroker father is ruined. Amelia is loved by William Dobbin but she marries George Osborne-he dies in the battle of Waterloo. Amelia's son is left into the care of his grandfather, who dies and leaves him a fortune. Amelia travels in the Continent with his brother and they meet Becky. Dobbin has returned from India and disapproves Amelia's kindness to Becky. Older and disillusioned, Dobbin and Amelia can marry. Becky regains her hold over Joseph, who dies in suspicious circumstances. Becky's husband Rowdon dies, and Becky ends the novel in the guise of a pious widow.-See also: Anthony Trollope, Michael Innes

Thackeray's increasing love for Jane Brookfield, the wife

of an old Cambridge friend, led to a rupture in their friendship. THE HISTORY OF HENRY ESMOND, ESQ., appeared in three volumes in 1852, and reflected the melancholic period in the life of the author. By the end of his career, Thackeray's disillusionment with contemporary culture seems to have deepened. In THE ADVENTURES OF PHILIP the protagonist, Philip, is out of place in a world that does not accommodate his vision of masculinity.

Thackeray said that he couldn't start a novel until he knew every aspect of his characters. He called Victorian times "if not the most moral, certainly the most squeamish." Once, as an editor, he rejected an Elizabeth Barrett Browning poem because it employed the word harlot. Thackeray became in 1860 the first editor of the Cornhill Magazine, for which he wrote his RAUNDABOUT PAPERS, LOVE THE WIDOWER, THE ADVENTURES OF PHILIP and the unfinished DENIS DUVAL. Less successful Thackeray was with his attempt to stand for Parliament. His contacts with friendly rival Charles Dickens ended in a quarrel, but their daughters continued to be friends. Thackeray died suddenly on Christams Eve 1863. Just before his death he he had reconciled with Dickens.

Thackeray was buried in Kensal Green Cemetery. His bust at the Westminster Abbey was made by the Italian sculptor Marachetti. The poet's daughter was not satisfied with the work and let another sculptor to modify her father's stone sideburns until they were the right length.

Selected Works:

The yellowplush papers, 1838

Catherine, 1839

The paris sketch book, 1840

The history of samuel titmarsh and the great hoggarty diamond, 1841-samuel titmarsh eli tarina isosta hoggartyn timantista

The iris sketch book, 1843

The luck of barry lyndon, 1844 rev. In 1856 as the memoirs of barry lyndon, esq.-film 1975, dir. By stanley kubrick, starring ryan o'neal, marisa berenson, patrick magee, hardy kruger.

Kubrick wanted to recreate on screen the look of 18th-century paintings and so set out to film the movie without any artifical lighting at all.

Notes of a jouney from cornhill to grand cairo, 1846

The book of snobs, 1848

Vanity fair, 1847-48-turhuuden turuilla-films: 1935, becky sharp, dir. By rouben mamoulian, starring miriam hopkins, cedric hardwicke, frances dee; 2004, dir. By mira nair, starring reese witherspoon, james purefoy, eileen atkins, gabriel byrne

The history of pendennis, 1848-50

Rebecca and rowena, 1850

The english humourists of the 18th century, 1851

The history of henry esmond, esq., 1852, 3 vol.-henry esmondin tarina hänen itsensä kertomana trans. By martta räsänen

The english humorists of the 18th century, 1853

The newcomes, 1853-55

The rose and the ring, 1855

Miscellanies, 4 vol., 1855-57

The virginians, 1857-59

The four georges, 1860

Lovel the widower, 1860

Poems and essays, 1860

The adventures of philip on his way through the world, 1862

Roundabout papers, 1860-63

Denis duval, 1864

Collected ed., 1867-69

Letters and private papers, 1945-46

Chapter 6

List of Characters

Miss Barbara Pinkerton	: Presiding over an Academy for Young Ladies.
Jemima Pinkerton	: her sister.
Amelia Sedley	: Afterwards Mrs. George Osborne, an accomplished young lady, yet with more heart than brains.
John Sedley	: Esq., of the Stock Exchange, father of Amelia.
Mrs. Sedley	: His wife.
Joseph Sedley	: Older brother of Amelia, in the East India Company's Civil Service.
Mrs. Blenkinsop	: Housekeeper of the Sedleys.
Sambo	: Coloured servant of the Sedleys.
Rebecca Sharp	: Afterwards Mrs. Rawdon Crawley, daughter of a poor English artist and a French dancer. A fascinating, clever and unscrupulous adventuress.
Miss Swartz	: A mulatto heiress from St. Kitt's, a school friend of Amelia's.
Sir Pitt Crawley	: A miserly, hard drinking, disreputable old baronet.
Rose Grawley	: Second wife of Sir Pitt—a colourless and neglected invalid.
Rose & Violet	: Daughters of Sir Pitt by his second wife.
Pitt Crawley	: A conventional prig—elder son of Sir Pitt by his first wife.
Rawdon Crawley	: Younger son of Sir Pitt Crawley by his first wife—a heavy young rake in the Dragoons.

Horrocks	:	Sir Pitt Crawley's butler.
Miss Horrocks	:	His daughter.
Rev. Bute Crawley	:	Younger brother of Sir Pitt Crawley a worldly minded country parson.
Mrs. Bute Crawley	:	His wife, a managing, scheming little woman.
James, Frank & Four Girls	:	Children of Bute Crawley.
Mr. Osborne	:	A prosperous merchant in the city, who owes his start in life to Mr. Sedley.
Jane	:	Spinster daughter and slave of Mr. Osborne.
Maria	:	Afterwards Mrs. Frederick Bullock, younger daughter of Mr. Osborne.
George Osborne	:	Son of Mr. Osborne, and godson of Mr. Sedley, a conceited young officer.
Miss Wirt	:	A "raw-boned vestal," governess to the Misses Osborne.
Miss Crawley	:	Half-sister to Sir Pitt Crawley, a shrewd rich old spinster.
Miss Briggs	:	Miss Crawley's companion.
Mrs. Firkin	:	Servant of Miss Crawley.
Bowls	:	Butler at Miss Crawley's.
Mr. Raggles	:	Former butler at Miss Crawley's, and owner of the house on Curzon St. rented by the Rawdon Crawleys.
Capt. William Dobbin	:	Afterwards Major and Lieutenant Colonel, good angel of George Osborne and Amelia Sedley.
Misses Dobbin	:	His sisters.
Countess Southdown	:	A strong-minded woman favourably known to the serious world.
Lady Emily Hornblower	:	Her daughter, "author of several delightful tracts."
Lady Jane Sheepshanks	:	Afterwards Mrs. Pitt Crawley, younger daughter of Countess Southdown.

Mr. Clapp	:	Mr. Sedley's clerk with whom he takes refuge after his failure.
Mrs. Clapp	:	His wife.
Miss Mary Clapp	:	Their daughter.
Frederick Bullock	:	Of the house of Bullock, Hulker & Bullock, who marries Maria Osborne.
Ensign Stubble & Ensign Simple	:	Subalterns in George Osborne's regiment.
Major O'dowd	:	Commander of Osborne's regiment at Waterloo.
Peggy O'dowd	:	His wife, commander of the Major.
Glorvina O'dowd	:	A good-natured Irish girl who fails to ensnare Major Dobbin.
George Osborne, JR	:	Son of Amelia and George Osborne.
Rawdon Crawley	:	JR., son of Rawdon Crawley and Becky Sharp.
George Gustavus	:	Marquess of Steyne, Earl of Gaunt, Viscount, Hellborough, Baron Pitchley and Grillsby, Knight of the Most Noble Order of the Garter, etc., etc., etc., an elderly roué
Lady Steyne	:	His wife.
Lady Gaunt	:	His daughter.
Mr. Moss	:	The bailiff.
Fifine	:	Becky Sharp's maid.
Capt. Macmurdo	:	Rawdon Crawley's friend in his affairs of honour.
Mr. Wenham	:	Lord Steyne's confidential friend.
Rev. Mr. Veal	:	Little George Osborne's tutor.
Rev. Beilby Binny	:	Curate of the District Chapel, an admirer of Mrs. Osborne.
Isidor	:	Belgian servant of Joseph Sedley.
Kirsch	:	Joseph Sedley's courier.
Fiche	:	Servant of Lord Steyne.
Doctors	:	Apothecaries, solicitors, clerks, officers, servants, gate keepers, German students, noblemen, auctioneers, school boys, etc.

Chapter 7

Character Analysis in Vanity Fair

Rebecca Sharp

Child of a poor artist and a French opera girl, Becky Sharp early learns to shift for herself. Her mother dead, Becky's father with "a great propensity for running into debt, and a partiality for the tavern" brings her up. From her mother she has a knowledge of French from her father the ability to ward off creditors. With this heritage of Bohemian blood, and a clever mind, Becky lives by her wits.

At her father's death two bailiffs quarrel over his corpse Becky is accepted at Miss Pinkerton's to teach French in exchange for schooling, free board and room, and a little money. Ingenious Rebecca manufactures a laudable ancestry for herself, and although she is at heart selfish and hostile, she can act the part of modesty, simplicity, gentleness, and untiring good humour. When she cares for the rich Miss Crawley who has 70,000 pounds Rebecca's "little nerves seemed to be of iron and she was quite unshaken by the duty and tedium of the sick chamber."

In addition to her mental endowment, Rebecca has physical charm, described by Dr. Squills as "Green eyes, fair skin, pretty figure, famous frontal development." Mrs. Bute Crawley laments Rebecca's physical attraction when she looks at her own dumpy, misshapen, blue-blooded daughters.

Becky has one determination: to carve out a place for herself in Vanity Fair. Although she hasn't blushed naturally since she was eight years old, she can blush at will. She exploits her aloneness and lack of protection. She can cry when she wants to, but the most genuine tears she sheds are those when she has to refuse marriage to the wealthy Sir Pitt Crawley, because she has already married his son, Rawdon.

When she and Rawdon are living on nothing a year, Rebecca deals with the creditors. It is she who starts the rumor that Rawdon has inherited from his rich aunt, and thereby gets out of Paris without paying any debts, since she has ordered a newly decorated apartment against her return. It is she who settles for a percentage of Rawdon's debts in England, so that he may return to London for a fresh start.

Among Rebecca's talents are music, both piano and voice. She can sketch, talk French like a native, dance, act, mimic. Not only her physical charm attracts Lord Steyne, but her wit and mimicry and her ability to get money out of him, even when he realizes she is outwitting him. The more money she wheedles out of him, the more amused he is, until the fatal day when Rawdon walks in on the two of them.

Rebecca's ambition is her outstanding characteristic. She sacrifices husband, child, friends to it; but she enjoys the battle. In a letter to Amelia, after Becky has gone to Queen's Crawley, she says, "At least I shall be amongst gentlefolks—and not with vulgar city people." This jibe refers to both the Sedleys and the Osbornes because George has thwarted her marriage with Joseph Sedley. She continues, "You might lodge all the people in Russell Square in the house, I think, and have space to spare."

Although Rebecca is a merciless social climber, has abandoned her child, whom she hates, has destroyed Rawdon and will destroy Joseph, yet it is she who brings Amelia to her senses, and who realizes that the one true gentleman in the whole of Vanity Fair is Dobbin. After eavesdropping on William's talk with Amelia, Becky says to herself, "What a noble heart that man has, and how shamefully that woman plays with it... if I could have had such a husband as that—a man with a heart and brains too! I would not have minded his large feet..." Rebecca determines to help William's cause with Amelia. For once she acts unselfishly. When she has destroyed the memory of George for Amelia, she soothes and kisses her, a "rare mark of sympathy with Mrs. Becky." Rebecca also protects Amelia from the two ruffian friends who follow Rebecca and are intent on exploiting Amelia.

Thackeray explains why Becky does what she does: "She was of a wild, roving nature, inherited from father and mother, who were both Bohemians, by taste and circumstance... " Becky succeeds in establishing herself in Vanity Fair, at the cost of the lives of two men and the alienation of all her friends and family. She serves as a direct contrast to Amelia.

Amelia Sedley

Exactly opposite from Rebecca, Amelia has many advantages. Miss Pinkerton describes her as industrious, obedient, sweet, and beloved. She has mastered these accomplishments: music, dancing, orthography, embroidery, and needlework. However, Miss Pinkerton suggests that she use a backboard for four hours each day for the next three years to improve her carriage, "so requisite for every young lady of fashion." The author indicates her need of "backbone" by suggesting the use of the backboard. Whereas Rebecca's chief quality is ruthless ambition, Amelia exhibits weak humility and blind loyalty. Only in protection and care of Georgy does she rise above her natural submission to defend her own ideas. Once she prevents her mother from giving Georgy medicine, causing a rift between herself and her mother. She objects when old Osborne wants Georgy. In both cases, she returns to a sweet and reasonable attitude when she has convinced herself of her own selfishness.

Protected by doting parents, Amelia leads a sheltered existence saddened by George's neglect and his apparent willingness to forget her when her fortune has vanished. Sweet, lovable, refreshing, she has not the sparkle nor the mentality of Becky. She does have the lifetime devotion of William Dobbin, who sees that George marries her; and looks after her when George dies. Amelia's loyalty and long, blind devotion to George amount almost to stupidity. Any fault in George she interprets as a fault in herself and accuses herself of guilty love to account for his having been killed. The fate of Europe is the fate of her lover to Amelia. Amelia's innocence and ready belief in other people make her unbelievably good in contrast to Becky's unbelievable duplicity. Both attract young men, but for different reasons. Becky's wit and physical charm win a following, whereas Amelia's goodness and sweetness charm all who meet her. Becky can cry when she wants to; Amelia cries over a dead canary, a mouse, the end of a stupid novel, or the slightest unkind word to her.

She remains blind to Dobbin's goodness throughout much of the book and although her eyes have been opened to a certain extent regarding Becky, yet when she thinks Becky needs a friend, she returns to comfort and help her. Amelia depends on others for her opinions, and this is why it takes a sharp companion like Becky to set her straight—to make her see realities. One negative reaction was jealousy of George, and she had ample reason for that emotion, but it did not lessen her love for him. At the end of the book Thackeray calls her a "tender little parasite." She has changed little from the beginning of the book. Sheltered as she has been, she has had little chance for growth.

George Osborne

George Sedley Osborne, John Sedley's godson, has been close to the Sedley family all his life. He and Joseph have gone to school together. Old Osborne has commanded him to marry Amelia, and this plan has been understood for years.

George Osborne belongs to Vanity Fair. As a boy he has been ashamed of William Dobbin, his protector at school, because he feels Dobbin is of a lower social status. His sisters convince him he is one of the most deserving characters in the British Army, and "he gave himself up to be loved with a great deal of easy resignation." George loves Amelia after his fashion, but he loves himself more; and often when his sisters think he is with Amelia, he is gambling, drinking or going to the theater. Popular with the men in the regiment because of his outstanding sportsmanship, he equally charms the ladies:

His whiskers had made an impression upon her... George had an air at once swaggering and melancholy, languid and fierce. He looked like a man who had passions, secrets, and private harrowing griefs and adventures. His voice was rich and deep. He would say it was a warm evening, or ask his partner to take an ice, with a tone as sad and confidential as if he were breaking her mother's death to her, or preluding a declaration of love. He trampled over all the young bucks of his father's circle, and was the hero among those third-rate men. Having a faithful and generous friend in William Dobbin, George does not appreciate him. Furious with Dobbin for telling the regiment about Amelia, George soon forgets his anger, borrows money from Dobbin to buy Amelia a gift, but purchases a pin for himself.

George courts the acquaintance of the nobility, as all true inhabitants of Vanity Fair, but he does not tell tales on ladies. Self-centered and selfish, he takes Amelia's love and loyalty as his due, and under Dobbin's pressure marries her. When disinherited, he blames Dobbin and says he has lost his money over stupid sentiment. But when his sisters talk against Amelia, he comes to her defence in spite of their glares and his father's anger. Infatuated with Becky, George asks her to run away with him, but the Battle of Waterloo intervenes. When George realizes he is going into battle and may never see Amelia again, he is overcome with remorse and charges William Dobbin to care for her. As an excuse for George's irresponsibility Thackeray points out that old Osborne's attitude has been lenient toward all sorts of the wildness that George displays. Old Osborne objects only to gambling, and George gambles on the sly. While Amelia considers George's death the greatest tragedy that could befall her, the reader realizes that, had he lived, her life would have been more sad. At times George rises to heroic proportions, as when he stands up for Amelia against his family. His inconsistency of character: The willingness to defy others in his beloved's behalf and also his willingness to betray her, mark his citizenship in Vanity Fair.

Joseph Sedley

Amelia's brother, a bachelor on service in India as the collector of Boggley Wollah, is twelve years older than she.

Of him Amelia says, "he is very kind and good, but he scarcely ever speaks to me." A "swell," Joseph loves fine clothes and worships the nobility. He earns his nickname "Waterloo Sedley" from his continuous tales of his association with the Duke of Wellington, whereas he trembled at the mere sound of the cannon. Joseph admires Lord Tapeworm, a low-class person, because he is nobility.

Joseph fears his father's coarse humour; timid around the ladies, he does not stay at home when he is in London. He is much too fat and occasionally he tries to reduce, but he loves eating, drinking, and sleeping too much to change. When his father's business fails, he sends money, but otherwise can't be bothered. His affections do not go deep. Rebecca finally entangles him with flattery, gains possession of his money, and hastens his death. Joseph's father characterizes him: "... if you, and I, and his sister were to die tomorrow he would say 'Good Gad!' and eat his dinner just as well as usual."

William Dobbin

Thackeray has called this book a novel without a hero. Actually the only gentleman in the book is William Dobbin, but as Thackeray takes pains to point out, his feet are too big for him to qualify in Vanity Fair. His name indicates a plodder—a workhorse—a dog, even; his devotion to Amelia is dog-like. But, in the end, even Becky, the most ardent admirer of Vanity Fair, wishes she might have had a man like Dobbin, in spite of his big feet.

Dobbin first appears in defence of little George Osborne, whereat George is shamed that his defender is not of a higher social status. Dobbin appears thereafter as the guardian of George's and Amelia's interests. It is he who sees that they marry, that George is more or less kind to Amelia; and after George's death, it is Dobbin who reconciles old Osborne to Amelia, whereby both Amelia and Georgy have position and wealth.

This is George's opinion of Dobbin: "There's not a finer fellow in the service, nor a better officer, though he is not an Adonis." Again he is described as "a lanky-gawky fellow ...

tumbles over everybody." Dobbin exerts a good influence over little George in that he gives him some values in place of those of Vanity Fair. When Georgy thinks it is vulgar to sit in the pit at the theater, Dobbin lets him sit where he likes but goes to the pit himself. Georgy soon follows. Dobbin is not only a favourite with Georgy but with all who know him.

Thackeray gives his definition of gentlemen and he means this to be a description of Dobbin: "... whose aims are generous, whose truth is constant, and not only constant in its kind, but elevated in its degree; whose want of meanness makes them simple: who can look the world honestly in the face with an equal manly sympathy for the great and the small..."

Dobbin's growth in character begins when he steps out of his habitual modesty and asserts himself. At the beginning when he is in school, shunned and scorned by others because of his awkwardness and because of his father's having furnished food to the establishment, he rises out of himself to defend George. He defeats the enemy, and thereby gains the respect of his fellow students and begins to show better scholarship.

The same kind of growth starts when he finally tells Amelia that she is not worthy of the kind of love he bears her. She begins to wake up, respect him, and has even sent for him before Becky disillusions her about George. Restrained, modest, loyal, and good, Dobbin merits the love of all.

Rawdon Crawley

Rawdon Crawley, younger son of Sir Pitt, has a commission in the Life Guards Green, bought for him by his indulgent aunt, Miss Crawley, when he has been asked to leave Cambridge. He stands six feet high, loves sports, gambling, and women. He detests his pious brother and his reprobate father but gets along well with young men. Thackeray describes him as a "heavy dragoon with strong desires and small brains, who had never controlled a passion in his life." But he is not too stupid to suspect that Mrs. Bute wants Rebecca ruined so that she cannot become Sir Pitt's third wife and inherit the Crawley money.

Rawdon's marriage and his love for Rebecca and little Rawdy, tame him. Rebecca's loyal slave, he does not see through her activities and explains to himself that she is made to shine in society. He gambles to make a living but regrets what he and Becky are doing to Raggles. He rises to magnificence when he makes himself Becky's watchdog and later when he confronts Lord Steyne and Rebecca. Although Rebecca has held Rawdon in contempt, she admires his authority in that difficult situation, and after she is alone, she wishes she had Rawdon again—"She thought about 'him' with great sadness, and perhaps longing—about his honest, stupid, constant kindness and fidelity: his never-ceasing obedience; his good humour; his bravery and courage." Rawdon's marriage is one of the most nearly honest actions in his life.

When he takes little Rawdy to school, he comes away "with a sadder, purer feeling in his heart than perhaps that poor battered fellow had ever known since he himself came out of the nursery." After being tamed by his affection for Rebecca and his bewilderment over her treatment of him, he would sit for hours in his brother's house: very silent, and thinking and doing as little as possible. He was glad to be employed of an errand: to go and make inquiries about a horse or a servant: or to carve the roast mutton for the dinner of the children. He was beat and cowed into laziness and submission. Delilah had imprisoned him and cut his hair off, too. The bold and reckless young blood of ten years back was subjugated, and was turned into a torpid, submissive, middle-aged, stout gentleman. Separated from wife and son, although sending money for both, Rawdon dies of yellow fever in Coventry Island.

Other Characters

Old John Osborne

George Osborne's father is a tyrant who rules his household with terror, but he does not intimidate George, nor in turn little Georgy. Mr. Osborne's idea of a hint that he doesn't want a footman around any more is to kick the fellow downstairs.

Old Osborne belongs in Vanity Fair. When John Sedley fails in business, Osborne, whom Sedley has helped, is the first to turn against Sedley. Osborne forbids George to marry Amelia unless she has ten thousand pounds. A name-dropper, Osborne wants his son to associate with nobility, but he objects to gambling. He commands his son to marry the wealthy mulatto heiress, Miss Swarts, but George marries Amelia and his father disowns him. Only long after George's death, and by the offices of William Dobbin, does old Osborne mellow and begin to redress his wrongs to his son's wife.

In his old age he becomes very fond of his grandson, although he fears him, and determines to make him a scholar. Dimly, he realizes some of the mistakes he made with the first George; he worries about the likeness of the second to the first George.

Marie Osborne

Maria Osborne, engaged to marry Frederick Bullock, hopes to get more money because of George's defection. When she marries Frederick, she feels obligated to scorn her own family, ruining her chances of getting more money out of them. When Amelia is restored to family favour, Maria patronizes her, and plans that one of her daughters should marry Georgy to get back the family money. Maria would have married anybody for money and position.

Frederick Bullock

Frederick Bullock delays marrying Maria Osborne in hopes of getting more money from her father. Delighted over George's disinheritance, Frederick hopes his Maria will be worth more now.

Jane Osborne

She once had a budding romance with an artist, but her father smashed that, ending Jane's only chance for life, although she hopes Dobbin may be getting romantic when he tries to tell her of George's marriage. Old Osborne makes her a slave, but through her, Georgy comes to live in Russell

Square. Georgy makes her old age happy. Neither of the Osborne sisters has ever thought Amelia worthy of their brother George.

John Sedley

Father of Joseph and Amelia, John Sedley is a British merchant who loves practical jokes. He gets Rebecca to eat curry, and while her mouth is afire, Joseph offers her a chili, which she thinks must be cold, but, of course, isn't. Sedley teases her about liking things from India, referring to her play for Joseph. He prefers Becky as a daughter-in-law to some native girl Jos might bring home.

John Sedley has little patience with Joseph's airs, but in his old age, he wants Joseph near. After his financial ruin, Mr. Sedley imposes on Amelia. Joseph, too indifferent for imposition, furnishes money but won't involve himself in his father's dubious wine venture.

The one argument that makes Sedley consent to Amelia's marriage is that old Osborne will be furious. Before his death, he apologizes to Amelia for his and his wife's unfairness to her. Old Sedley dies in poverty.

Mrs. John Sedley

At first a kind, good-natured woman eager to keep her place in Vanity Fair, she loses her good temperament with the onset of poverty. Critical of Amelia's love for Georgy, she quarrels with her daughter. However, in her final illness she enjoys Amelia's constant devotion and care.

Georgy Osborne

Son of George Osborne and Amelia Sedley Osborne, little Georgy is orphaned before he is born. Brought up to believe he is the most important creature on earth, he gravitates to the values of Vanity Fair. But for William Dobbin, he might have remained entirely selfish. Popular, intelligent, lovable, Georgy inherits half the Osborne fortune and, at the end of the book, appears to be a better man than either his father or grandfather.

Rawdy Crawley

Son of Rawdon Crawley and Rebecca Sharp Crawley, little Rawdy is his father's treasure, the bane of his mother, who hates him. He goes away to school as the protégé of his mother's "protector," Lord Steyne. After the separation of his parents, he spends his leisure time with his aunt, Lady Jane. After the death of his cousin and his uncle, he inherits Queen's Crawley. Although he does not see his mother, he provides for her. The reader believes that Rawdon, like George, is a better man than his father or grandfather.

Mrs. Blenkinsop

Two characters have this name. One is the Sedley's housekeeper and confidante of Amelia. Having lived so long with the Sedleys, she stays with them in their poverty, tends them, and grumbles about them.

The other Mrs. Blenkinsop is a banker's wife who cuts Rebecca.

Mr. Clapp

Mr. Clapp has been Sedley's clerk for years. He takes the Sedleys into his home after their financial failure.

Mrs. Clapp

Mrs. Clapp of Vanity Fair gives Amelia a hard time over rents; but after Amelia has money, Mrs. Clapp fawns on her.

Mary Clapp

Sometimes called Polly, Miss Clapp loves Amelia and "Major Sugar-plums," as she calls Dobbin.

John

John is the Sedleys' groom, who is rude to Becky when he drives her to Sir Pitt's house. Amelia has given Becky some clothes John has wanted for his girl friend.

Mr. Sambo

Mr. Sambo is the good-natured, bandy-legged servant of the Sedleys, who doubles as coachman, butler, or waiter.

Sir Pitt Crawley

Son of Walpole Crawley, first baronet, of the Tape and Sealing Wax office, Sir Pitt has a celebrated genealogy. His first wife, sixth daughter of Lord Binkie, gave birth to two sons, Pitt and Rawdon. His second wife, Rose, daughter of an ironmonger, has two daughters. The reader first meets him when he carries in Rebecca's trunks and does not offer her any food. Becky characterizes him as "... old, stumpy, short, vulgar, and very dirty man, in old clothes and shabby old gaiters, who smokes a horrid pipe, cooks his own horrid supper in a saucepan. He speaks with a country accent, and swore a great deal..." He talks of himself all the time, sometimes in coarse and vulgar accents, sometimes affecting the tone of a man of the world. He has been on parliamentary lists for years.

Stingy, dirty, disreputable, and vulgar, "whatever Sir Pitt Crawley's qualities might be, good or bad, he did not make the least disguise of them." His affinity for Vanity Fair is evidenced by the fact that though he eats boiled mutton, he has three footmen to serve it.

Sir Pitt becomes very fond of Becky and after Rose dies, he comes to Miss Crawley's, where Rebecca is taking care of her, and asks Becky to marry him. In this humorous scene Rebecca has to refuse. Sir Pitt, in a fury, goes home and tears up Rebecca's belongings. After Becky is lost to him, he takes up with Miss Horrocks, the butler's daughter, and horrifies all his relatives by taking her about the country and drinking with her. He might have married her, but his illness and death prevent marriage.

Tipsy, but still stingy, he is such a sharp landlord that he can't find good tenants; so close, he grudges seed for planting. He dies unmourned.

Pitt Crawley

Pitt, the older son of Sir Pitt, pompous and pious as an undertaker, is always reading sermons and saying prayers. He insists on manners. His father doesn't swear at Lady Crawley when his son is in the room. At Eton he has been called "Miss Crawley":

At college his career was of course highly creditable. he never advanced any sentiment or opinion which was not perfectly trite and stale, and supported by a Latin quotation; yet he failed somehow, in spite of a mediocrity which ought to have insured any man a success...

Pitt marries Lady Jane Sheepshanks, Lord Southdown's third daughter, and because of Rawdon's unfortunate marriage and Mrs. Bute's domineering, Pitt inherits from Miss Matilda Crawley. At his father's death, he inherits a seat in Parliament and Queen's Crawley. He grows up to his position, although too stingy to give away any money. He is kind to Rawdon and Rebecca. When they part, he takes over little Rawdon. Even though he is a stingy hypocrite, Pitt has some admirable traits.

Bute Crawley

Rector of Crawley-cum-Snailby, brother to the baronet, Sir Pitt Crawley, Bute likes all sports, drinking, eating, and gambling. In debt, he hopes to inherit from Aunt Matilda. He has one son, James, and four ugly daughters.

Mrs. Bute Crawley

Sometimes Barbara, sometimes Martha, Mrs. Bute won't call on Sir Pitt's second wife because she is the daughter of an ironmonger. Mrs. Bute manages her husband and the rectory, and lets Bute dine out to save money. She spies on the relatives, hopes to undermine Becky.

When she nurses Aunt Matilda, she instills all possible prejudice against Rawdon and Becky. But she domineers and bores Aunt Matilda almost to death. The doctors have to intervene and get Aunt Matilda out of the house. Then Bute breaks his collar-bone and Mrs. Bute has to go home, and never gets another chance at the fortune.

She moves in on Sir Pitt as soon as he is unconscious, routs the hopeful Miss Horrocks. After the new Sir Pitt takes over, the Bute Crawleys come to Queen's Crawley for festivities.

James Crawley

Son of the Bute Crawleys, he gets thrown out of Aunt

Matilda's through Pitt's duplicity, but later Pitt encourages him to pay court to one of Pitt's half sisters, and arranges for him to be rector following Bute.

Miss Matilda Crawley

Sir Pitt's unmarried half sister has inherited her mother's large fortune. She sends Rawdon, her favourite, to Cambridge, buys him a commission, and plans to make him her heir. She dislikes Pitt, the milksop pious brother. An old reprobate, Aunt Matilda eats and drinks too much.

Her wealth and her health are of great importance to her eager relatives, who act loving to her and to each other when she visits. Thackeray describes her, "no lady of fashion in London who would desert her friends more complacently as soon as she was tired of their society, and though few tired of them sooner, yet as long as her engouement lasted her attachment was prodigious... "

Rawdon spoils his chances of inheriting by marrying Rebecca. Mrs. Bute domineers and bores the old lady. Eventually, through the sweetness of Lady Jane, Pitt's intended, and the diplomacy of Pitt himself, he inherits the bulk of Miss Crawley's wealth.

Miss Rosalind and Miss Violet Crawley

Half sisters to Pitt and Rawdon, these girls like Rebecca as governess, tolerate her as sister-in-law.

Firkin and Briggs

Two of Miss Crawley's maids, Firkin never likes Rebecca, but Briggs is taken in, loans Becky her money, is finally provided for by Lord Steyne. Briggs is one of the few admirable persons in the book.

The Countess Matilda Southdown

This "tall and awful missionary of the truth," is mother to Lady Jane Sheepshanks, who marries Pitt, and to Lady Emily Homblower, author of the Washerwoman of Finchley Common, a tract the countess forces on everyone.

Charles Raggles

Butler for Miss Crawley, he owes his start in life to the Crawleys. Rawdon and Rebecca cheat and ruin him, and he ends in debtors' prison.

Lord of Steyne

Lord Steyne, ugly and depraved, has won his wife at a gaming table. He takes Rebecca as protégé until Rawdon catches them. Through him she is presented at Court. He gives her money, position. Ordinarily his greatest fun is to torture his wife and family, but he appreciates his wife's defence of Rebecca. One of his sons is insane; the other has no children. The threat of madness hanging over the house may account for Steyne's excesses. Never forgiving an insult, he will not be reconciled to Becky. Of Vanity Fair, he represents the landed aristocracy of his time.

The Marchioness of Steyne

Wife of Lord Steyne, of excellent family, she becomes silent, superstitious, religious. She shows her innate kindness to Rebecca.

Young Lord Gaunt

Son of Lord Steyne, he marries Lady Blanche Thistlewood of the House of Bareacres. They have no children.

George Gaunt

He marries the Honorable Joan of John Johnes, first Baron of Helvellyn. They have children, but George is insane, gets the order of the "Strait Waistcoat!"

Wenham

Wenham is Lord Steyne's man who prevents a duel with Rawdon and ruins Becky's reputation with Sir Pitt.

Colonel Michael O'Dowd

This valiant soldier receives the rank of major-general after Tiptoff's death. He has served in all parts of the world and is Dobbin's commanding officer. He obeys his wife.

Peggy O'Dowd

Wife of Colonel Michael O'Dowd, "she was the best of comforters, in good fortune the most troublesome of friends; having a perfectly good opinion of herself always, and an indomitable resolution to have her own way." Peggy who loves everything Irish, is determined to marry off her sister, Glorvina.

Horrocks

Horrocks is Sir Pitt's butler and drinking partner. His daughter, Miss Horrocks or "Ribbons," hopes to be the third Lady Crawley.

Miss Barbara Pinkerton

Manager and owner of the academy on Chiswick Mall, she and her sister, Miss Jemima, educate young ladies. Miss Pinkerton hates Rebecca, always talks of her idol, Dr. Johnson.

Space does not permit mention of all the minor characters. Some of the more amusing names will be found under The Use of Names.

Chapter 8

Themes in Vanity Fair

Vanity

Vanity, which takes a variety of forms, is a major motivation of individuals and characterizes society. Consider the following definitions of vanity from the OED: "Vain and unprofitable conduct or employment of time"; "The quality of being foolish or of holding erroneous opinions"; "The quality of being personally vain; high opinion of oneself; self-conceit and desire for admiration." Another meaning of vanity could possibly be the vanity mirror; this meaning relates to the use of mirrors in the text and the drawings.

Society's Values

Individuals and society are driven by the worship of wealth, rank, power, and class and are corrupted by them. Consequences of this worship are the perversion of love, friendship, and hospitality and the inability to love.

Selfishness

Everyone is selfish in varying degrees. As little Georgy ironically writes in an essay. "An undue love of Self leads to the most monstrous crime and occasions the greatest misfortunes both in States and Families". The selfishness of characters like Becky, Jos Sedley, and Lord Steyne is obvious; however, even apparently selfless characters like Amelia, Dobbin, and Lady Jane are selfish.

Illusion and Reality

Is it possible to distinguish between illusion and reality?

Motivated by self-interest, the characters practice hypocrisy, they misrepresent themselves both to others and to themselves, and they lie. Some characters deliberately choose their illusions or fantasies over the truth. Thus, every character deludes others and/or is self-deluded does this pattern include the narrator?.

Heroism

Men and women are not heroic; the heroic poses and pretenses of characters, literature, and society are consistently deflated.

Fiction Versus Reality

The false portrayal of human nature and activities in novels, romance, and literary conventions is distinguished from real life. The subtitle, A Novel Without a Hero; Thackeray's identifying various characters as the hero or heroine; the marriages of Amelia and Becky early in the novel—all violate novelistic conventions. George Osborne parodies the conventional hero. Is Thackeray's shifting narrator a satire of the literary convention that "novelists know the truth about everything" ?

Married and Parental Relationships

In a novel of domestic life, there are no happy marriages because of the egotism, selfishness, folly, and false values of individuals and of society. Similarly, selfishness, vanity, snobbery, and/or materialism affect every child-parent relationship.

The Gentleman

Thackeray rejects the older concept of a gentleman as a man of rank and leisure, i.e., a member of the gentry or aristocracy. The true gentleman, as well as the true lady, is recognized by moral character, being considerate, benevolent, and diligent. Amelia, Lady Jane, and Dobbin are among the few real ladies and gentlemen in this novel.

Time

Thackeray's concern with time has caused him to be called the novelist of memory. The action is set in the past, and the narrator compares and contrasts the past with the present as he moves between them; occasionally he tells us a future event or outcome. The characters' memories of the past help to characterize them in the present. Thackeray shows the effect which the passage of time has on the characters. The concern with time is reflected in the structure; the narrator occasionally interrupts the chronology, jumps back in time, and returns to the point where he stopped the chronology.

Chapter 9

Short Summary of Vanity Fair

Vanity Fair by William Makepeace Thackeray

A FTER six years at Miss Pinkerton's school, Amelia Sedley went home, guaranteed a polished and refined young lady. Amelia was a dear little creature, all rosy health and bright good humour, though the silly thing would cry over a dead canary-bird or a mouse the cat had seized upon. She was accompanied by her dear friend, Becky Sharp, who was to make a short visit at the Sedley home before beginning her career of self-support as a governess.

Becky was small, pale, and sandy-haired, with eyes habitually cast down; when they looked up they were large, odd, and attractive. As Miss Sharp's father had been an artist and a drunkard, and her French mother an opera girl, it is not sur- prising that Rebecca asserted she had never been a girl-she had been a woman since she was eight years old.

At the Sedley home, Becky met Amelia's brother Joseph, a stout, puffy man, who wore buckskins and Hessian boots, several immense neckcloths, a red striped waistcoat, and an apple-green coat. He was lazy, peevish, a glutton, and a hard drinker, but Rebecca decided instantly to set her cap for him and began by whispering to Amelia, rather loud, "He's very handsome!" Rebecca's plans, however, were foiled by George Osborne, an admirer of Amelia, and Miss Sharp took her departure from the Sedley house.

She went to be governess in the home of Sir Pitt Crawley, which place, in her letters to Amelia, she dubbed Humdrum Hall. There were many Crawleys, the most important being

Sir Pitt's spinster sister, and his second son, Rawdon Crawley. The old lady possessed seventy thousand pounds, and had almost adopted Rawdon, who was her favourite nephew, while several members of the family fought to supplant him in her favour. Captain Rawdon Crawley was a large young dandy, who spoke with a great voice and swore a good deal. He remarked of the demure Rebecca, "By Jove, she's a neat little filly ! " and both he and his aunt took a decided fancy to the clever and fascinating little governess, though, indeed, she made conquest of pretty much whomsoever she chose.

Now we must flit back to London to see what has become of Miss Amelia. Far less interesting than Becky, and with nothing but her wax-doll face to recommend her, yet all the young men clustered round her chair and battled for a dance with her. She was now engaged to George Osborne, albeit his sisters wondered, "What could George find in that creature?" So much did they wonder this, that it affected George, and he concluded he was throwing himself away on the chit. But poor little Amelia adored him, and Captain Dobbin, who favored Amelia himself, kept Osborne up to the mark in his attentions. The infatuated girl cared nothing about the Napoleonic war that was raging, the fate of Europe was to her only Lieutenant George Osborne; while he, often away with his regiment, the Horse Guards, read her letters hastily, murmuring, "Poor little Emmy-how fond she is of me! and gad! what a headache that mixed punch has given me!"

About this time Miss Crawley returned from visiting her brother and brought back with her to her house in Park Lane no less a personage than Miss Rebecca Sharp, who, so well had she played her cards, was now Miss Crawley's much cherished companion. Whereupon Captain Rawdon Crawley be-came a frequent visitor at his aunt's home. Incidentally, Lady Crawley died-so incidentally that Miss Crawley merely said, pettishly, "I suppose I must put off my party for the third!" Immediately upon the death of his wife, Sir Pitt came to his sister's house and endeavored to retrieve his lost Becky as governess."I daren't. I don't think it would be right to be alone-with-you, sir," she replied, seemingly in great agitation.

"Come as Lady Crawley, then ! There, will that satisfy you?" and the vulgar, ill-bred old M. P. fell down on his knees and leered at her like a satyr. Rebecca, in real consternation at her lost chance, wept genuine tears, as she exclaimed, "Oh, Sir Pitt-oh, sir -I-I'm married already!"

When it further transpired that the bride-groom of Becky's secret marriage was the brass-spurred and long-mustachioed Captain Rawdon Crawley, there were two cataclysms, one in which Miss Crawley went from one fit of hysterics into another, and one where the frenzied old Sir Pitt went wild with hatred and insane with baffled desire. But the bridegroom captain remarked to his wife: "You're sure to get us out of the scrape, Beck. I never saw your equal, and I've met with some clippers in my time, too ! "

George Osborne, though dependent on his mercenary, low-bred father, despised him, and when the elder Osborne forbade George to marry our little Amelia the young man broke over the traces and married her out of hand. The marriage was egged on and managed by the faithful Dobbin; and, radiant in her straw bonnet with pink ribbons and a white-lace veil, little Emmy went off with her husband to Brighton for the honey-moon. Here they fell in with the Rawdon Crawleys. Becky, mistress of a fine establishment and surrounded by respectful admirers, was so adroit at wheedling tradesmen and standing off creditors, that she made it possible for them to maintain a fine social position on nothing a year.

Soon after this, among the brilliant train of camp-followers that hung around the Duke of Wellington's army, our friends were all in Brussels. George, now desperately infatuated with Becky, and neglecting his six weeks' wife shamefully, slipped a note in a bouquet at a ball, begging Becky to elope with him. But before the note was answered came the call to arms, and Lieu-tenant Osborne, forgetting all love and intrigue, kissed his Amelia and marched away-marched, alas ! to his death on the field of Waterloo.

Colonel Rawdon Crawley, promoted for gallantry, returned in triumph, and he and his wife passed the winter of 1815 in Paris in much splendor and gaiety. Becky's salon became famous, and great people hobnobbed there. Colonel Crawley's dexterity at cards and billiards became so marked that he constantly won from his guests, and under Becky's tutelage he became a clever and successful gambler, and thus aided in their fortune of nothing a year.

Amelia, now the widow of Osborne, and with a small son, Georgy, was in sad penury, her father-in-law refusing to see her at all, and her own father and mother dependent upon her. Becky, too, was the mother of a son, but she cared nothing for her child, nor for her husband; indeed, she so far forgot her wifely duty as to be guilty of an intrigue with the rich old Lord Stevne. Colonel Crawley discovered this, thrashed the nobleman, and left his wife. Then Becky, following her own devious ways, became an undisguised adventuress and neglected to care for her reputation. She bobbed about from one city to another, now hounded by creditors; now cared for by some rich admirer.

At last, when poor Becky had fallen very low in funds and in repute, she was found by Joseph Sedley and his sister Amelia. The old acquaintance was renewed, and gentle, generous Amelia took her one-time bosom friend into her heart and home. Major Dobbin strongly disapproved, and denounced Becky for what she was in her very presence. Amelia resented this, and Dobbin then begged Amelia, once again, to marry him-a plea he had often before made. On her refusal, Dobbin went off, vowing never to return, leaving Amelia alone with her fealty to her dead George. Whereupon, Becky, learning the state of things, told Amelia of George's note to her asking her to elope with him, and contrasting the faithless George most unfavorably with the patient and long-suffering Dobbin. So Amelia re-called Dobbin, married him, and they lived happy ever after.

Mrs. Rawdon Crawley then attached her-self to Joseph Sedley, though not by any legal bonds. He was her utter slave and insured his life heavily for her benefit-and benefit she did, for he died soon after.

Rawdon Crawley died, too, and the son Rawdon refused ever to see his mother again.

Rebecca lived at Bath or Cheltenham, where some excellent people considered her a most injured woman. She devoted her life to works of piety and charity, and though when she met Amelia and her husband once they turned quickly away, Becky only cast down her eyes demurely and smiled.

Vanitas vanitatum! Which of us is happy in this world? Let us shut up the box and the puppets-our play is played out.

Chapter 10

Summary and Commentaries

Chapters 1-4

Summary

Miss Amelia Sedley and Becky Sharp prepare to leave Chiswick Mall for Amelia's home. Miss Pinkerton, who runs the academy, autographs a copy of Dr. Johnson's dictionary for Amelia, whose father is rich. The orphaned Becky, having neither money nor position does not rate one.

Miss Pinkerton writes Amelia's mother a stilted and complimentary letter in regard to Amelia, and adds a postscript that Miss Sharp should stay only ten days, as she has a position in a family of distinction. With this tender missive, she includes Amelia's bill.

Miss Jemima, sister of Miss Pinkerton, tries to give Becky a dictionary, but Becky throws it into the garden as the girls' coach drives off. Everyone loves Amelia; no one cares for Becky. Becky's look of hatred and her vindictive smile as she hurls the book horrify Amelia. When Becky wishes that Miss Pinkerton were at the bottom of the Thames, Amelia remonstrates with her. Becky replies that revenge may be wicked, but it's natural.

Miss Pinkerton has taken Becky into the academy and given her free board and lodging, and the chance to learn what she can plus a few guineas a year. In return, Becky is to teach French. When Miss Pinkerton wants Becky to give free piano lessons, Becky defies and refuses. Becky hates Miss Pinkerton, ridicules her, feels no gratitude.

At night when Becky has walked the floor and sobbed, both she and her acquaintances think it is grief for her father, but actually it is resentment at being confined, without position or money. When Miss Pinkerton can stand Becky no longer, she secures a position for her with Sir Pitt Crawley.

Becky finds out that Amelia's brother, Joseph, is not married. She determines to marry him, if possible, and never go on to the Crawleys. Joseph's obesity, emphasized by his loud and sporty clothes, makes people think of an elephant. His shyness stymies his ambition to be a lady-killer. With affected dignity he extends two fingers for his sister to shake.

Becky makes an impression, saying aloud how handsome Joseph is, then acting "timid as a fawn," and casting her eyes down and not daring to look at him. Joseph, flushed with embarrassment, pulls the bell rope loose.

Mr. Sedley, an aggressive tease, comes in "rattling his seals like a true British merchant." He goads Joseph into taking Becky down to dinner and urges Becky to eat curry, which is very hot. While her mouth is afire, Joseph asks her if she wants a chili, which she thinks must be cool because of its name. Becky's near strangulation amuses Mr. Sedley and Joseph.

When Joseph absents himself for two or three days, Becky endears herself to the Sedley household. On the night Amelia, Becky, George Osborne, and Joseph plan to go to Vauxhall, it rains. They stay home, visit, sing, and reminisce. Joseph tells Rebecca stories about India and almost proposes to her; but food is served, and appetite and slumber come before the passion of love with Joseph, the Collector of Boggley Wollab. The next day when Joseph brings flowers, Becky gets him to hold her knitting yarn for her.

Commentary

The social strata and the situation in Vanity Fair are made clear. Miss Pinkerton, a snob and name-dropper, honors only those who have money and position. Thackeray outlines Becky's background and her position at Miss Pinkerton's, and reveals something of her temperament when she routs the old lady by speaking to her in French and by refusing to be intimidated. Her triumph over Miss Pinkerton indicates her ability to take care of herself. Thackeray's fine hand at characterization is apparent in this conversation.

Miss Pinkerton says, "I never have seen the individual who has dared in my own house to question my authority. I have nourished a viper in my bosom." Becky answers, "A viper—a fiddlestick... You took me because I was useful... Get me a situation—we hate each other and I am ready to go."

On the other hand, here is Rebecca being coy: "Starting back as timid as a fawn. She had previously made a respectful virgin-like curtsy to the gentleman, and her modest eyes gazed so perseveringly on the carpet that it was a wonder how she should have found an opportunity to see him."

The reader gets a view of Joseph—vain, overweight, bashful, and lonely in these ironic lines: "Being an invalid, Joseph Sedley contented himself with a bottle of claret, besides his madeira at dinner, and he managed a couple of plates full of strawberries and cream and twenty-four little rout cakes that were lying neglected in a plate near him."

The author makes particular fun of mothers anxious to marry off their daughters, and pities Becky who has no help in this area. From the first scene of this book, Thackeray begins his revelation and evaluation of the false values of Vanity Fair.

Chapters 5-7

Summary

This installment begins with a flashback about Dr. Swishtail's school. Students have snubbed William Dobbin because his father is a retail grocer. Dobbin has crossed Cuff, the bully of the school, when he tries to take Dobbin's letter away from him. Later Dobbin stops Cuff from beating George Sedley Osborne. In the ensuing fight young Dobbin defeats Cuff.

Dobbin's victory over Cuff has gained his acceptance by the students and the lifelong friendship of George Osborne. This history explains why George invites William, now of His Majesty's ____th Regiment of Foot, to the Sedley house the night of the party at Vauxhall. Dobbin's father has become a rich alderman, consequently he and his family are respected everywhere.

As the evening progresses, Becky catches George admiring himself in the mirror. Joseph Sedley assumes a courteous manner and opens the door with the "most killing grace." All three are actors in Vanity Fair.

Chapter 6 opens with the author making fun of writers. He then describes the evening at Vauxhall, when everyone thinks Joseph will propose to Becky. Mr. Sedley, contemptuous of his son, thinks Becky better than a black daughter-in-law. Amelia has discussed the affair with Mrs. Blenkinsop, the housekeeper, and everyone talks of Joseph's marriage. At Vauxhall, Dobbin carries the shawls; the others pair off. Joseph drinks too much and makes a fool of himself. George takes the girls home; Dobbin takes Joseph home.

The next day Joseph has a terrible hangover. George, Dobbin, and Sedley's valet make him think he has been a veritable lion the night before. Then Osborne tells him the truth, that he was maudlin and couldn't stand up. George mimics Joseph's treatment of Rebecca. George later tells Dobbin that he would rather have a lady for a sister-in-law, that Rebecca should know her station, and that Dobbin can make love to her. When George returns to Sedleys and says Joseph isn't coming, Becky recognizes that George is her enemy. Amelia sends a messenger to Joseph and finds he is ill.

On the arrival of Joseph's letter saying that he is leaving for Scotland, Rebecca knows she is beaten. Blenkinsop, the housekeeper, consoles Amelia by telling her that Becky has read Mrs. Sedley's mail and stolen a ribbon. In vain Amelia defends Rebecca. Everyone, except Amelia, knows it is time for Rebecca to go. On Amelia's insistence Mr. Sedley and George give Becky presents; she departs for the Crawleys, who are supposed to be of a higher status than the Sedleys.

Rebecca is trying to visualize a baronet, Sir Pitt Crawley, when they arrive at Great Gaunt Street. The coachman hates Rebecca because she does not tip and because Amelia has given her some dresses he hoped his girl friend would get. He tells the old fellow who is looking out of the Crawley's window to unload Becky's trunks. The old fellow who turns out to be Sir Pitt, the baronet, helps. Tinker, the housekeeper, and stingy Sir Pitt eat, but do not ask Becky to join them.

Rebecca tries in vain to get information from Tinker. The next morning Rebecca and Sir Pitt catch the stagecoach for Queen's Crawley.

Commentary

This installment begins with a flashback about Dr. Swishtail's school. Students have snubbed William Dobbin because his father is a retail grocer. Dobbin has crossed Cuff, the bully of the school, when he tries to take Dobbin's letter away from him. Later Dobbin stops Cuff from beating George Sedley Osborne. In the ensuing fight young Dobbin defeats Cuff.

Dobbin's victory over Cuff has gained his acceptance by the students and the lifelong friendship of George Osborne. This history explains why George invites William, now of His Majesty's ____th Regiment of Foot, to the Sedley house the night of the party at Vauxhall. Dobbin's father has become a rich alderman, consequently he and his family are respected everywhere.

As the evening progresses, Becky catches George admiring himself in the mirror. Joseph Sedley assumes a courteous manner and opens the door with the "most killing grace." All three are actors in Vanity Fair.

Chapter 6 opens with the author making fun of writers. He then describes the evening at Vauxhall, when everyone thinks Joseph will propose to Becky. Mr. Sedley, contemptuous of his son, thinks Becky better than a black daughter-in-law. Amelia has discussed the affair with Mrs. Blenkinsop, the housekeeper, and everyone talks of Joseph's marriage. At Vauxhall, Dobbin carries the shawls; the others pair off. Joseph drinks too much and makes a fool of himself. George takes the girls home; Dobbin takes Joseph home. The next day Joseph has a terrible hangover. George, Dobbin, and Sedley's valet make him think he has been a veritable lion the night before. Then Osborne tells him the truth, that he was maudlin and couldn't stand up. George mimics Joseph's treatment of Rebecca. George later tells Dobbin that he would rather have a lady for a sister-in-law, that Rebecca should know her station, and that Dobbin can make love to her. When George returns to Sedleys and says Joseph isn't coming, Becky recognizes that George is her enemy. Amelia sends a messenger to Joseph and finds he is ill.

On the arrival of Joseph's letter saying that he is leaving for Scotland, Rebecca knows she is beaten. Blenkinsop, the housekeeper, consoles Amelia by telling her that Becky has read Mrs. Sedley's mail and stolen a ribbon. In vain Amelia defends Rebecca. Everyone, except Amelia, knows it is time for Rebecca to go. On Amelia's insistence Mr. Sedley and George give Becky presents; she departs for the Crawleys, who are supposed to be of a higher status than the Sedleys.

Rebecca is trying to visualize a baronet, Sir Pitt Crawley, when they arrive at Great Gaunt Street. The coachman hates Rebecca because she does not tip and because Amelia has given her some dresses he hoped his girl friend would get. He tells the old fellow who is looking out of the Crawley's window to unload Becky's trunks. The old fellow who turns out to be Sir Pitt, the baronet, helps. Tinker, the housekeeper, and stingy Sir Pitt eat, but do not ask Becky to join them.

Rebecca tries in vain to get information from Tinker. The next morning Rebecca and Sir Pitt catch the stagecoach for Queen's Crawley.

Chapter 5 shows that snobbery begins early in Vanity Fair. Dobbin's schoolmates shun and laugh at him because his tuition is paid in goods. Osborne thinks himself better than Dobbin because Osborne's father is a gentleman and keeps a carriage. Even when Dobbin fights for Osborne, the latter is ashamed of him.

After Dobbin whips the bully, Dobbin improves in scholarship; his father, for the first time, respects him and publicly gives him money. Still snobbish as a young man, George says he doesn't want a governess for a sister-in-law.

Although he may have been joking when he suggests Becky is good enough for Dobbin, the reader may feel that George's real attitude toward Dobbin is condescension even though Dobbin's father is now a knighted alderman. Becky sees that George has prevented her marriage and "she loved George Osborne accordingly." Aside from Dobbin, the only admirable person so far is Amelia, and she appears too simple and innocent to be interesting.

Thackeray lets his characters reveal themselves by words. Mr. Sedley remarks that if all the family should die, Joseph would say, "Good Gad!" and go ahead with his dinner. Thackeray also shows them in action. "Jos squeezed through the gate into the gardens." Rebecca flirts with Joseph; when someone steps on her foot she falls "back with a little shriek into the arms of Mr. Sedley, and this little incident increased the tenderness and confidence of that gentleman to such a degree, that he told her several of his favourite Indian stories over again for, at least, the sixth time." Amelia looks "as happy as a rose-tree in sunshine." Thackeray points out that Rebecca cries only so long as the Sedleys can see her; she despises them now that she has failed to get Joseph.

Loathsome as Sir Pitt is, he has the refreshing characteristic of making no pretenses, and in this, he is something like Mr. Sedley. Both have enough money to scorn the opinion of society. Characteristic of Thackeray's frequent reversion to the essay, he begins Chapter 6 with rambling observations directed to the reader, telling how he might have changed the story; he closes the installment with a discourse on how times have changed.

Part of the conflict in Vanity Fair arises from the frantic, often questionable, struggle of all characters, except Dobbin, Amelia, and Briggs who will be introduced later to rise in social and financial power. Plot centers around conflict; Thackeray loses no opportunity to point out this struggle. He satirizes the naming of children after celebrities, and mentions the Crawley ancestor, the first baronet of the Tape and Sealing-Wax Office, who was impeached for embezzlement—as were other honest gentlemen.

Chapters 8-11

Summary

Rebecca writes to Amelia describing her sadness at their separation, relating in detail the coach trip, and ridiculing Sir Pitt. She describes the Crawley family, dwells on Sir Pitt's crudeness and stinginess, saying that he even counts the grapes on the vines. At the close of the letter, the author notes that Rebecca reveres only money and success. He says he will tell the truth, and it will not be beautiful.

After the death of his highbred first wife, Sir Pitt has married Rose Dawson, the daughter of an ironmonger. Rose, happy to be Lady Crawley, has given up the man she loved and the friends of her youth, as they cannot be received by one of her station. To her sorrow she finds that no one of her new rank will associate with her. Her only good quality, her beauty, soon fades; she continuously mourns its loss.

Young Pitt Crawley, a very correct person, is attentive to the schooling of the two Crawley girls, his half sisters. Rebecca is to be their governess.

The late Walpole Crawley, beloved by all for his drunkenness and hospitality, has left the family estate financially embarrassed because of a fine incurred for embezzlement. Sir Pitt is too stingy to hire honest workmen and is swindled by the dishonest. He buys cheap horses and loses them by starvation. He will not pay his debts, even those owed his son from the mother's estate. His rich half sister won't loan him money. However, he loves show and will not drive without four horses; and although he eats boiled mutton, he has three footmen to serve it.

Rebecca wins her way into the affections of those who count in this household. She asks Mr. Pitt to translate French for her, though she knows it better than he. She sighs and cries over his pious discourses and tells him she is descended from the Montmorency family, but omits the detail that her mother was an actress. Rebecca plays backgammon with Sir Pitt. She copies his letters, corrects his spelling, reads his law papers, learns about running the estate, and wins the baronet's confidence to the degree that he begins to depend on her advice. Sir Pitt's sons, Pitt and Rawdon, hate each other. Miss Crawley, the rich aunt, has sent Rawdon, her favourite, to Cambridge. After two years he is expelled, and she buys him a commission in the Life Guards Green where he is a dandy and fights duels. Pitt Crawley objects to visits from his rich aunt because he can't pray and read his sermons. She won't leave him money anyhow, having a weakness for Rawdon's wild, unorthodox, and radical ways, and calling Pitt a "puling hypocrite."

After his description of the honest folk at Queen's Crawley, Thackeray introduces the Reverend Bute Crawley, who bets on the races, boxes, eats, drinks, sings, fishes, follows the hounds, and is generally popular in the area. His wife writes his sermons, runs the house, and lets him go as he pleases, knowing every meal he eats elsewhere saves her money. Bute, in debt from a wild racing bet, thinks his rich sister must leave him half her money. Sir Pitt and Bute quarrel and spy on each other continually, but when their rich sister visits, they love each other and wait on her like toadies.

Snoopy Mrs. Bute writes Miss Pinkerton for information about Becky, and gets plenty. Rebecca writes Amelia about Humdrum Hall Queen's Crawley and of Rawdon and how he prefers to dance with her. Horrocks, the butler, tells Sir Pitt he thinks Becky a match for Rawdon, and the author adds, for Rawdon's father too.

The subject of Miss Matilda Crawley's death is hopefully discussed among her loving relatives who want her money. Chapter 11 comments on how people will pretend and flatter to get money.

The atmosphere at Queen's Crawley shows in the following conversation. Sir Pitt says, "How's Buty, Hodson? I'm afraid he's better, Sir Pitt."

Sir Pitt brags that there is timber worth six thousand pounds along his driveway and immediately has two little boys flogged for gathering sticks. Although Sir Pitt isn't fit for anything he can neither read nor spell, yet he is courted by ministers and statesmen. He rates high in Vanity Fair.

Part of the twist of Thackeray's plot is that the always correct and stuffy Pitt Crawley, who frowns on his half sisters' laughter, who will neither let them play cards nor escape household prayers at ten, is the instrument of introducing Becky into the household.

Often the author intrudes to tell the reader what to think. He says this installment is mild, but that he must tell things as he sees them. Rebecca is bad. Some people are "Faithless, Hopeless, Charityless: let us have at them, dear friends, with might and main. Some there are, and very successful too, mere quacks and fools; and it was to combat and expose such as those, no doubt, that Laughter was made." With cutting sarcasm Thackeray points out the foibles of a noble family. Miss Crawley is well treated "for she had a balance at her banker's which would have made her beloved anywhere."

Thackeray wishes someone would send him a rich old aunt, whom he would treat with all kindness, money being all-important in Vanity Fair. He says, "I, for my part, have known a five-pound note to interpose and knock up a half-century's attachment between two brethren; and can't but admire, as I think what a fine and durable thing Love is among worldly people." And he adds, "What a charming reconciler and peacemaker money is."

Following the publication of the preceding chapters, some readers wrote that they could see nothing in Amelia. Thackeray says this is the greatest compliment one woman can pay another. With men around, no woman gives another credit for anything. The Osborne girls are jealous of their brother. Miss Maria Osborne's special friend, Mr. Bullock, has danced with Amelia, which attention makes Maria jealous, although she pretends joy.

Osborne is humiliated by the way his fellow soldiers kid him about Amelia's letters. He horrifies Dobbin by lighting his cigar with one. Dobbin hears the men gossiping about Osborne's wild life. Irate, he tells them Osborne is engaged to Miss Sedley. When this revelation angers George, Dobbin asks him if he is ashamed of his engagement. Osborne says he doesn't want his business to be everybody's business and he wants his little fling. Dobbin begs him to make Amelia happy, and Osborne says he will take her a present. Dobbin loans him money, but Osborne buys himself a diamond shirt-pin.

Delighted to see Osborne, Amelia doesn't think of gifts. She has been picturing him tending wounded or performing other rigorous duties. Amelia thinks Lieutenant Osborne the most wonderful man in the world and he agrees with her. She visits the Osborne home in Russell Square. Old Osborne comes home in bad humour, sees Amelia there, glares at her, and complains about the meal.

When George comes home late for supper, his father tells him he can't marry Amelia unless she has ten thousand pounds, and the elder Osborne suspects Sedley's financial condition is shaky. He promises George money, as he wants him to go about in good society, which he believes can do no wrong, but he insists that George must never gamble. Relieved that his father hasn't heard of some of his activities, George seems reconciled to break with Amelia, but he does not tell her. The scene shifts to Matilda Crawley's home, where Miss Sharp has come home with Miss Crawley to care for her. Rawdon Crawley suddenly becomes much interested in his aunt's health and visits her often. All of the Crawleys are afraid that Miss Matilda will get well. Rawdon loves Rebecca and "raves about her in uncouth convulsions." Sir Pitt raves because she has left his household.

When Miss Matilda is well enough, Becky takes her to visit Amelia. Miss Crawley likes Amelia and invites her and George Osborne to her home. George tries to patronize Rebecca, but she squelches him by asking what his grandfather did, then reassuring him that he can't help his pedigree.

In the meantime Lady Crawley dies, unmourned except by her stepson, Pitt Crawley, who has been her sole comfort. Almost immediately after her death, Sir Pitt comes to Miss Crawley's house and proposes to Becky, who has to refuse because she is already married.

The atmosphere at Queen's Crawley shows in the following conversation. Sir Pitt says, "How's Buty, Hodson? I'm afraid he's better, Sir Pitt."

Sir Pitt brags that there is timber worth six thousand pounds along his driveway and immediately has two little boys flogged for gathering sticks. Although Sir Pitt isn't fit for anything he can neither read nor spell, yet he is courted by ministers and statesmen. He rates high in Vanity Fair.

Part of the twist of Thackeray's plot is that the always correct and stuffy Pitt Crawley, who frowns on his half sisters' laughter, who will neither let them play cards nor escape household prayers at ten, is the instrument of introducing Becky into the household.

Often the author intrudes to tell the reader what to think. He says this installment is mild, but that he must tell things as he sees them. Rebecca is bad. Some people are "Faithless, Hopeless, Charityless: let us have at them, dear friends, with might and main. Some there are, and very successful too, mere quacks and fools; and it was to combat and expose such as those, no doubt, that Laughter was made." With cutting sarcasm Thackeray points out the foibles of a noble family. Miss Crawley is well treated "for she had a balance at her banker's which would have made her beloved anywhere."

Thackeray wishes someone would send him a rich old aunt, whom he would treat with all kindness, money being all-important in Vanity Fair. He says, "I, for my part, have known a five-pound note to interpose and knock up a half-century's attachment between two brethren; and can't but admire, as I think what a fine and durable thing Love is among worldly people." And he adds, "What a charming reconciler and peacemaker money is."

Chapters 12-14

Summary

Following the publication of the preceding chapters, some readers wrote that they could see nothing in Amelia. Thackeray says this is the greatest compliment one woman can pay another. With men around, no woman gives another credit for anything. The Osborne girls are jealous of their brother. Miss Maria Osborne's special friend, Mr. Bullock, has danced with

Amelia, which attention makes Maria jealous, although she pretends joy. Osborne is humiliated by the way his fellow soldiers kid him about Amelia's letters. He horrifies Dobbin by lighting his cigar with one. Dobbin hears the men gossiping about Osborne's wild life.

Irate, he tells them Osborne is engaged to Miss Sedley. When this revelation angers George, Dobbin asks him if he is ashamed of his engagement. Osborne says he doesn't want his business to be everybody's business and he wants his little fling. Dobbin begs him to make Amelia happy, and Osborne says he will take her a present. Dobbin loans him money, but Osborne buys himself a diamond shirt-pin. Delighted to see Osborne, Amelia doesn't think of gifts.

She has been picturing him tending wounded or performing other rigorous duties. Amelia thinks Lieutenant Osborne the most wonderful man in the world and he agrees with her. She visits the Osborne home in Russell Square. Old Osborne comes home in bad humour, sees Amelia there, glares at her, and complains about the meal. When George comes home late for supper, his father tells him he can't marry Amelia unless she has ten thousand pounds, and the elder Osborne suspects Sedley's financial condition is shaky. He promises George money, as he wants him to go about in good society, which he believes can do no wrong, but he insists that George must never gamble. Relieved that his father hasn't heard of some of his activities, George seems reconciled to break with Amelia, but he does not tell her.

The scene shifts to Matilda Crawley's home, where Miss Sharp has come home with Miss Crawley to care for her. Rawdon Crawley suddenly becomes much interested in his aunt's health and visits her often. All of the Crawleys are afraid that Miss Matilda will get well. Rawdon loves Rebecca and "raves about her in uncouth convulsions." Sir Pitt raves because she has left his household.

When Miss Matilda is well enough, Becky takes her to visit Amelia. Miss Crawley likes Amelia and invites her and George Osborne to her home. George tries to patronize Rebecca, but she squelches him by asking what his grandfather did, then reassuring him that he can't help his pedigree. In the meantime Lady Crawley dies, unmourned except by her stepson, Pitt Crawley, who has been her sole comfort. Almost immediately after her death, Sir Pitt comes to Miss Crawley's house and proposes to Becky, who has to refuse because she is already married.

Commentary

This number starts with biting comment on women and their relationship to each other. "To be despised by her sex is a very great compliment to a woman." Lady Crawley "showed her friendship by abusing all her intimate acquaintances to her new confidante than which there can't be a more touching proof of regard." Rich people like Lady Crawley take needy people's services as their due. Even Rawdon realizes that his aunt Mrs Bute Crawley is trying to entangle him with Rebecca so that she won't become the third wife of Sir Pitt.

Of Amelia's blind love for George Thackeray says that she doesn't care about the war in Europe but when Napoleon abdicates she throws herself into George's arms because he won't have to go overseas. "The fate of Europe was Lieutenant George Osborne to her." The Misses Osborne do not know such tender passion as does Amelia, and they think her stupid and without charm.

Becky, also in contrast to Amelia, weeps "some of the most genuine tears that ever fell from her eyes," when she has to refuse the proposal of the rich Sir Pitt.

Thackeray contrasts George and William. George reveals himself when he lights his cigars with Amelia's letters, buys himself a pin with money borrowed to get Amelia a present, and wants to sow wild oats. In one thought he observes how much Amelia loves him and how dreadfully his head aches from the wine. By his conduct William betrays his feeling for Amelia and the loyalty of his character. Even though his mouth is full, he bursts out at mealtime in defence of Miss Sedley. He loans George money to buy Amelia a gift, worries about her, and interrogates George as to his intentions.

A minor character, Mrs. Major O'Dowd, manager and

meddler, thinks George an elegant fellow; but when she hears he is engaged, she writes her sister Glorvina not to come for a visit. Peggy O'Dowd's recurring and amusing attempts to marry off Glorvina will appear throughout the book.

Conflict arises between William and George because of George's neglect of Amelia. Conflict arises between George and his father because Amelia's fortune has vanished, and with it her charm, so far as the elder Osborne is concerned.

In an earlier chapter the reader has seen George ruin Rebecca's chances to marry Joseph; now he sees George repaid by Rebecca's generous assurance that he can't help his pedigree.

Chapters 15-18

Summary

The mystery of Becky's refusal of Sir Pitt, her consequent embarrassment and tears, the deepening attachment of Miss Crawley's household for the poor child, start this number off with excitement. The author shows the pace by an essay on the probability of a gentleman's marrying a maidservant. "If people only made prudent marriages, what a stop to population there would be!"

Becky begins work on plans for her own and Rawdon's future. When she joins Rawdon, Mrs. Bute Crawley moves in on Miss Crawley. Sir Pitt returns and, finding out about Becky and Rawdon, goes into a rage.

Now the author begins a dissertation about attending sales. He takes the reader to the auction of the Sedley estate and gives details of the varied reactions of people at a sale. When Jos Sedley hears of his father's business failure, he tells his parents to draw on his agents for money, and then continues his way unconcerned.

At the sale Becky buys a picture of Joseph, and Dobbin buys Amelia's piano and sends it to her. Meanwhile Miss Crawley has not come through with money for Rawdon, who wishes for a few card games with George to replenish his cash. Rawdon realizes that Mrs. Bute is poisoning Miss Crawley's mind, but he does not regret his marriage; Becky humors him and makes him happy. At this point an essay shows how Napoleon's actions affect little Amelia Sedley's happiness. Napoleon's activities are blamed for Mr. Sedley's failure and the subsequent breaking up of the Sedley household, the rupture with the Osbornes, and the attempt by old Osborne to break George's attachment to Amelia.

Although all the gossips of Vanity Fair agree that Amelia does not merit George, William Dobbin defends her. At first George has little interest in the misfortunes of the Sedleys; but when he realizes that Amelia may be out of reach, his interest reawakens.

Commentary

Everyone in Miss Crawley's household is putting on an act. Rebecca schemes how she and Rawdon can win forgiveness from Sir Pitt and Miss Crawley.

There is humour in Miss Crawley's hurrying up to see Sir Pitt on his knees; she is bewildered at Rebecca's refusal and tears. Thackeray says Rebecca "wept there so naturally that the old lady, surprised into sympathy, embraced her with an almost maternal kindness... I am sure our friend Becky's disappointment deserves and will command every sympathy."

The irony of Vanity Fair is that the people pretend to feel emotions until their pocketbooks, passions, or family names are touched; then they revert to savagery. The worship of money shows in Mrs. Bute Crawley's taking charge of the household ostensibly to protect Miss Crawley, actually to get her money. The worship of name and position shows in the horror the Crawleys feel because Rawdon has married a governess. Becky's friends say her mother was of a fine French family; her enemies say she was an opera girl. However, if a person has money, like Sir Pitt, he may marry whomever he likes, and the family will conceal its disapproval.

Many incidents of this stage of the story will figure later in the plot: the purchase of Jos' picture by Becky; Dobbin's purchase of the piano for Amelia; the Osborne reaction to Sedley's failure; Rawdon's willingness to live on nothing. William Dobbin, "the uproused British lion," brings about the reconciliation of George and Amelia and sets the stage for further developments. George, having neglected to find out what has happened to Amelia, feels shame for having forgotten her. Selfish as he is, he can feel embarrassment over his own cruelty. However, as the reader will see, he does not stop being selfish.

Chapters 19-22

Summary

Summary Commentary Thackeray contrasts Mrs. Bute Crawley's flattery of the servants with Rawdon's blunt treatment, and concludes that soft words take a person further than unkind ones. Mrs. Bute Crawley establishes herself in Miss Crawley's house, makes friends of Firkin and Briggs, and digs in for battle, suspecting that Rawdon will try for reconciliation. Mrs. Bute wants to protect Miss Crawley "from the arts of those unprincipled people." Mrs. Bute makes such a fuss over Miss Crawley's illness that she frightens the poor woman. Thackeray observes that the tinsel of Vanity Fair does not persist in the lonely hours of illness and sorrow.

Mrs. Bute would like to convert Miss Crawley and starts out by making her hate all of Rawdon's sins. Thackeray observes that one's relatives can abuse one's reputation worse than anyone else. By making Rawdon and Rebecca as disreputable as possible, Mrs. Bute hopes to prevent Miss Crawley's ever seeing Rawdon again.

But Mrs. Bute is over-jealous and over-zealous. The doctor insists that Miss Crawley have some fresh air. Her guardian is afraid Miss Crawley will see Rawdon and forgive him, although what Mrs. Bute says is that the sight of him will kill the invalid. Dr. Squill and Mr. Clump see through Mrs. Bute's machinations. As for the patient, she hates Mrs. Bute and would like to be free of her. One day Mrs. Bute and Miss Crawley meet Rawdon, but Miss Crawley doesn't speak; triumphant for the moment, Mrs. Bute sees danger in future meetings. Meanwhile Dobbin helps Amelia and George marry. George, touched by Amelia's sorrow and devotion, is willing to marry her in spite of her loss of fortune and feels himself quite generous. Both fathers oppose the marriage, but Mr. Sedley becomes reconciled when he thinks that the match will make Osborne furious.

Old Osborne wants George to marry Miss Swartz, the rich "Black Princess." He thinks he can starve George into the marriage by withholding money, but if George marries Amelia, his father will disinherit him. Miss Swartz doesn't know what old Osborne has in mind, but she thinks George attractive. George is praising Amelia when his father comes in, eyes afire, but George outglares him, goes back to Dobbin and tells him that he has broken with his father and that he will marry Amelia the next day, which he does. The scene shifts to Brighton where Joseph, Rawdon, and George watch the crowd and the sea. Rawdon makes a little cash by gambling with Jos. Dobbin, coming in on the coach, is welcomed by everyone. He says he has seen old Osborne but does not reveal what the old man has said. He asks about Amelia, then shocks them all by saying they're ordered to Belgium.

Commentary

Thackeray leaves no doubt of Mrs. Bute's motivations in regard to Miss Crawley's money; but greed is nothing new in

Vanity Fair. Commenting on how much his sisters think of Miss Swartz, George tells Amelia, "My dear child, they would have loved you if you had had two hundred thousand pounds."

Thackeray says, "I know some respectable people who don't consider themselves at liberty to indulge in friendship for any individual who has not a certain competency, or place in society... People in Vanity Fair fasten on to rich folks quite naturally."

The action of the story is forwarded by the marriage of George and Amelia, their removal to Brighton, their meeting with Becky and Rawdon who are in Brighton because Miss Crawley is there, and the final orders for Belgium. William Dobbin reveals himself not only capable of suffering for Amelia and stimulating George to honorable actions, but of feeling shame and remorse for Mr. Sedley and his desolation.

Thackeray points out other practices in Vanity Fair: "I knew once a gentleman, and very worthy practitioner in Vanity Fair, who used to do little wrongs to his neighbours on purpose, and in order to apologize for them in an open and manly way afterwards—and what ensued? My friend Crocky Doyle was liked everywhere, and deemed to be rather impetuous—but the honestest fellow."

"How well those live who are comfortably and thoroughly in debt... Long custom, a manly appearance, faultless boots and clothes, and a happy fierceness of manner, will often help a man as much as a great balance at the banker's."

Chapters 23-25

Summary

An essay on friendship explains why Dobbin is so bold for George's interest, whereas he does nothing for himself. In time, now, the reader goes back to Dobbin before his arrival in Brighton.

Dobbin's nervous behaviour when he has visited Russell Square has made Miss Lane Osborne think that he is about to propose to her. Finally, Dobbin has come out with the news about George's and Amelia's marriage. When Frederick Bullock hears this, he rejoices because he thinks Maria will inherit more, and when he points out this possibility to the sisters, they rise in their own esteem.

Dobbin has gone to inform Mr. Osborne of George's marriage and has suggested that any differences between father and son should be straightened out because the regiment has been ordered to the Continent. Mr. Osborne, however, has refused reconciliation and has disinherited George. While Dobbin prepares to go to Brighton, Miss Jane waits in vain for his return. Alone with George in Brighton, Dobbin gives him a letter from old Osborne stating that he is cut off with two thousand pounds from his mother's estate. George blames Dobbin for the outcome and says, "A beggar, by Jove, and all in consequence of my d—d sentimentality." Finally George gets through berating Dobbin for being instrumental in bringing about the marriage and forgives him.

Rebecca outshines Amelia in every way. She charms George, in fact all the men except honest Dobbin. When Rebecca tells George how she plans to trap Briggs for a talk, George's laugh upsets Amelia, who goes off whimpering, feeling she has lost George. When she questions her husband she finds out about his disinheritance and feels better, thinking that money is their only problem and that George is worried about her. In varying degrees of excitement and anxiety the principal characters prepare to go to Brussels.

The scene shifts back to Miss Crawley. Becky has talked to Briggs and discovered that all the servants rebel against Mrs. Bute's dictatorship. Fortunately, the Reverend Bute breaks his collar bone and his wife has to go home; this is the opportunity that the Rawdon Crawleys have wished for. Immediately they write to Miss Crawley, but she laughs at their letter and sees through their designs. She does, however, agree to meet Rawdon by himself, at which interview he gains a token twenty pounds. Becky laughs at his unhappiness; he has hoped for two hundred.

Commentary Thackeray's humour shows as he describes William trying to break the news of George's marriage to Miss

Jane Osborne, while she thinks he is trying to propose. Turning to irony he shows Mr. Bullock in his visit with the Osborne sisters: "A delightful throb of expectation lighted up his little eyes, and caused him to smile on his Maria, as he thought that by this piece of folly of Mr. George's she might be worth thirty thousand pounds more." And the Osborne sisters, when Fred points out the possibilities of money, "had risen not a little in their own esteem." Thackeray says this respect for money is human, that children follow the one who has the money, the candy, or the possessions.

After Dobbin breaks the news of George's marriage to Mr. Osborne, the latter scratches George's name out of the family Bible. If there is a chance of reconciliation, Dobbin loses it by not proposing to Miss Jane. Old Osborne is agreeable so long as he gets his own way—that is, he is friendly to Dobbin until he realizes he can't manage him. Osborne rules his household with a "loud grating pompous voice." Thackeray has shown Osborne's character through his actions.

The action now moves away from Brighton toward Brussels. Both George and Rawdon are disappointed in their money settlements: George with two thousand and Rawdon twenty. This blocking of hope creates tensions in the plot. Her mind only on George, Amelia begins to suspect Becky, but does not blame George. He has been noble, Amelia thinks, to marry her.

With a cold appraising eye, Becky sees her companions clearly and fears only the honest Dobbin. She displays her forethought by sending the family possessions on ahead, when it is not certain Rawdon will have money to pay lodgings, and by taking a devious route through London to avoid previous creditors. Becky is skillful in finding out the family secrets by choosing the same apothecary as Miss Crawley, and too skillful in helping Rawdon write the letter to his aunt. Becky's mind, constantly on one goal—a booth in Vanity Fair—searches for opportunities to advance. Although Becky is the villainess, the reader will admire her resourcefulness, her intelligence, and her unfailing drive toward her goal. Those who already have a place in Vanity Fair, like the Osborne sisters, display negative natures most of the time, which do not arouse interest like the wicked but positive Becky. Death lies outside Vanity Fair. Of the approaching death of Aunt Crawley, Thackeray writes, "The last scene of her dismal Vanity Fair comedy was fast approaching; the tawdry lamps were going out one by one; and the dark curtain was almost ready to descend."

Chapters 26-29

Summary This installment begins with a description of the style of living practiced by George and Amelia. When Amelia wants to visit her mother, George goes to the theater. Here Thackeray interposes an essay on mothers.

Amelia, married nine days, feels apprehensive rather than happy. "Something which, when obtained, brought doubt and sadness rather than pleasure... harmless lost wanderer in the great struggling crowds of Vanity Fair." George gets his money from his father's solicitor; the clerks there prophesy no good end for him. Certain that the outcome of the war will be good, George sends Amelia out to buy dresses and gimcracks. Dobbin's fine military appearance causes Jos to feel friendly, and George's regiment thinks more highly of him after meeting his attractive wife. Mrs. O'Dowd takes Amelia under her protection and begins to connive how she can marry Glorvina to Jos. As usual she talks about Ireland.

The regiment departs for Belgium, Jos and the ladies following in grand style. Jos' pseudo-military appearance makes a great impression, the impression he desires. The gaiety of Brussels with its gambling, feasting, and dancing, entertains Amelia until Crawley's regiment arrives. For reasons she cannot define, Amelia's heart fails.

With the coming of the Rawdon Crawleys, the banterings and courtesies so often a prelude to love begin between George and Becky. Though Amelia does not understand exactly why, she is unhappy. Meanwhile, Becky also plays up to General Tufto. Dobbin tries to persuade George to quit gambling. At a brilliant ball, George, enamored of Becky, leaves a note in her bouquet. Wretched and depressed, Amelia has gone home to bed. That night the marching orders come. George, overcome by remorse, wishes he hadn't flirted with Becky, hadn't wounded Amelia, hadn't spent money so recklessly, nor quarreled with his father. In shame and remorse, he embraces Amelia.

Commentary With such an interrelated play of characters in this section, the reader will find it simpler to regard each individual without concern for chronology. Amelia's viewpoint is not that of Vanity Fair; her happiness is centered neither in turtle soup nor pompous show. "Love has been her faith hitherto... took her opinions from those people who surrounded her, such fidelity being much too humble-minded to think for itself." Later the author calls her a parasite. Popular with the regiment, Amelia blossoms until Becky comes, begins flirting with George, and shows even the gentle Amelia that Becky cannot be trusted.

Even minor characters reflect Vanity Fair. The valet is ashamed of Amelia's address. Greed appears in Bullock, whose "yellow face was over a ledger... happened to be in the banking room when George entered. His yellow face turned to a more deadly colour... " The family of Bareacres "flung off that happy frigidity and insolence of demeanour which occasionally characterizes the great at home... and... condescended to mingle with the rest of the company whom they met there... 'we needn't know them in England, you know.'"

A true son of Vanity Fair, George insists that Amelia attend the O'Dowd party, although he is ashamed of Mrs. O'Dowd. He cultivates the Lady Bareacres, who will cut him if she ever sees him in London. Later George boasts to Rawdon of his friendship with the Bareacres and tolerates Mrs O'Dowd because she keeps Amelia out of his way. He lets the General assume that he George Osborne is of the Peciage Osbornes. He feels himself kind because he lets Amelia buy new clothes

But George has better moments When the call to battle comes he regrets his involvement with Becky: "Oh how he wishes that night's work undone! and that with a clear conscience... he might say farewell to the tender and guileless being by whose love he has set such little store."

Another loyal citizen of Vanity Fair, Joseph is proud to

speak to Dobbin when the latter appears important in military uniform. Joseph assumes an air of authority, gives out military information and bravado. He likes the Belgian servant to call him "my lord."

The plot moves forward when Becky conquers General Tufto and begins to flirt with George. Meanwhile she hoodwinks her husband, who condones his wife's behaviour and thinks himself too dull for her.

Rawdon shows his better qualities by friendliness to the Osbornes when they first arrive—Becky barely nods—and by talking to Amelia when she is otherwise neglected.

Becky hints at her Montmorency ancestry, criticizes Amelia, works at climbing toward that booth in Vanity Fair. It makes no difference that Amelia is the victim. "Women only know how to wound so. There is a poison on the tips of their little shafts, which stings a thousand times more than a man's blunter weapon. Our poor Emmy, who had never hated, never sneered all her life, was powerless in the hands of her remorseless little enemy."

To reinforce the wholesome character of Amelia, as opposed to Becky, Thackeray brings in Dobbin, the foil for George and Joseph. Dobbin befriends Amelia, tries to influence George to stop gambling, and acts as a balance wheel for tfle whole group. Dobbin, undoubtedly, is the hero of the novel, but since this is Vanity Fair, Thackeray points out that Dobbin's feet are too big; he has neither the physical charm nor the duplicity required of the dwellers in Vanity Fair.

Chapters 30-32

Summary

This section opens with the O'Dowds discussing the forthcoming battle and making preparations for the major's march. After his departure Mrs. O'Dowd reads a book of sermons.

Rawdon, more affected than Becky at their parting, shows his love and worship for her by his concern for her welfare. "She had known perpetually how to divert him; and he had found his house and her society a thousand times more pleasant than any place or company..." Becky's thought, however, concerns how much security she has and what she can do in the event Rawdon doesn't come back.

George tells Amelia goodbye, and departs with a sigh of relief. Dobbin wakes the sleepy Jos to charge him to take care of Amelia, and is pained by Amelia's grief.

Joseph, proud to be left in charge of the women, reassures them. Isidor, his valet, hopes the British will be defeated so he can have Jos' possessions. As if to further his interests, he demoralizes Jos with bad news.

Becky, wanting to make sure of a retreat in case of bad news, flatters Jos by begging him not to go and join the troops, to stay and protect the ladies. If Jos has a carriage, Becky expects to share it should flight become necessary.

Amelia finally accuses Rebecca of being a false friend and a false wife. In spite of Amelia's accusations, Rebecca, touched at her grief, tries to reassure her. Since Amelia, obviously, doesn't want Becky around, Becky suggests to Peggy O'Dowd that she stay. Peggy, not liking Becky, answers with sarcasm, but she stays with Amelia.

Suddenly the sound of cannons frightens everyone. Jos wants to flee; Mrs. O'Dowd scorns his cowardice. The cook's soldier-friend comes with the tale that George's company is cut in pieces. Terrified, Jos gives the eager Isidor his military-looking coat and dresses himself in somber civilian garb so that he looks almost like a clergyman. Lady Bareacres wants to leave but has no horses for her carriage. She tries to buy Rebecca's but receives only scorn; instead, Rebecca sells her horses to the fearful Jos for a fortune.

Amelia wants to go to the army and begs Jos to take her. However, her attention is diverted by the arrival of the wounded ensign, Tom Stubble, who announces that George is safe. Peggy and Amelia nurse Tom Stubble.

Convinced by the rumors of English defeat, Jos rides off, leaving Amelia behind. Becky thinks Amelia stupid to grieve over George. She dreams of what she might do if Rawdon doesn't come back: She might become a duchess. Mrs. O'Dowd watches her patient, reads sermons, mispronounces words, and prays for the Major. Again the cannons roar. George finally dies in the battle of Waterloo.

Commentary The reader will notice a striking contrast in the reaction of the women whose husbands are called to battle. Peggy O'Dowd, completely devoted to army life, prepares her husband's things, gives him coffee and sweets. Amelia, stricken, can do nothing. Becky figures up her financial status, but shows some kind of loyalty to Amelia.

Rawdon's better self shows in that he, "who had seldom thought about anything but himself, until the last few months of his life, when Love had obtained the mastery over the dragoon... went off on his campaign with a kit as modest as that of a sergeant, and with something like a prayer on his lips for the woman he was leaving."

The action in this section shows Jos left in charge, Amelia's prostration, her final accusation of Rebecca, Rebecca's flattery of and power over Jos.

Jos' character shows in his love for eating, his susceptibility to Rebecca's flattery, his brave talk, and his actual cowardice. These traits will lead to the final complication and resolution of the Becky-Joseph relationship. The author excuses Jos' susceptibility: "From Solomon downwards, have not wiser men than he been cajoled and befooled by women?"

But in defence of women Thackeray says; "It was the women's tribute to the war. It taxes both alike, and takes the blood of the men, and the tears of the women."

Tongue-in-cheek, the author makes this comment on Vanity Fair, that when the cannon was heard, "even great English lords and ladies condescended to speak to persons whom they did not know."

Chapters 33-35

Summary

Back in England Miss Crawley hears about Rawdon and thinks what a good marriage for money he could have made. Rawdon, through Rebecca, sends his aunt gifts from the battlefield and anecdotes—both the product of Becky's imagination.

At Queen's Crawley, Miss Horrocks, the butler's daughter, accompanies Sir Pitt as he goes about drinking with all the common people. Sir Pitt's relatives hear about his activities with disgust.

All the family send tokens of love to Miss Crawley. Pitt frequents Brighton courts Lady Jane Sheepshanks, and tells Countess Southdown, Lady Jane's mother, of the advantages there would be in Miss Crawley's friendship. The countess immediately plans to convert the old lady and to dose her with medicine. Pitt restrains his future mother-in-law by cautioning gentleness, lest Aunt Crawley be offended, mentioning that she has seventy thousand pounds. The countess agrees to moderation. Briggs gives a favorable report about Pitt and Lady Jane to Miss Crawley, who invites them to visit her, whereupon Lady Jane wins the old lady's heart.

Mrs. Bute has made the fatal mistake of boring Miss Crawley. In a last attempt to court her favour, the Bute Crawleys send their son James to visit the rich aunt. Encouraged by the double-crossing Pitt, James drinks too much, makes a fool of himself, and finally smokes a pipe in the house. Miss Crawley invites him to leave.

Meanwhile Becky and Rawdon live in Paris in splendor on the money Rebecca has received from Jos for the horses. Proud of Becky's business ability, Rawdon "believed in his wife as much as the French soldiers in Napoleon." One of the French ladies writes Miss Crawley about Rebecca, so "soon to be a mother." "To hear her speak of you, her protectress, her mother, would bring tears to the eyes of ogres. How she loves you! How we all love our admirable, our respectable, Miss Crawley!"

The letter angers Miss Crawley because she thinks Rebecca has used her name to get into French society. She writes to the French lady, who doesn't understand English and can't read the letter. In turn the French lady reports a fine letter from Miss Crawley, and the hopes of the Rawdon Crawleys rise.

On March 26, 1816, Becky has a son. When Miss Crawley

hears of it, she instructs Pitt to marry Lady Jane, declaring that she will leave them her money. War news brings to the Osbornes the shock of George's death. Old Osborne tries to think the death a judgment on the boy for disobedience. Bowed under the weight of the fact that there is no chance now for reconciliation, old Osborne can neither forgive nor receive an apology. Three weeks after George's death, Sir William Dobbin calls on Mr. Osborne with a note George has written before dawn on the day of the battle. George asks protection for his wife and child and thanks his father for his former kindness.

The first indication that old Osborne has even thought about George comes in the special monument that appears in the church about two months later. Then Mr. Osborne goes to visit the battleground and his son's burial place. When he meets Amelia, he does not speak; he blames her for everything. Dobbin tries to reason with him and says he has a message from George. Old Osborne will not make any provision for his grandchild.

Amelia has nearly lost her sanity at the news of George's death but recovers when little George is born. Dobbin takes her to her mother in England. For a while he stays near and visits Amelia daily, then he rejoins his regiment.

Commentary

As usual the topic of discussion and chief preoccupation of Vanity Fair is MONEY. Miss Crawley thinks of how Rawdon might have married a brewer's daughter with a quarter of a million. Miss Crawley's relatives try to keep in her favour by sending tokens of affection. Later when Countess Southdown is eager to convert and cure Miss Crawley, Pitt says, "Remember she has seventy thousand pounds; think of her age, and her highly nervous and delicate condition: I know that she has destroyed the will which was made in my brother's favour: it is by soothing that wounded spirit that we must lead it into the right path, and not by frightening it..."

The author adds, "Lady Southdown, we say, for the sake of the invalid's health, or for the sake of her soul's ultimate welfare, or for the sake of her money, agreed to temporize."

Pitt Crawley reveals diplomacy and duplicity in getting rid of James. In calling him Machiavel, Thackeray has hinted at his double dealing. Pitt uses psychology and charm on Miss Briggs, and he wins the inheritance. As Bute Crawley says to his wife, "You are a clever woman, but you manage too well, you know." She has outmanaged herself.

Thackeray says of Lady Jane's character and attachment to Miss Crawley, "The young lady herself had never received kindness except from this old spinster, and her brother and father: and she repaid Miss Crawley's engollement by artless sweetness and friendship." This reflects the author's opinion of Lady Jane's tract-scattering, medicine-dosing mother.

Rebecca has shown by this time that she can make money and spend it. She can also climb into society. As for Amelia, her only friend is Dobbin, but she neither realizes nor appreciates his devotion.

Old Osborne, still convinced he is right, refuses any help to Amelia or little George.

The reader will remember that it was at Pitt's insistence that some education be provided for his half sisters, and as a result, Becky came into the Crawley family. Although Pitt has many selfish characteristics, this motive, at least, was generous. In spite then, of all the unworthy motives he has, Pitt does inherit Aunt Crawley's money. Whether, in the long analysis, he is a better man than Rawdon, the reader must decide.

At the end of this section, the inheritance of Miss Crawley's fortune is no longer a factor in the struggle; Dobbin has had no luck in pushing Amelia's cause with her father-in-law; Becky still climbs, with Rawdon's full belief reinforcing her.

Chapters 36-38

Summary

Thackeray starts this section with an essay on how people live on nothing. He then talks about Rawdon and Rebecca, who are settled in Mayfair, entertain all the time, yet have no money, except what Rawdon makes by gambling.

The story reverts to the time in Paris when Rawdon has gambled with other soldiers. Colonel O'Dowd has warned Spooney about gambling with Rawdon, at which Becky and Peggy O'Dowd have quarreled. Only Rebecca's intervention with General Tufto has prevented Rawdon's being returned to England.

Rebecca makes Crawley sell out of the Guards so they can return to England to pursue his fortune. Becky spreads the news that Rawdon will inherit from his dying aunt; she orders mourning for herself and little Rawdon. She then skips out on her hotel bill, goes to England, and arranges with her husband's creditors to settle for a percentage of what is owed. Becky then goes back to the Continent, rejoins her son and husband; and the three return to London.

They hire a house from Mr. Raggles, formerly Miss Crawley's butler. This business arrangement is Raggles' downfall, for he is not able to collect the rent and ends up in Fleet Prison because he can't pay his debts. Here Thackeray moralizes on how the gentry rob the servants. Rawdon and Rebecca patronize all Miss Crawley's former tradesmen and pay nobody.

When Pitt inherits Miss Crawley's fortune, Becky insists Rawdon congratulate him and ingratiate himself into his brother's good graces. Rebecca determines that Lady Jane shall sponsor her in London society.

Rebecca secures a woman for her "house-dog" and companion. She neglects little Rawdon but hires a French maid to take care of him. The boy becomes a great favourite with his father, who brings him toys and plays with him. Rawdon takes the boy to see his old trooper friends. One Sunday morning Rawdon and the boy meet Georgy Osborne, who is walking with his grandfather, Mr. Sedley. Georgy and little Rawdon become friends.

The reader is now brought up to date on Amelia, Dobbin, and Jos. After leaving Brussels, Jos has returned to India, where, because of his many tales, he has earned the name of "Waterloo Sedley."

Amelia has continued to pine for George and has devoted

all her time and thought to little George whom she sees as an improved edition of his father. When Mrs. Sedley has attempted to give Georgy some medicine, Amelia has objected and the two women have quarreled.

Mr. Sedley has suspected Dobbin of trickery over the money that has been supposedly left at George's death. Actually the money has come from Dobbin's own pocket because of his love for Amelia. Amelia has accepted whatever Dobbin has told her and has not known how much she owes him. Dobbin is always sending gifts for her and Georgy. Dobbin's sisters have told Amelia that Dobbin is to marry Glorvina O'Dowd. Amelia has protested her happiness about it, but tears have clouded her eyes. Mrs. Sedley knows that Dobbin loves Amelia, but Amelia won't talk of it.

Commentary

The subterfuges Becky has learned from her poverty-stricken father come into play here, not only in her dealing with creditors but in her beginning affair with Lord Steyne. She foresees the necessity of protecting her reputation by hiring a female companion. The greatest flaw in Becky's character and the one which will contribute to her downfall is her neglect of little Rawdon. She has no affection for him and scorns Rawdon's paternal love for the boy. Thackeray presents both the dark and the light aspects of his characters. In answer to those critics who think Thackeray too cynical, one should examine the development of Rawdon from a coarse soldier to a devoted husband and father, albeit not a provider. He considers himself too dull for his wife and lets her have her own way. Although he does not realise it, he has become known as "Mrs. Crawley's husband." Thackeray also shows the better side of the braggart Jos. He does provide money for his parents, but his pride and better judgment do not permit him to be taken in by his father's attempt to force him into participation in the questionable wine business. Even the gentle Amelia rises to an unsuspected height of spirit when she defies her mother's medication of Georgy. And although Thackeray does not permit the reader inside Amelia's mind, he lets him see the tears when she hears Dobbin will marry Glorvina. The honest Dobbin, although not of Vanity Fair, practices deception in keeping the Sedleys from knowing how much he has done for Amelia.

Chapters 39-42

Summary

The story goes back to the relatives who hoped to benefit by Miss Crawley's death. Bute has been mourning because he has received five thousand pounds instead of the expected thirty thousand. Mrs. Bute has redoubled her efforts to make good marriages for her daughters.

There is a flashback to Pitt's and Lady Jane's visit to Sir Pitt. Sir Pitt has liked Lady Jane and has given her pearls but has refused to discuss the degeneration of the family estate with his son. Neither has he allowed them to stay with him. Miss Horrocks, the butler's daughter, reigns at Queen's Crawley and Pitt fears his father will marry her. One evening Miss Horrocks tries to play and sing; the kitchen maid whom she has promoted encourages her. Sir Pitt thinks her attempts to be a lady are very funny. He drinks too much and becomes seriously ill.

Within an hour Mrs. Bute and family enter the house, surprise Miss Horrocks trying to pilfer Sir Pitt's desks. Mrs. Bute chases Miss Horrocks out with a threat of jail. She also sends word to Pitt and takes over the household from whence the Horrocks have fled. Sir Pitt lingers for months but never regains lucidity. Young Pitt moves into Queen's Crawley and takes over

After the death of the old baronet, the new Sir Pitt decides to send for Rawdon and Rebecca. Since Rawdon sees no possibility of money forthcoming from the visit, he is not eager to go. But Rebecca, delighted at the invitation, sees all the intricate possibilities of advancement in Vanity Fair. She pictures Rawdon in Parliament and herself presented in Court as a result of the influence of Lord Steyne and Sir Pitt.

Now comes a flashback on the fortunes of Briggs since

the death of Aunt Crawley. After various experiences, Briggs has come to be Becky's "housedog." Before six months have passed, the Rawdon Crawleys have borrowed much of her life's savings on pretext of investment.

The author then describes Rawdon's and Becky's trip to Queen's Crawley where they are well received, and Becky exerts herself to make a good impression.

The reader is next taken back to the Osborne family. Mr. Osborne's bitterness has not improved his temper. After much bargaining over the marriage of Maria to Frederick Bullock, who has been holding out for more dowry, the match has been made. Old Osborne keeps the other daughter, Jane, as a slave at home. Popular little Georgy visits many people. Inevitably becomes in contact with his maiden aunt, Jane, whom he charms. Later at her father's questioning, she bursts into tears and says little George is beautiful as an angel and just like his father. Old Osborne trembles but says nothing.

Commentary "A Cynical Chapter" brings the action up to Sir Pitt's final illness. Thackeray's cynicism expresses itself in such lines as these about Mrs. Bute: who could have guessed from her frequent appearance in public how she pinched and starved at home... I know no sort of lying which is more frequent in Vanity Fair than this: and it may be remarked how people who practise it take credit to themselves for their hypocrisy, and fancy that they are exceedingly virtuous and praiseworthy, because they are able to deceive the world with regard to the extent of their means... Mrs. Bute certainly thought herself one of the most virtuous women in England. What will not a mother do for the benefit of her beloved ones?

Miss Horrocks has hoped to become Lady Crawley, but "fate intervened enviously, and prevented her from receiving the reward due to such immaculate love and virtue." Miss Horrocks begs mercy from Mrs. Bute, "but those who know a really good woman are aware that she is not in a hurry to forgive, and that the humiliation of an enemy is a triumph to her soul."

A cynical example of Vanity Fair shows in the kitchen maid whom Miss Horrocks has promoted. First she praises

Miss Horrocks' pitiful attempt at music; then when Sir Pitt falls ill and Mrs. Bute takes over, the maid turns against Miss Horrocks.

When Becky is recognized as part of the family by the new Sir Pitt's invitation, she takes another step toward establishment in Vanity Fair. The description of Becky's reaction to Lady Jane's kindness makes the reader wonder if Rebecca is acting or is feeling something like sentiment. "The embrace somehow brought tears into the eyes of the little adventuress—which ornaments, as we know, she wore very seldom. The artless mark of kindness and confidence touched and pleased her." When Becky remarks that she could be good for five thousand a year, the author points out that temptation may have something to do with goodness: ... who knows but Rebecca was right in her speculations—and that it was only a question of money and fortune which made the difference between her and an honest woman? If you take temptations into account, who is to say that he is better than his neighbour? A comfortable career of prosperity, if it does not make people honest, at least keeps them so.

It does appear that the good fortune of the young Sir Pitt helps him to become kinder, more of a gentleman.

The erratic treatment of the dying Sir Pitt by nurse Hester gives rise to the ironic comment of the author:

What love, what fidelity, what constancy is there equal to that of a nurse with good wages?... we quarrel with them because, when their relations come to see them once a week, a little gin is smuggled in in their linen-basket. Ladies, what man's love is there that would stand a year's nursing of the object of his affection? Whereas a nurse will stand by you for ten pounds a quarter, and we think her too highly paid.

Thackeray's comment on the end of life in Vanity Fair is: "For this was all that was left after more than seventy years of cunning and struggling, and drinking, and scheming, and sin, and selfishness—a whimpering old idiot put in and out of bed and cleaned and fed like a baby."

Thackeray makes some pointed comments on governesses keeping their places, on death and funerals, and on the conscience of Vanity Fair. He points out that there are things Vanity Fair cannot buy. Old Osborne's character hasn't changed. When he kicks Miss Wirt's trunks downstairs, tramples her hand luggage, and shakes his fist at her departing hackney-coach, he exhibits the same character he showed in Chapter 21, where the author says, "He called kicking a footman downstairs, a hint to the latter to leave his service."

Chapters 43-46

Summary

The reader now goes to the Madras division in the Indian Empire, where Sir Michael O'Dowd commands Dobbin's regiment. Mrs. O'Dowd, kind, impetuous, and eager, tyrannizes her husband, bosses the ladies of the regiment, and mothers the young men. She decides Glorvina should marry Dobbin, who, of course, dreams only of Amelia.

When Amelia's letter of congratulation on his marriage to Glorvina comes, Dobbin despairs because he sees Amelia doesn't love him. Then, when he receives a letter from his sister telling him that Amelia may give up Georgy, as she is marrying the Reverend Mr. Binney, Dobbin rushes to Sir Michael and demands leave to return to England.

The scene moves to Great Gaunt Street, the location of the Crawleys' family house which is being renovated. Becky has originated the plan as part of her scheme to get into Vanity Fair. Becky has hinted to Sir Pitt that she and Rawdon need money, but he doesn't respond.

Little Rawdon has grown into a fine boy, generous and soft-hearted, but he has no affection for his mother. Her hatred toward him has destroyed his love. When the Rawdon Crawleys go to Queen's Crawley for Christmas, they are greeted cordially. Sir Pitt has improved the old home place and is repairing the popularity of the Crawleys by making friends in the area.

Becky, as usual, ingratiates herself with all who are important. She even courts the favour of Countess Southdown and shows affection to Mrs. Bute. Her attentions to Sir Pitt flatter him but make Lady Jane suspicious. Two incidents chill Lady Jane's feeling toward Becky. First, Little Rawdon says he always eats in the kitchen at home, and second, when his mother tries to show off by kissing him, he tells her she never kisses him at home. Rawdon appreciates Lady Jane's attention to his son. Little Rawdon enjoys the affection of all. When the vacation ends, Rawdon and his son are loath to leave, but Becky wants to return to London.

When Parliament opens and Sir Pitt comes to London, Rawdon and his son spend time with Lady Jane and the children, but Rebecca fawns on Sir Pitt and Lady Jane becomes more jealous. Meanwhile Christmas at the Sedleys must be celebrated without much joy. They have no money. Georgy distinguishes himself with many honors at the Reverend Mr. Binney's school, and Amelia hopes he will be great and famous. Miss Jane Osborne thinks often of little George. When she speaks up to her father at his question about her gold watch and chain, she defends herself by saying she bought it with her own money. The old man knows she has given it to Georgy and tells her to go buy herself another one.

The Dobbin sisters keep urging Amelia to let Georgy visit them, hoping thereby to reconcile him with his grandfather. Mr. Osborne finally offers to take Georgy on the condition he live entirely with his grandfather, seeing his mother only occasionally at her place. If such arrangements are made he will give Amelia an allowance. Furious, Amelia accuses the old man of trying to buy the child. Credit becomes difficult for the Sedleys. No money comes from Joseph. All bills are due. Amelia has a quarrel with her parents over the use of her own money. Mrs. Sedley so browbeats Amelia that the latter gives up all her money to her parents.

Commentary

Here is an example of the confusion possible in this narrative. The author has Georgy tell his mother that he has seen Sir William, and Mr. Dobbin, who have promised to show him the Tower of London. According to the previous narrative, Dobbin has just asked leave to return from Madras to London.

He does not arrive, according to the account that follows, until Georgy has gone to his grandfather's place and is established in the Reverend Mr. Veal's school. Thackeray does not always keep time, place, sequence, and names in their proper places. Dobbin measures Amelia's feeling for him by his thought on her letters "how cold, how kind, how hopeless, how selfish they were!"

Thackeray characterizes Peggy O'Dowd: "In a word, in adversity she was the best of comforters, in good fortune the most troublesome of friends; having a perfectly good opinion of herself always, and an indomitable resolution to have her own way." She has determined to get Glorvina a husband, and she will succeed. As for Glorvina, her great desire is to be admired, possibly the reason for her "forty or fifty previous defeats" in matrimonial endeavor.

Becky crawls up the social ladder with every opportunity. But her hatred for little Rawdon—she realizes his potential danger to her double life—begins to undermine Becky's relation with Lady Jane. Thackeray compares Becky's social climb under the eyes of knowing servants to a spider's efforts: "So you see Molly, the housemaid, of a morning, watching a spider in the doorpost lay his thread and laboriously crawl up it, until, tired of the sport, she raises her broom and sweeps away the thread and the artificer." The analogy foreshadows what will happen to Rebecca.

While Rebecca gains favour with Sir Pitt, and loses the confidence of Lady Jane, Rawdon gains Lady Jane's affection—leading eventually to Rebecca's catastrophe.

Amelia, the victim of her own soft heart and the crushing poverty that brings out the selfishness and senility of her parents, perceives that Georgy's welfare demands his transferal to his grandfather Osborne. The softening process in old Osborne, seen when he does not rave about Miss Jane's having given Georgy a watch, will continue rapidly when he has Georgy near him.

One of the few characters untouched by Vanity Fair is loyal Mr. Clapp, who remains faithful to the Sedleys, no matter what their financial condition.

Chapters 47-50

Summary

This installment opens with a description of Great Gaunt Street from the viewpoint of Tom Eaves. Tom thinks that in rich families the sons and fathers naturally hate each other. The son wishes the father would die so he may inherit; the younger sons wish the older son dead so they may inherit. The insanity of Lord Steyne's son and the fear of its transmission to his grandchildren grieve Lord Steyne. He tries to forget his troubles through pleasure and fabulous parties to which everyone longs to go, although everyone deplores his morals.

Becky finally is presented at Court—the height of her ambition. Lady Jane remarks on the beauty and quality of Becky's gown, and Rawdon questions her about her jewels. She does not reveal that she stole the gown material from the Crawley's house in Great Gaunt Street nor that the jewels are gifts from both Sir Pitt and Lord Steyne.

After Becky's presentation at Court, the Marchioness of Steyne and the Countess of Gaunt invite her to dine. Becky's triumph in view of this advancement is not dimmed by Lord Steyne's conviction that she cannot hold her place in Vanity Fair without money. Lord Steyne wants Becky to get rid of Briggs in order that he can have more time alone with his favourite. Becky cries, saying that she owes Briggs money and can't pay it. Lord Steyne gives her a draft for the amount she specifies which is twice what she owes Briggs. Becky pays a little on the most pressing bills and conceals the rest in her private hiding place.

The reader now gets a flashback of Lord Steyne's bullying the women of his house into inviting Becky. Lady Blanche is one of the Bareacres ladies whom Becky has insulted in Brussels. At first the ladies have refused to invite Becky, but Lord Steyne has overcome their reluctance by the most brutal methods.

The story continues with an account of the illustrious people Becky meets at the Steyne's home, and the glowing newspaper account of Becky's charm, which publicity fills Mrs. Bute's heart with rage. Actually the ladies at the party ignore Becky, but she is befriended by Lady Steyne, who feels sorry for her. Becky sings religious songs for the old lady, songs which bring nostalgic tears to Lady Steyne. The night ends in triumph for Becky.

The story returns to the Sedleys, who are near starvation. Mrs. Sedley has turned against everyone. Emmy tries to do art work for money, but fails; she seeks private tutoring to no avail. She realizes she must part with Georgy. Thackeray discloses that Joseph hasn't neglected his parents, but Mr. Sedley has sold the annuity as backing for one of his haphazard business schemes. Old Osborne rejoices that Amelia has been starved out—he had hoped to do the same to George—starvation is one of the weapons of Vanity Fair. He sends for Georgy but gives orders that Amelia is not to come to Russell Square. Two days after his rise to affluence, little Georgy begins to patronize his mother.

Amelia walks to Russell Square and watches the light go out in Georgy's room, prays for him, and walks home in silence. Once she sees Georgy and his aunt going to church. A chimney sweep asks for charity and the footman tries to drive him away, but Georgy gives him money. This kind, impulsive action cheers his mother; she goes into the church and watches little Georgy's head and, above it, the monument to his father.

Commentary The author offers some excuse for Lord Steyne's dissoluteness by telling of his anxiety over the family insanity. Lord Steyne seeks to forget it through sensuous pleasure; his wife seeks refuge in religion. The inhabitants of Vanity Fair are willing to shut their eyes to Lord Steyne's immoralities because he has both money and position. This fact should be remembered later when Rebecca meets catastrophe.

Tom Eaves, a combination of eavesdropper and Peeping Tom, thinks he knows everything and judges with a cynical eye, yet he too, bows before a "great man" and having put all his money into an annuity, does not hate his relatives and has no "feeling with regard to his betters, but a constant and generous desire to dine with them." Lord Steyne's prediction that Becky can't stay at the top of Vanity Fair society proves prophetic. Circumstances are closing in about Becky: the cache in her desk will betray her. At first, only the servants have talked about her; now the people at Court notice Lord Steyne's absorbed attention to her. Although she has been invited to Lord Steyne's home by his ladies, and she seems at the culmination of success, the potential of her destruction grows stronger. The author, presenting the good and the bad, allows the reader to admire Lord Steyne in one incident, at least. Although he is in the best humour when he is torturing his wife and daughter-in-law; yet when his wife rescues Becky, he is grateful and tells his wife. Becky too, shows a moment of human kindness when she appreciates Lady Steyne's kindness in speaking to her and asking her to sing.

Speaking of Amelia's final surrender of Georgy, Thackeray says, "Poverty and misery for all, want and degradation for her parents, injustice to the boy—one by one the outworks of the little citadel were taken, in which the poor soul passionately guarded her only love and treasure." Thackeray discourses on the subject of men and women. While the following comment fits Amelia, it could not be altogether true of Becky: I know few things more affecting than that timorous debasement and self-humiliation of a woman. How she owns that it is she and not the man who is guilty: how she takes all the faults on her side and persists in shielding the real culprit! It is those who injure women who get the most kindness from them—they are born timid and tyrants, and maltreat those who are humblest before them. By heavens it is pitiful, the bootless love of women for children in Vanity Fair. Both Amelia and Becky maltreat those who are humblest before them.

Chapters 51-53

Summary

Thackeray begins this installment with a discourse on how all the doors of fashion now open for Becky and how vain it all is. He lists the important people and places she visits. Becky continues to charm people; the women try to snub Becky but she bests them.

Vanity Fair wonders where Becky gets money to entertain. Some say she begs; some say she levies it. The author says, "The truth is that by economy and good management—by a sparing use of ready money and by paying scarcely anybody—people can manage, for a time at least, to make a great show with very little means."

Charades are popular at this time and Becky urges Lord Steyne to present some. She outshines all the other women in the character of Clytemnestra, and at supper sits with the royal personage in attendance. Becky's triumphs alarm Rawdon; they seem to separate her from him. On the way home from the charade party, Rawdon is arrested by two bailiffs and taken to jail for debts.

A flashback now shows the reader that Lord Steyne has insisted on sending little Rawdon away to a special school. His father has grieved at his departure, but his mother has wanted to be rid of him. Little Rawdon gets on well at school. As Lord Steyne's protege, Sir Pitt's nephew, and the son of a colonel, he has both position and money.

Steyne next has proposed to get rid of Briggs. Failing in this, he has suspected that the money he has given Becky to pay Briggs has been used for something else. He has questioned Briggs and confirmed his suspicions. He has solved the Briggs problem by giving her a position at Gauntly Hall. Becky has attributed her failure in paying Briggs to Rawdon's demands that he have the money himself, telling his wife that he would pay Briggs.

Rawdon, delighted that Briggs has security, has begun to feel uneasy over Becky. Lady Jane and Sir Pitt have protested that Becky shouldn't be allowed to go about without a companion. They have urged Rawdon to go with her. Becky's failure to pay attention to Sir Pitt's remonstrances has resulted in strained relations between the two families. Rawdon has become Becky's watchdog, and her charm has lulled his suspicion.

Now the reader returns to Rawdon, who is not too depressed by his situation. He has been locked up before. But when time passes, and he does not get a reply from his letter to Becky, he wonders. When he finally receives word that Becky will get money from Lord Steyne, all his suspicions return. He writes a note addressed to Sir Pitt or Lady Jane imploring assistance. Lady Jane comes within an hour. Rawdon's violent appreciation startles Lady Jane, and she goes home to pray for him.

Rawdon hurries home and finds Lord Steyne and Becky together. Rawdon strikes Lord Steyne, throws a diamond pin at him, which cuts him on the forehead, leaving a permanent scar. Becky pleads innocence, but Lord Steyne thinks the two of them have laid a trap and he condemns Becky. Taking Becky's keys, Rawdon ransacks her possessions and discovers her secret hoard. Becky admits the thousand pound note has come from Lord Steyne. Rawdon determines to return it, and to pay off creditors with the other money. Even while Becky protests her innocence, Rawdon leaves her. The French maid comes in, comforts Becky, puts her to bed, and gathers up the jewels.

Commentary

Of Becky's rise and fall, Thackeray says it has all happened before and will again. But he admits there are advantages in Vanity Fair: "What well-constituted mind, merely because it is transitory, dislikes roast beef?" It is vanity but one should enjoy it. Thackeray says Becky's brief triumph should be enjoyed because it is brief. "Glory like this is said to be fugitive." Becky, at the height of her ambition, plays the part of Clytemnestra, a symbolic choice, for she has been having an affair with Lord Steyne, even as Clytemnestra had with Aegisthus. Becky would sacrifice Rawdon as quickly as Clytemnestra did Agamemnon. The role of the nightingale contrasts to that of murderess. Thackeray has again shown both the dark and the light of human nature, for Becky fills both roles. Thackeray describes the portals of society as being guarded by "grooms of the chamber with flaming silver forks with which they prong all those who have not the right of the entrée... the honest newspaper-fellow who sits in the hall... dies after a little time. He can't survive the glare of fashion long. It scorches him up, as the presence of Jupiter in full dress wasted that poor imprudent Semele—a giddy moth of a creature who ruined herself by venturing out of her natural atmosphere." Semele, a mortal beloved of Jupiter, was induced by Juno, Jupiter's wife, to ask Jupiter to approach her as he did Juno—with full majesty. The splendor burned Semele up. Thackeray is suggesting that Becky is in the same position.

Thackeray comments on society: "... all the delights of life, I say,—would go to the deuce, if people did but act upon their silly principles, and avoid those whom they dislike and abuse."

Becky's catastrophe comes about through Lord Steyne's getting Briggs and little Rawdon out of the house, causing Rawdon to take over as watchdog. If Becky had let Rawdon have the money to bail himself out, he would not have been suspicious. If Rawdon hadn't formed a friendship for Lady Jane, she wouldn't have rescued him. If Rawdon had been less a man, Becky could have kept her treasures. If Becky hadn't implicated Rawdon in her failure to pay Briggs, Steyne might have backed up her protestations of innocence. But Steyne had had too much experience in Vanity Fair.

In the space of forty-eight hours Becky has reached the height of society and fallen into its depths. The title of Chapter 52 is ironic: "In Which Lord Steyne Shows Himself in a Most Amiable Light." He provides for little Rawdon's education and Briggs' future, but his motives are not philanthropic.

Becky shows her femininity by liking Rawdon better when he bosses her and insists on obedience. However, the desire for wealth makes Lord Steyne imperative to her interests, and she has to get rid of Rawdon one way or another—while she caters to Lord Steyne. When Rawdon realizes that Becky has betrayed him, he wishes to be a better person. Becky thinks only of what she has lost—her status in Vanity Fair.

Chapters 54-56

Summary Commentary When Rawdon goes to see his older brother, Pitt thinks him drunk, then believes Rawdon wants money and offers many excuses. When Rawdon says he does not want money, Pitt sighs with relief. Rawdon tells all that has happened and says he may be killed in a duel with Steyne. Rawdon asks only that little Rawdon be cared for and Pitt promises. Rawdon secures an old soldier friend, Macmurdo, as second. Macmurdo tries to convince Rawdon that there is a reasonable doubt of Becky's guilt, but his words are wasted.

Meanwhile Becky sleeps until afternoon. When she rings for her servants, no one answers. She goes downstairs to find the servants sitting around drinking. Insolent, they refuse to obey her. Only Raggles is courteous; he laments because of his financial ruin.

Becky leaves the house and tries to get Sir Pitt to promise a reconciliation with Rawdon. Becky is kneeling before Pitt, kissing his hand when Lady Jane comes in. Irate at last, Jane tells Sir Pitt he can choose between them and sweeps out of the room. Sir Pitt promises to try to mediate peace between Rebecca and Rawdon. She has told Sir Pitt of Rawdon's appointment and how it was to be a surprise and how she knew Lord Steyne favored her; but she accepted and encouraged his attention only for Rawdon's sake. She says she couldn't trust Rawdon with money, as he is a spendthrift.

The scene shifts to Rawdon breakfasting with Macmurdo and other officers. When the two go the club, men start congratulating Rawdon. They have been talking about him and his wife's influence. Rawdon discovers he has been appointed governor of Coventry Island. Lord Steyne's man, Wenham, comes to talk to Rawdon, avoiding the subject of the duel as long as possible and regretting that he and his wife were unable to accept an invitation to the Crawleys that fatal night because Mrs. Wenham had a headache and couldn't go.

He says Lord Steyne wants to forget the whole thing. Rawdon doesn't believe the story, but Macmurdo urges him to accept it. Rawdon takes the position provided by Lord Steyne because he thinks it will infuriate Steyne to have Rawdon living off his influence. Once established, Rawdon sends gifts to his friends, makes an annuity to Becky, and writes his son regularly, meanwhile sending money to his brother for Rawdon's keep. Little Rawdon spends his holidays with Lady Jane and rides to the hounds at Queen's Crawley. His mother makes no attempt to see him.

Little Georgy, established in his grandfather's home, merits all the pride his father had won. Old Osborne plans to make little Georgy an educated gentleman. While both his grandfather and Aunt Jane adore him, his aunt, Mrs. Bullock, hates him for having taken the inheritance she has coveted for her own children.

Georgy's mother makes friends with the schoolmaster in order to see Georgy, who, quick of mind, well dressed, and flush with money, domineers everyone. In Russell Square everyone fears old Osborne, but he fears Georgy. He tries by over-indulgence to make amends to his grandson, trying to forget the harshness to his son.

Mrs. Sedley, who has been under Amelia's constant care, dies. Now Amelia devotes all her time to her father. One day two gentlemen come to school to see Georgy. They are Major Dobbin and a stout gentleman. Georgy recognizes Dobbin who asks him if his mother has mentioned Dobbin. Georgy assures him that his mother has talked of Dobbin hundreds of times.

Commentary

Sir Pitt reacts with his father's stinginess when his first thought is that Rawdon's trouble must be money. When his pocketbook isn't touched, he can relent and promise protection to little Rawdon, although after Rawdon goes to Coventry Island, he remits regularly to his brother, a consideration which shows how much Rawdon has grown in character.

Rawdon wins the reader's sympathy when he shows Macmurdo the thousand pound note and says:

This is what he gave her, Mac: and she kep' it unknown to me: and with this money in the house, she refused to stand by me when I was locked up!" The captain could not but own that the secreting of the money had a very ugly look.

The reader wonders if the withholding of the money proves to Rawdon his wife's infidelity with Lord Steyne. In

Vanity Fair, the money would come first, and although Rawdon's values have changed, Rebecca's have not. One of the most touching word pictures of the whole book is: "He covered his face with his black hands; over which the tears rolled and made furrows of white..." Rawdon has been too disturbed to think of washing, or even of changing from his party clothes, which he was wearing when thrown into detention. Lady Jane, sympathetic, can't bear going to church after seeing Rawdon's agony.

In keeping with the pretense of Vanity Fair, Becky tells Sir Pitt a logical and convincing story of the tragic night. Wenham makes a virtuous case for Lord Steyne and Becky when he talks to Rawdon. Later, he will tell Pitt enough to estrange him forever from Becky.

In spite of the fact that Macmurdo and Rawdon are planning a duel with Lord Steyne, they pretend gaiety with their companions. Thackeray's comments, "Feasting, drinking, ribaldry, laughter, go on alongside of all sorts of other occupations in Vanity Fair..." A good example of contrast between those of and those not of Vanity Fair shows in Hester's care of the dying Sir Pitt and Amelia's care of her parents.

Thackeray uses a Biblical metaphor in his reference to Georgy's visiting his mother: "but when her Samuel came to see the widow..." Amelia has felt it a religious duty to let old Osborne have little Georgy.

Chapters 57-60

Summary

Old Osborne likes to think of Sedley's being forced to accept charity from him. He hints to Georgy that his mother's father is a wretched old bankrupt, whereupon Georgy patronizes the old man.

Amelia's nature is to sacrifice herself and to think herself guilty of selfish love, thereby accounting for her punishment through loss of the first George and surrender of the second. She devotes herself to her mother. After her mother's death, she takes care of her father, who becomes very fond of her.

Amelia has the consolation of doing her duty. Major Dobbin, upon getting leave to go home, has become ill and at Madras the attendants despair of his life. He has made his will with a request that a hair chain of Amelia's hair be buried with him. Finally, he has been put aboard a homeward bound ship, which has Joseph Sedley as a passenger. Jos, wealthy, is returning to England for his health. Dobbin continually discusses Amelia with Joseph. When Joseph proves to Dobbin's satisfaction that Amelia is not planning on marriage, Dobbin swiftly recovers. He exults in high spirits and is depressed only when the ship is delayed.

Dobbin and Joseph descend from the boat amid cheers. The major wants to leave immediately for London, but Jos wants a good night's sleep. Dobbin, ready to leave early the next morning, departs without the sleepy Jos. Dobbin flings money about to hurry the trip. He goes to his old haunt, the Slaughters', where the old waiter remembers which room he always had and his other preferences. Dobbin recalls his days there with George. The old waiter asks about Mrs. George Osborne.

Dobbin dresses carefully, thinking that if the old waiter recognizes him, Amelia will. Dobbin trembles as he nears Amelia's home. The little girl who used to call him Major Sugarplums comes to the door and recognizes him. He hugs and kisses her; he is so glad to be back. The Clapps bring him up to date on news, but he is afraid to ask if Amelia is married. Miss Polly Clapp offers to take him to find Amelia and her father in Kensington Gardens. On the way they meet the Reverend Mr. Binney walking with his wife and sister. At Polly's explanation that the reverend has married Miss Grits, Dobbin is delighted.

When they see Amelia and her father, Dobbin sends Polly ahead to tell Amelia he is there. At first Amelia thinks there is something wrong about Georgy. Then, when she sees Dobbin, she begins to cry, runs to him. They hold hands. Dobbin misses his cue to take her in his arms and reports he has another arrival to announce. She asks if it is his wife. Horrified at this suggestion, Dobbin says it is Jos. Emmy runs to tell her father, who is much delighted. Although Dobbin has claimed to be in a hurry, he has time to go back to tea, his eyes always on Amelia, dreaming of her as he has always done. Amelia shows him Georgy's miniature and praises the child. Dobbin tells Mr. Sedley that Jos has come home particularly to see him, because Dobbin wants the Sedley family on good terms among themselves. When Mr. Sedley dozes, Amelia talks more about Georgy, claiming that he is the image of his father. Dobbin won't allow himself to be jealous of her eternal devotion to George but believes that George didn't prize her enough.

Old Mr. Sedley can't rest for putting his papers in order for Jos. On his part Jos is delayed because he has to buy a couple of splendid, colorful vests before he goes to London. On the third day the fashionably attired "Waterloo Sedley" drives to London, stopping to eat and drink every time he has a chance. Dobbin has made Jos promise he will make a home for Amelia and their father, and Joseph tells them they will never want again.

When they move to the new home, Amelia takes her pictures and the piano that she thought George had sent, after the family's financial failure. Dobbin is delighted with her attachment to the piano, even though Amelia thinks George, instead of Dobbin, sent it. Amelia guesses the truth from his expression, and thereafter the piano loses its value for her. She apologizes to William for not appreciating his gift, and he can't stand it any longer. He declares his love, but Amelia loves only George. After Jos comes home, fortune smiles on the Sedleys. Little Georgy likes and respects Dobbin and learns some new values—not those of Vanity Fair. Georgy mimics Uncle Jos, who doesn't appreciate the humour.

Commentary

Thackeray comments on life: think how mysterious and often unaccountable it is—that lottery of life which gives to this man the purple and fine linen, and sends to the other rags for garments and dogs for comforters. And so, if you properly tyrannize over a woman, you will find a halfp'orth of kindness act upon her, and bring tears into her eyes, as though you were an angel benefiting her. Oh, be humble, my brother, in your prosperity!... whose virtue is a deficiency of temptation, whose success may be a chance, whose rank may be an ancestor's accident, whose prosperity is very likely a satire.

Some examples of Thackeray's figures of speech are: "To a traveller returning home it the English landscape looks so kind it seems to shake hands with you as you pass through it." Dobbin's dream of Amelia is a "bread-and-butter paradise." Joseph's Indian servant's brown face is the "colour of a turkey's gizzard." William sighing over Amelia's indifference is like "... the poor boy at school who has no money may sigh after the contents of the tartwoman's tray."

Thackeray uses names to characterize. Some of the names in this section are: Little Ricketts, who has fevers; Fogle, Fake & Cracksman, a business firm; Baron Bandanna; The Reverend Felix Rabbits, who has fourteen daughters.

"Waterloo Sedley," unchanged since the reader met him, shows his character by vanity in dress and in the tales of himself and great personages, and in his love of nobility; but he is generous with his family when he is forced to see their need. He can't stand Georgy's making fun of him. He has books but never reads them, gifts for people he hasn't yet met. He loves to eat, sleep, and talk.

Dobbin shows his ability to manage little George when the latter doesn't want to go into the pit at the theatre because it's vulgar. Dobbin leaves Georgy where he wants to sit and goes into the pit himself. Soon shamefaced Georgy joins him. Georgy is growing up—a cause for optimism.

Thackeray says of Dobbin, "I am ashamed to say that the major stretched the truth so far as to tell old Mr. Sedley that it was mainly a desire to see his parent which brought Jos once more to Europe." The difference between Dobbin's deceptions and those of Vanity Fair is that Dobbin acts out of unselfish motives, whereas citizens of Vanity Fair think first of themselves. Dobbin even lacks personal vanity to the extent that he is not jealous of the attention young officers pay Amelia. He thinks they are showing good judgment.

Of Amelia the author says, "Emmy was very ignorant, and

that is a pity, some people are so knowing." Although Amelia is still the gentle comforter who wipes away her father's tears and kisses him, she has acquired more character. Mrs. Clapp, one of the lower class who still lives in Vanity Fair, wants to fawn on Amelia, but "in the vulgar sycophant who now paid court to her, Emmy always remembered the coarse tyrant who had made her miserable many a time." In regard to Thackeray's technique, his time sequences are not always clear—sometimes his flashbacks aren't identified, as in Chapter 59 Joseph assures his father and sister they shall never want again. Five paragraphs later, Amelia gets a letter from Jos saying he will be delayed. He hasn't yet left Southampton.

Summary

This section starts with an essay describing the appearance and use of the second-floor arch of a London house where, among other things, the undertaker's men rest the coffin of a deceased person in the household. The subject of this essay leads to Thackeray's revelation that old Mr. Sedley is dying. Before he dies he tells Amelia that he and her mother have been unkind and unjust to her. She prays with him.

After Sedley dies, old Osborne points out his own success and tells Georgy, "He was a better man than I was, this day twenty years-a better man I should say by ten thousand pound." Old Osborne, at first inclined to underrate Dobbin, begins to hear of his fame from members of his own society. Sir William, Dobbin's father, praises him. Dobbin's name appears in parties of nobility. Then Osborne discovers that Dobbin has in part supported Amelia and Georgy. Dobbin says it was his responsibility that George married Amelia and he felt obligated.

Osborne says he is an honest fellow. They discuss Georgy, who is so much like his father. Old Osborne is softening. He sends a card for Mr. Joseph Sedley and defends Dobbin when his daughter Jane belittles him. He asks about Amelia and says he will be reconciled to her, but Mr. Sedley's illness and death prevent. Meanwhile Osborne changes his will, and before he can be reconciled to Amelia, he dies. Frederick Bullock fears that Osborne has left half his property to his grandson, and he has, with prevision for Amelia and a legacy for Dobbin. Amelia is guardian of Georgy; Dobbin is executor. Amelia is grateful to Dobbin, but grateful only, for the reconciliation which he has effected.

After Amelia has money, the servants respect her; people who never thought of her before visit her now and patronize her, especially Mrs. Frederick Bullock, her sister-in-law. Amelia does not enjoy these people.

The house at Russell Square is dismantled and things put in storage until Georgy's majority. When Joseph, Amelia and Georgy, and Dobbin go to the continent, Joseph eats and sleeps, Amelia sketches Dobbin and Georgy act as her attendants. Amelia hears good music for the first time, likes Mozart, and wonders if it's wicked to be so happy. She begins to appreciate Dobbin, who is the first gentleman she has known despite his large feet and hands.

The author claims to have seen the party at Pumpernickel, to have witnessed Amelia's delight in the opera, Jos interest in nobility, and to have admired Amelia himself. Joseph, greatly impressed by Lord Tapeworm and his doctor and the mineral springs, decides to stay at Pumpernickel. He thinks he will grow young and thin. Lord Tapeworm believes he has impressed Amelia, whereas he has only bewildered her. The group is presented at Court. The duchy stretches about ten miles but managed with in its small area to offer "famous" theatre, marriage "fêtes" on a grand scale, and moderate despotism; even factional politics was thoroughly entrenched in Pumpernickel—"the society was divided in its allegiance to those two great nations the French and the English." In short a variety of experiences, frequently available only in much larger places, was available in the small duchy of Pumpernickel.

Amelia entertains, speaks French, sings, and charms the German ladies. Jos is enamored of Fanny de Butterbrod, a canoness and countess, but during the festival of a royal marriage, Becky shows up She spies Joseph, flatters him, asks him to visit her.

Commentary

Some of Thackeray's figures are: "... whilst the sands of life were running out in the old man's glass upstairs... The velvet-footed butler brought them their wine... She walks into the room as silently as a sunbeam."

The following passage has beautiful description: "At this time of summer evening, the cows are trooping down from the hills, lowing and with their bells tinkling, to the old town, with its old moats, and gates, and spires, and chestnut trees, with long blue shadows stretching over the grass; the sky and the river below flame in crimson and gold; and the moon is already out, looking pale towards the sunset. The sun sinks behind the great castle-crested mountains, the night falls suddenly, the river grows darker and darker, lights quiver in it from the windows in the old ramparts, and twinkle peacefully in the villages under the hills on the opposite shore."

Grandfather Osborne tries to mold little George in the shape of Vanity Fair when he measures grandfather Sedley's goodness by the amount of money he has had. Bullock shows his greed when his first interest at his father-in-law's death is how much money Georgy has inherited.

The lawyers of Vanity Fair smile, but they note their visits in their bills. The people of Vanity Fair now see Amelia, whereas they didn't before:... in this vast town one has not the time to go and seek one's friends; if they drop out of the rank they disappear, and we march on without them. Who is ever missed in Vanity Fair?

Mrs. Frederick Bullock patronizes Amelia and entertains her "with faint fashionable fiddlefaddle and feeble Court slipslop." Joseph, of Vanity Fair himself, likes this Court gossip, but Dobbin is bored. He can't stand the woman with her "twopenny gentility."

Thackeray here offers this definition of gentlemen:... men whose aims are generous, whose truth is constant, and not only constant in its kind, but elevated in its degree; whose want of meanness makes them simple: who can look the world honestly in the face with an equal manly sympathy for the great and the small.

William Dobbin qualifies as a gentleman, with the following, basic to his philosophy:... beauty of art or nature made him thankful as well as happy; and that the pleasure to be had in listening to fine music, as in looking at the stars in the sky, or at a beautiful landscape or picture, was a benefit for which we might thank Heaven as sincerely as for any other worldly blessing.

Thackeray's humour shows in these examples: Marshal Tiptoff, "died in this year full of honours, and of an aspic of plovers' eggs..." Although the duchy of Pumpernickel is only ten miles long, Joseph is much excited over its nobility, particularly over Lord Tapeworm. "Mr. Jos had the honour of leading out the Countess of Schlüsselback, an old lady with a humpback, but with sixteen good quarters of nobility, and related to half the royal houses of Germany." Another jibe at Vanity Fair comes in this description of a palace:... the delighted people are permitted to march through room after room of the grand ducal palace, and admire the slippery floor, the rich hangings, and the spittoons at the doors of all the innumberable chambers... The army consisted of a magnificent band that also did duty on the stage...

Georgy shows an endearing quality when he climbs the pole, wins a prize sausage, and then gives it to a peasant who has nearly grasped it.

Chapters 64-67

Summary

Becky's life, after Rawdon leaves her, consists at first in trying to stay respectable, but just when she has built up a new circle of friends, someone informs about her and she is left alone. She tries at first to get Sir Pitt to listen to her, but Wenham, Lord Steyne's man, has told Pitt too much about her.

Becky wanders about the Continent, fleeing creditors, gambling, and acting as boarding house queen. Vagabond blood flows in her veins. She writes her son once, when, on the death of Sir Pitt's only son, little Rawdon becomes the heir of Queen's Crawley. Little Rawdon is not impressed with his mother's attention; it comes too falsely and too late. In Rome Becky sees Lord Steyne and hopes to regain his favour, remembering how her wit has amused him and what good fun they have had, but Steyne sends his man to threaten her with death. Steyne has been offended and he never forgets. He dies in 1830, much praised and lamented.

In the course of her travels Becky arrives at Brussels and remembers George, Amelia, and Joseph, and thinks, "they were kind simple people." And then, as the reader has seen, Becky meets Joseph and the others in Pumpernickel.

Joseph, as Becky has requested, goes to her hotel, a dirty refuge which suits Rebecca. She is on good terms with all there; they are her kind of people.

Becky convinces Jos that she has been wronged, that Rawdon and his family have torn her child from her, and that Jos was and is her first and only real love. Joseph goes home and convinces Amelia of Becky's innocence and need. Dobbin objects, never having been taken in by Becky. He says Amelia wasn't always fond of Becky referring to her jealousy over George. Angered, Amelia says she will never forgive him.

Triumphant, Becky moves in. Dobbin, after a last protest about letting Becky stay, reproves Amelia as not being worthy of his love and devotion. Much to Georgy's sorrow and Amelia's regret, Dobbin departs to join his regiment. Becky takes over Joseph's house, winning Amelia by praise of Major Dobbin. A couple of Becky's disreputable friends move in and connive to exploit Amelia. Although she has no idea of what they are planning, Amelia abhors them and writes to ask William Dobbin to come back.

That same day Becky decides she should protect Amelia and tells her that Joseph is too weak, that she should send for William. When Amelia starts the old line about her only being able to love George, Becky shows her the note George has written on the eve of Waterloo asking Becky to run away with him. Amelia cries—for many reasons—but she now feels free to love William.

In two days William returns to marry Amelia. Becky departs during the wedding days, returns and fastens herself on Joseph, and gets all his money. The last time William sees him, Joseph is both fascinated and terrified by Becky, but he won't leave her. Three months later he dies, the implication being that Becky has hastened his ruin as she did Rawdon's. Rawdon dies of yellow fever. Sir Pitt dies. Rawdon, Becky's son, inherits Queen's Crawley. The Dobbins, happy in marriage and their two children, George and Janey, live nearby and are friends of the family at Queen's Crawley.

None of them has anything to do with Rebecca, although her son makes her an allowance. She seems to have plenty of money, lives a respectable life, goes to church, and engages in all sorts of charities.

Commentary

In this section all the story ends are tied together, and the reader knows what happens to all the main characters. Becky has achieved what she set out to do: occupy a booth in Vanity Fair. Her son owns Queen's Crawley where she went first as governess.

Dobbin has Amelia and a daughter, both of whom rejoice his heart. Amelia has married a gentleman, at last, and appreciates him. George, who might have grown up without conscience, without any standards but those of Vanity Fair, has learned from Dobbin that there are other values. Lady Jane has young Rawdon and her own child with Amelia as friend. Becky has destroyed both Rawdon and Joseph. She has played Clytemnestra twice, as Thackeray says. As she began with entangling Joseph in her silken thread, so she ends engaged in the same manner. The plot has rounded into a full circle.

Although the true winners in the book are those who do not have their souls for barter in Vanity Fair, yet Thackeray allows Becky, his chief protagonist for Vanity Fair, to show some genuine feeling. For example, it is Becky who realizes that Dobbin is a gentleman in spite of his big feet; and it is she who brings Amelia to her senses in regard to her endless worship of George. Becky sees things clearly, uses everything to her advantage, but usually is honest with herself—and once in a while with Amelia and Dobbin. Thackeray defends his method of presentation by saying that he has only hinted "at the existence of wickedness in a light, easy, and agreeable manner, so that nobody's fine feelings may be offended." He calls Becky "Clytemnestra" and "Circe", allusions that leave no doubt as to her character. He compares Becky to a siren or mermaid or monster. "When they sink into their native element, depend on it those mermaids are about no good, and we had best not examine the fiendish marine cannibals, reveling and feasting on their wretched pickled victims." Another figure describes Becky in her attempt to be considered respectable, to a drowning man who will hang on to anything so long as there is hope.

Thackeray compares lying to being in debt. If one lie comes due, the liar has to make up a new one to take the place of the old one. As time passes both the number of fibs and the danger of their detection increases.

Amelia tyrannizes Dobbin, Thackeray says, as if he were a dog. She makes him "fetch and carry," and he likes to jump when she speaks and "trot behind her with her reticule in his mouth." Thackeray takes his analogies from many sources:

As the most hardened Arab that ever careered across the Desert over the hump of a dromedary, likes to repose sometimes under the date-trees by the water; or to come into the cities, walk in the bazaars, refresh himself in the baths, and say his prayers in the Mosques, before he goes out again marauding: Jos' tents and pilau were pleasant to his little Ishmaelite. She picketed her steed, hung up her weapons, and warmed herself comfortably by his fire. The halt in that roving, restless life was inexpressibly soothing and pleasant to her.

Thackeray's implication is that as soon as she becomes bored, she will go marauding again.

In a paragraph regarding Dobbin's victory, Thackeray calls Amelia a vessel, a prize, a bird, and a parasite:

The vessel is in port. He has got the prize he has been trying for all his life. The bird has come in at last. There it is with its head on his shoulder, billing and cooing close up to his heart, with soft outstretched fluttering wings... Grow green again, tender little parasite, round the rugged old oak to which you cling! Examples of Thackeray's humour follow: When Joseph arrives to see Becky, she puts a rouge-pot, a brandy bottle, and a plate of broken meat into her bed. She sits on the bed to keep Joseph from sitting on the objects. When Becky begins to move around in her excitement about how Rawdon and his family have torn little Rawdy from her arms, "The brandy-bottle inside clinked up against the plate which held the cold sausage. Both were moved, no doubt, by the exhibition of so much grief."

Dobbin amuses himself with a cigar, "that pernicious vegetable." Becky mourns about Rawdy, but she eats "a very good dinner." After Dobbin has gone, Thackeray says, "As for Emmy, had she not done her duty? She had her picture of George for a consolation."

Some of Thackeray's observations on human nature are: "When a traveller talks to you perpetually about the splendour of his luggage, which he does not happen to have with him; my son, beware of that traveller! He is, ten to one, an imposter."—"She wished to give him nothing, but that he should give her all. It is a bargain not infrequently levied in love." As Thackeray made allowances for Lord Steyne's depravity, he excuses Becky, "She was of a wild, roving nature, inherited from father and mother, who were both Bohemians by taste and circumstance..." And Dobbin, an honest gentleman to the last, tells Becky when he objects to her staying at Joseph's house, "I beg your pardon, ma'am, but I am bound to tell you that it is not as your friend that I am come here now." And Becky respects him for his honesty.

Chapter 11

Complete Text of W.M. Thackeray's Vanity Fair

William Makepeace Thackeray
Vanity Fair
CHAPTER I
Chiswick Mall

While the present century was in its teens, and on one sunshiny morning in June, there drove up to the great iron gate of Miss Pinkerton's academy for young ladies, on Chiswick Mall, a large family coach, with two fat horses in blazing harness, driven by a fat coachman in a three-cornered hat and wig, at the rate of four miles an hour. A black servant, who reposed on the box beside the fat coachman, uncurled his bandy legs as soon as the equipage drew up opposite Miss Pinkerton's shining brass plate, and as he pulled the bell at least a score of young heads were seen peering out of the narrow windows of the stately old brick house. Nay, the acute observer might have recognized the little red nose of good-natured Miss Jemima Pinkerton herself, rising over some geranium pots in the window of that lady's own drawing-room.

"It is Mrs. Sedley's coach, sister," said Miss Jemima. "Sambo, the black servant, has just rung the bell; and the coachman has a new red waistcoat."

"Have you completed all the necessary preparations incident to Miss Sedley's departure, Miss Jemima?" asked Miss Pinkerton herself, that majestic lady; the Semiramis of Hammersmith, the friend of Doctor Johnson, the correspondent of Mrs. Chapone herself. "The girls were up at four this morning, packing her trunks, sister," replied Miss Jemima; "we have made her a bow-pot."

"Say a bouquet, sister Jemima, 'tis more genteel."

"Well, a booky as big almost as a haystack; I have put up two bottles of the gillyflower water for Mrs. Sedley, and the receipt for making it, in Amelia's box."

"And I trust, Miss Jemima, you have made a copy of Miss Sedley's account. This is it, is it? Very good—ninety-three pounds, four shillings. Be kind enough to address it to John Sedley, Esquire, and to seal this billet which I have written to his lady."

In Miss Jemima's eyes an autograph letter of her sister, Miss Pinkerton, was an object of as deep veneration as would have been a letter from a sovereign. Only when her pupils quitted the establishment, or when they were about to be married, and once, when poor Miss Birch died of the scarlet fever, was Miss Pinkerton known to write personally to the parents of her pupils; and it was Jemima's opinion that if anything could console Mrs. Birch for her daughter's loss, it would be that pious and eloquent composition in which Miss Pinkerton announced the event.

In the present instance Miss Pinkerton's "billet" was to the following effect:—

The Mall, Chiswick, June 15, 18

MADAM,—After her six years' residence at the Mall, I have the honour and happiness of presenting Miss Amelia Sedley to her parents, as a young lady not unworthy to occupy a fitting position in their polished and refined circle. Those virtues which characterize the young English gentlewoman, those accomplishments which become her birth and station, will not be found wanting in the amiable Miss Sedley, whose INDUSTRY and OBEDIENCE have endeared her to her instructors, and whose delightful sweetness of temper has charmed her AGED and her YOUTHFUL companions.

In music, in dancing, in orthography, in every variety of embroidery and needlework, she will be found to have realized her friends' fondest wishes. In geography there is still much to be desired; and a careful and undeviating use of the backboard, for four hours daily during the next three years, is recommended as necessary to the acquirement of that dignified DEPORTMENT AND CARRIAGE, so requisite for every young lady of FASHION.

In the principles of religion and morality, Miss Sedley will be found worthy of an establishment which has been honoured by the presence of THE GREAT LEXICOGRAPHER, and the patronage of the admirable Mrs. Chapone. In leaving the Mall, Miss Amelia carries with her the hearts of her companions, and the affectionate regards of her mistress, who has the honour to subscribe herself,

Madam, Your most obliged humble servant, BARBARA PINKERTON

P.S.—Miss Sharp accompanies Miss Sedley. It is particularly requested that Miss Sharp's stay in Russell Square may not exceed ten days. The family of distinction with whom she is engaged, desire to avail themselves of her services as soon as possible.

This letter completed, Miss Pinkerton proceeded to write her own name, and Miss Sedley's, in the fly-leaf of a Johnson's Dictionary— the interesting work which she invariably presented to her scholars, on their departure from the Mall. On the cover was inserted a copy of "Lines addressed to a young lady on quitting Miss Pinkerton's school, at the Mall; by the late revered Doctor Samuel Johnson." In fact, the Lexicographer's name was always on the lips of this majestic woman, and a visit he had paid to her was the cause of her reputation and her fortune.

Being commanded by her elder sister to get "the Dictionary" from the cupboard, Miss Jemima had extracted two copies of the book from the receptacle in question. When Miss Pinkerton had finished the inscription in the first, Jemima, with rather a dubious and timid air, handed her the second.

"For whom is this, Miss Jemima?" said Miss Pinkerton, with awful coldness. "For Becky Sharp," answered Jemima, trembling very much, and blushing over her withered face and neck, as she turned her back on her sister. "For Becky Sharp:

she's going too." "MISS JEMIMA!" exclaimed Miss Pinkerton, in the largest capitals. "Are you in your senses? Replace the Dixonary in the closet, and never venture to take such a liberty in future."

"Well, sister, it's only two-and-ninepence, and poor Becky will be miserable if she don't get one."

"Send Miss Sedley instantly to me," said Miss Pinkerton. And so venturing not to say another word, poor Jemima trotted off, exceedingly flurried and nervous.

Miss Sedley's papa was a merchant in London, and a man of some wealth; whereas Miss Sharp was an articled pupil, for whom Miss Pinkerton had done, as she thought, quite enough, without conferring upon her at parting the high honour of the Dixonary. Although schoolmistresses' letters are to be trusted no more nor less than churchyard epitaphs; yet, as it sometimes happens that a person departs this life who is really deserving of all the praises the stone cutter carves over his bones; who IS a good Christian, a good parent, child, wife, or husband; who actually DOES leave a disconsolate family to mourn his loss; so in academies of the male and female sex it occurs every now and then that the pupil is fully worthy of the praises bestowed by the disinterested instructor. Now, Miss Amelia Sedley was a young lady of this singular species; and deserved not only all that Miss Pinkerton said in her praise, but had many charming qualities which that pompous old Minerva of a woman could not see, from the differences of rank and age between her pupil and herself.

For she could not only sing like a lark, or a Mrs. Billington, and dance like Hillisberg or Parisot; and embroider beautifully; and spell as well as a Dixonary itself; but she had such a kindly, smiling, tender, gentle, generous heart of her own, as won the love of everybody who came near her, from Minerva herself down to the poor girl in the scullery, and the one-eyed tart-woman's daughter, who was permitted to vend her wares once a week to the young ladies in the Mall. She had twelve intimate and bosom friends out of the twenty-four young ladies. Even envious Miss Briggs never spoke ill of her; high and mighty Miss Saltire Lord Dexter's granddaughter allowed that her figure was genteel; and as for Miss Swartz, the rich woolly-haired mulatto from St. Kitt's, on the day Amelia went away, she was in such a passion of tears that they were obliged to send for Dr. Floss, and half tipsify her with salvolatile. Miss Pinkerton's attachment was, as may be supposed from the high position and eminent virtues of that lady, calm and dignified; but Miss Jemima had already whimpered several times at the idea of Amelia's departure; and, but for fear of her sister, would have gone off in downright hysterics, like the heiress who paid double of St. Kitt's. Such luxury of grief, however, is only allowed to parlour-boarders. Honest Jemima had all the bills, and the washing, and the mending, and the puddings, and the plate and crockery, and the servants to superintend. But why speak about her? It is probable that we shall not hear of her again from this moment to the end of time, and that when the great filigree iron gates are once closed on her, she and her awful sister will never issue therefrom into this little world of history.

But as we are to see a great deal of Amelia, there is no harm in saying, at the outset of our acquaintance, that she was a dear little creature; and a great mercy it is, both in life and in novels, which and the latter especially abound in villains of the most sombre sort, that we are to have for a constant companion so guileless and good-natured a person.

As she is not a heroine, there is no need to describe her person; indeed I am afraid that her nose was rather short than otherwise, and her cheeks a great deal too round and red for a heroine; but her face blushed with rosy health, and her lips with the freshest of smiles, and she had a pair of eyes which sparkled with the brightest and honestest good-humour, except indeed when they filled with tears, and that was a great deal too often; for the silly thing would cry over a dead canary-bird; or over a mouse, that the cat haply had seized upon; or over the end of a novel, were it ever so stupid; and as for saying an unkind word to her, were any persons hard-hearted enough to do so—why, so much the worse for them. Even Miss Pinkerton, that austere and godlike woman, ceased scolding her after the first time, and though she no more comprehended sensibility than she did Algebra, gave all masters and teachers particular orders to treat Miss Sedley with the utmost gentleness, as harsh treatment was injurious to her.

So that when the day of departure came, between her two customs of laughing and crying, Miss Sedley was greatly puzzled how to act. She was glad to go home, and yet most woefully sad at leaving school. For three days before, little Laura Martin, the orphan, followed her about like a little dog. She had to make and receive at least fourteen presents—to make fourteen solemn promises of writing every week: "Send my letters under cover to my grandpapa, the Earl of Dexter," said Miss Saltire who, by the way, was rather shabby. "Never mind the postage, but write every day, you dear darling," said the impetuous and woolly-headed, but generous and affectionate Miss Swartz; and the orphan little Laura Martin who was just in round-hand, took her friend's hand and said, looking up in her face wistfully, "Amelia, when I write to you I shall call you Mamma." All which details, I have no doubt, JONES, who reads this book at his Club, will pronounce to be excessively foolish, trivial, twaddling, and ultra-sentimental. Yes; I can see Jones at this minute rather flushed with his joint of mutton and half pint of wine, taking out his pencil and scoring under the words "foolish, twaddling," &c., and adding to them his own remark of "QUITE TRUE." Well, he is a lofty man of genius, and admires the great and heroic in life and novels; and so had better take warning and go elsewhere.

Well, then. The flowers, and the presents, and the trunks, and bonnet-boxes of Miss Sedley having been arranged by Mr. Sambo in the carriage, together with a very small and weather-beaten old cow's-skin trunk with Miss Sharp's card neatly nailed upon it, which was delivered by Sambo with a grin, and packed by the coachman with a corresponding sneer—the hour for parting came; and the grief of that moment was considerably lessened by the admirable discourse which Miss Pinkerton addressed to her pupil. Not that the parting speech caused Amelia to philosophise, or that it armed her in any way with a calmness, the result of argument; but it was intolerably dull, pompous, and tedious; and having the fear of her schoolmistress greatly before her eyes, Miss Sedley did not venture, in her presence, to give way to any ebullitions of private grief. A seed-cake and a bottle of wine were produced in the drawing-room, as on the solemn occasions of the visits of parents, and these refreshments being partaken of, Miss Sedley was at liberty to depart.

"You'll go in and say good-by to Miss Pinkerton, Becky!" said Miss Jemima to a young lady of whom nobody took any notice, and who was coming downstairs with her own bandbox.

"I suppose I must," said Miss Sharp calmly, and much to the wonder of Miss Jemima; and the latter having knocked at the door, and receiving permission to come in, Miss Sharp advanced in a very unconcerned manner, and said in French, and with a perfect accent, "Mademoiselle, je viens vous faire mes adieux."

Miss Pinkerton did not understand French; she only directed those who did: but biting her lips and throwing up her venerable and Roman-nosed head on the top of which figured a large and solemn turban, she said, "Miss Sharp, I wish you a good morning." As the Hammersmith Semiramis spoke, she waved one hand, both by way of adieu, and to give Miss Sharp an opportunity of shaking one of the fingers of the hand which was left out for that purpose.

Miss Sharp only folded her own hands with a very frigid smile and bow, and quite declined to accept the proffered honour; on which Semiramis tossed up her turban more indignantly than ever. In fact, it was a little battle between the young lady and the old one, and the latter was worsted. "Heaven bless you, my child," said she, embracing Amelia, and scowling the while over the girl's shoulder at Miss Sharp. "Come away, Becky," said Miss Jemima, pulling the young woman away in great alarm, and the drawing-room door closed upon them for ever.

Then came the struggle and parting below. Words refuse to tell it. All the servants were there in the hall—all the dear friend—all the young ladies—the dancing-master who had just arrived; and there was such a scuffling, and hugging, and kissing, and crying, with the hysterical YOOPS of Miss Swartz, the parlour-boarder, from her room, as no pen can depict, and as the tender heart would fain pass over. The embracing was over; they parted—that is, Miss Sedley parted from her friends. Miss Sharp had demurely entered the carriage some minutes before. Nobody cried for leaving HER.

Sambo of the bandy legs slammed the carriage door on his young weeping mistress. He sprang up behind the carriage. "Stop!" cried Miss Jemima, rushing to the gate with a parcel.

"It's some sandwiches, my dear," said she to Amelia. "You may be hungry, you know; and Becky, Becky Sharp, here's a book for you that my sister—that is, I—Johnson's Dixonary, you know; you mustn't leave us without that. Good-by. Drive on, coachman. God bless you!"

And the kind creature retreated into the garden, overcome with emotion.

Rebecca's Farewell

But, lo! and just as the coach drove off, Miss Sharp put her pale face out of the window and actually flung the book back into the garden.

This almost caused Jemima to faint with terror. "Well, I never"— said she—"what an audacious"—Emotion prevented her from completing either sentence. The carriage rolled away; the great gates were closed; the bell rang for the dancing lesson. The world is before the two young ladies; and so, farewell to Chiswick Mall.

William Makepeace Thackeray

Vanity Fair

CHAPTER XII

Quite a Sentimental Chapter

We must now take leave of Arcadia, and those amiable people practising the rural virtues there, and travel back to London, to inquire what has become of Miss Amelia "We don't care a fig for her," writes some unknown correspondent with a pretty little handwriting and a pink seal to her note. "She is fade and insipid," and adds some more kind remarks in this strain, which I should never have repeated at all, but that they are in truth prodigiously complimentary to the young lady whom they concern. Has the beloved reader, in his experience of society, never heard similar remarks by good-natured female friends; who always wonder what you CAN see in Miss Smith that is so fascinating; or what COULD induce Major Jones to propose for that silly insignificant simpering Miss Thompson, who has nothing but her wax-doll face to recommend her?

What is there in a pair of pink cheeks and blue eyes forsooth? these dear Moralists ask, and hint wisely that the gifts of genius, the accomplishments of the mind, the mastery of Mangnall's Questions, and a ladylike knowledge of botany and geology, the knack of making poetry, the power of rattling sonatas in the Herz-manner, and so forth, are far more valuable endowments for a female, than those fugitive charms which a few years will inevitably tarnish. It is quite edifying to hear women speculate upon the worthlessness and the duration of beauty.

But though virtue is a much finer thing, and those hapless creatures who suffer under the misfortune of good looks ought to be continually put in mind of the fate which awaits them; and though, very likely, the heroic female character which ladies admire is a more glorious and beautiful object than the kind, fresh, smiling, artless, tender little domestic goddess, whom men are inclined to worship—yet the latter and inferior sort of women must have this consolation—that the men do admire them after all; and that, in spite of all our kind friends' warnings and protests, we go on in our desperate error and folly, and shall to the end of the chapter. Indeed, for my own part, though I have been repeatedly told by persons for whom I have the greatest respect, that Miss Brown is an insignificant chit, and Mrs. White has nothing but her petit minois chiffonne, and Mrs. Black has not a word to say for herself; yet I know that I have had the most delightful conversations with Mrs.

Black of course, my dear Madam, they are inviolable: I see all the men in a cluster round Mrs. White's chair: all the young fellows battling to dance with Miss Brown; and so I am tempted to think that to be despised by her sex is a very great compliment to a woman.

The young ladies in Amelia's society did this for her very satisfactorily. For instance, there was scarcely any point upon which the Misses Osborne, George's sisters, and the Mesdemoiselles Dobbin agreed so well as in their estimate of her very trifling merits: and their wonder that their brothers could find any charms in her. "We are kind to her," the Misses Osborne said, a pair of fine black-browed young ladies who had had the best of governesses, masters, and milliners; and they treated her with such extreme kindness and condescension, and patronised her so insufferably, that the poor little thing was in fact perfectly dumb in their presence, and to all outward appearance as stupid as they thought her. She made efforts to like them, as in duty bound, and as sisters of her future husband.

She passed "long mornings" with them—the most dreary and serious of forenoons. She drove out solemnly in their great family coach with them, and Miss Wirt their governess, that raw-boned Vestal. They took her to the ancient concerts by way of a treat, and to the oratorio, and to St. Paul's to see the charity children, where in such terror was she of her friends, she almost did not dare be affected by the hymn the children sang. Their house was comfortable; their papa's table rich and handsome; their society solemn and genteel; their self-respect prodigious; they had the best pew at the Foundling: all their habits were pompous and orderly, and all their amusements intolerably dull and decorous. After every one of her visits and oh how glad she was when they were over! Miss Osborne and Miss Maria Osborne, and Miss Wirt, the vestal governess, asked each other with increased wonder, "What could George find in that creature?"

How is this? some carping reader exclaims. How is it that Amelia, who had such a number of friends at school, and was so beloved there, comes out into the world and is spurned by her discriminating sex? My dear sir, there were no men at Miss Pinkerton's establishment except the old dancing-master; and you would not have had the girls fall out about HIM? When George, their handsome brother, ran off directly after breakfast, and dined from home half-a-dozen times a week, no wonder the neglected sisters felt a little vexation. When young Bullock of the firm of Hulker, Bullock & Co., Bankers, Lombard Street, who had been making up to Miss Maria the last two seasons, actually asked Amelia to dance the cotillon, could you expect that the former young lady should be pleased? And yet she said she was, like an artless forgiving creature. "I'm so delighted you like dear Amelia," she said quite eagerly to Mr. Bullock after the dance. "She's engaged to my brother George; there's not much in her, but she's the best-natured and most unaffected young creature: at home we're all so fond of her." Dear girl! who can calculate the depth of affection expressed in that enthusiastic SO?

Miss Wirt and these two affectionate young women so earnestly and frequently impressed upon George Osborne's mind the enormity of the sacrifice he was making, and his romantic generosity in throwing himself away upon Amelia, that I'm not sure but that he really thought he was one of the most deserving characters in the British army, and gave himself up to be loved with a good deal of easy resignation.

Somehow, although he left home every morning, as was stated, and dined abroad six days in the week, when his sisters believed the infatuated youth to be at Miss Sedley's apron-strings: he was NOT always with Amelia, whilst the world supposed him at her feet. Certain it is that on more occasions than one, when Captain Dobbin called to look for his friend, Miss Osborne who was very attentive to the Captain, and anxious to hear his military stories, and to know about the health of his dear Mamma, would laughingly point to the opposite side of the square, and say, "Oh, you must go to the Sedleys' to ask for George; WE never see him from morning till night." At which kind of speech the Captain would laugh in rather an absurd constrained manner, and turn off the conversation, like a consummate man of the world, to some topic of general interest, such as the Opera, the Prince's last ball at Carlton House, or the weather—that blessing to society.

"What an innocent it is, that pet of yours," Miss Maria would then say to Miss Jane, upon the Captain's departure. "Did you see how he blushed at the mention of poor George on duty?" "It's a pity Frederick Bullock hadn't some of his modesty, Maria," replies the elder sister, with a toss of he head.

"Modesty! Awkwardness you mean, Jane. I don't want Frederick to trample a hole in my muslin frock, as Captain Dobbin did in yours at Mrs. Perkins'."

"In YOUR frock, he, he! How could he? Wasn't he dancing with Amelia?" The fact is, when Captain Dobbin blushed so, and looked so awkward, he remembered a circumstance of which he did not think it was necessary to inform the young ladies, viz., that he had been calling at Mr. Sedley's house already, on the pretence of seeing George, of course, and George wasn't there, only poor little Amelia, with rather a sad wistful face, seated near the drawing-room window, who, after some very trifling stupid talk, ventured to ask, was there any truth in the report that the regiment was soon to be ordered abroad; and had Captain Dobbin seen Mr. Osborne that day?

The regiment was not ordered abroad as yet; and Captain Dobbin had not seen George. "He was with his sister, most likely," the Captain said. "Should he go and fetch the truant?" So she gave him her hand kindly and gratefully: and he crossed the square; and she waited and waited, but George never came.

Poor little tender heart! and so it goes on hoping and beating, and longing and trusting. You see it is not much of a life to describe. There is not much of what you call incident in it. Only one feeling all day—when will he come? only one thought to sleep and wake upon. I believe George was playing billiards with Captain Cannon in Swallow Street at the time when Amelia was asking Captain Dobbin about him; for George was a jolly sociable fellow, and excellent in all games of skill.

Once, after three days of absence, Miss Amelia put on her bonnet, and actually invaded the Osborne house. "What! leave our brother to come to us?" said the young ladies. "Have you had a quarrel, Amelia? Do tell us!" No, indeed, there had been no quarrel. "Who could quarrel with him?" says she, with her eyes filled with tears. She only came over to—to see her dear friends; they had not met for so long. And this day she was so perfectly stupid and awkward, that the Misses Osborne and their governess, who stared after her as she went sadly away, wondered more than ever what George could see in poor little Amelia. Of course they did. How was she to bare that timid little heart for the inspection of those young ladies with their bold black eyes? It was best that it should shrink and hide itself. I know the Misses Osborne were excellent critics of a Cashmere shawl, or a pink satin slip; and when Miss Turner had hers dyed purple, and made into a spencer; and when Miss Pickford had her ermine tippet twisted into a muff and trimmings, I warrant you the changes did not escape the two intelligent young women before mentioned.

But there are things, look you, of a finer texture than fur or satin, and all Solomon's glories, and all the wardrobe of the Queen of Sheba—things whereof the beauty escapes the eyes of many connoisseurs. And there are sweet modest little souls on which you light, fragrant and blooming tenderly in quiet shady places; and there are garden-ornaments, as big as brass warming-pans, that are fit to stare the sun itself out of countenance. Miss Sedley was not of the sunflower sort; and I say it is out of the rules of all proportion to draw a violet of the size of a double dahlia.

No, indeed; the life of a good young girl who is in the paternal nest as yet, can't have many of those thrilling incidents to which the heroine of romance commonly lays claim. Snares or shot may take off the old birds foraging without—hawks may be abroad, from which they escape or by whom they suffer; but the young ones in the nest have a pretty comfortable unromantic sort of existence in the down and the straw, till it comes to their turn, too, to get on the wing.

While Becky Sharp was on her own wing in the country, hopping on all sorts of twigs, and amid a multiplicity of traps, and pecking up her food quite harmless and successful, Amelia lay snug in her home of Russell Square; if she went into the world, it was under the guidance of the elders; nor did it seem that any evil could befall her or that opulent cheery comfortable home in which she was affectionately sheltered. Mamma had her morning duties, and her daily drive, and the delightful round of visits and shopping which forms the amusement, or the profession as you may call it, of the rich London lady. Papa conducted his mysterious operations in the City—a stirring place in those days, when war was raging all over Europe, and empires were being staked; when the "Courier" newspaper had tens of thousands of subscribers; when one day brought you a battle of Vittoria, another a burning of Moscow, or a newsman's horn blowing down Russell Square about dinner-time, announced such a fact as—"Battle of Leipsic—six hundred thousand men engaged—total defeat of the French—two hundred thousand killed." Old Sedley once or twice came home with a very grave face; and no wonder, when such news as this was agitating all the hearts and all the Stocks of Europe.

Meanwhile matters went on in Russell Square, Bloomsbury, just as if matters in Europe were not in the least disorganised. The retreat from Leipsic made no difference in the number of meals Mr. Sambo took in the servants' hall; the allies poured into France, and the dinner-bell rang at five o'clock just as usual. I don't think poor Amelia cared anything about Brienne and Montmirail, or was fairly interested in the war until the abdication of the Emperor; when she clapped her hands and said prayers—oh, how grateful! and flung herself into George Osborne's arms with all her soul, to the astonishment of everybody who witnessed that ebullition of sentiment. The fact is, peace was declared, Europe was going to be at rest; the Corsican was overthrown, and Lieutenant Osborne's regiment would not be ordered on service. That was the way in which Miss Amelia reasoned. The fate of Europe was Lieutenant George Osborne to her. His dangers being over, she sang Te Deum. He was her Europe: her emperor: her allied monarchs and august prince regent. He was her sun and moon; and I believe she thought the grand illumination and ball at the Mansion House, given to the sovereigns, were especially in honour of George Osborne.

We have talked of shift, self, and poverty, as those dismal instructors under whom poor Miss Becky Sharp got her education. Now, love was Miss Amelia Sedley's last tutoress, and it was amazing what progress our young lady made under that popular teacher. In the course of fifteen or eighteen months' daily and constant attention to this eminent finishing governess, what a deal of secrets Amelia learned, which Miss Wirt and the black-eyed young ladies over the way, which old Miss Pinkerton of Chiswick herself, had no cognizance of! As, indeed, how should any of those prim and reputable virgins? With Misses P. and W. the tender passion is out of the question: I would not dare to breathe such an idea regarding them. Miss Maria Osborne, it is true, was "attached" to Mr.

Frederick Augustus Bullock, of the firm of Hulker, Bullock & Bullock; but hers was a most respectable attachment, and she would have taken Bullock Senior just the same, her mind being fixed—as that of a well-bred young woman should be—upon a house in Park Lane, a country house at Wimbledon, a handsome chariot, and two prodigious tall horses and footmen, and a fourth of the annual profits of the eminent firm of Hulker & Bullock, all of which advantages were represented in the person of Frederick Augustus.

Had orange blossoms been invented then those touching emblems of female purity imported by us from France, where people's daughters are universally sold in marriage, Miss Maria, I say, would have assumed the spotless wreath, and stepped into the travelling carriage by the side of gouty, old, bald-headed, bottle-nosed Bullock Senior; and devoted her beautiful existence to his happiness with perfect modesty—only the old gentleman was married already; so she bestowed her young affections on the junior partner. Sweet, blooming, orange flowers! The other day I saw Miss Trotter, arrayed in them, trip into the travelling carriage at St. George's, Hanover Square, and Lord Methuselah hobbled in after. With what an engaging modesty she pulled down the blinds of the chariot—the dear innocent! There were half the carriages of Vanity Fair at the wedding.

This was not the sort of love that finished Amelia's education; and in the course of a year turned a good young girl into a good young woman—to be a good wife presently, when the happy time should come. This young person erhaps it was very imprudent in her parents to encourage her, and abet her in such idolatry and silly romantic ideas loved, with all her heart, the young officer in His Majesty's service with whom we have made a brief acquaintance. She thought about him the very first moment on waking; and his was the very last name mentioned m her prayers. She never had seen a man so beautiful or so clever: such a figure on horseback: such a dancer: such a hero in general.

Talk of the Prince's bow! what was it to George's? She had seen Mr. Brummell, whom everybody praised so. Compare such a person as that to her George! Not amongst all the beaux at the Opera and there were beaux in those days with actual opera hats was there any one to equal him. He was only good enough to be a fairy prince; and oh, what magnanimity to stoop to such a humble Cinderella! Miss Pinkerton would have tried to check this blind devotion very likely, had she been Amelia's confidante; but not with much success, depend upon it. It is in the nature and instinct of some women. Some are made to scheme, and some to love; and I wish any respected bachelor that reads this may take the sort that best likes him.

While under this overpowering impression, Miss Amelia neglected her twelve dear friends at Chiswick most cruelly, as such selfish people commonly will do. She had but this subject, of course, to think about; and Miss Saltire was too cold for a confidante, and she couldn't bring her mind to tell Miss Swartz, the woolly-haired young heiress from St. Kitt's. She had little Laura Martin home for the holidays; and my belief is, she made a confidante of her, and promised that Laura should come and live with her when she was married, and gave Laura a great deal of information regarding the passion of love, which must have been singularly useful and novel to that little person. Alas, alas! I fear poor Emmy had not a well-regulated mind.

What were her parents doing, not to keep this little heart from beating so fast? Old Sedley did not seem much to notice matters. He was graver of late, and his City affairs absorbed him. Mrs. Sedley was of so easy and uninquisitive a nature that she wasn't even jealous. Mr. Jos was away, being besieged by an Irish widow at Cheltenham. Amelia had the house to herself—ah! too much to herself sometimes—not that she ever doubted; for, to be sure, George must be at the Horse Guards; and he can't always get leave from Chatham; and he must see his friends and sisters, and mingle in society when in town he, such an ornament to every society!; and when he is with the regiment, he is too tired to write long letters. I know where she kept that packet she had—and can steal in and out of her chamber like Iachimo—like Iachimo? No—that is a bad part. I will only act Moonshine, and peep harmless into the bed where faith and beauty and innocence lie dreaming.

But if Osborne's were short and soldierlike letters, it must be confessed, that were Miss Sedley's letters to Mr. Osborne to be published, we should have to extend this novel to such a multiplicity of volumes as not the most sentimental reader could support; that she not only filled sheets of large paper, but crossed them with the most astonishing perverseness; that she wrote whole pages out of poetry-books without the least pity; that she underlined words and passages with quite a frantic emphasis; and, in fine, gave the usual tokens of her condition. She wasn't a heroine. Her letters were full of repetition. She wrote rather doubtful grammar sometimes, and in her verses took all sorts of liberties with the metre. But oh, mesdames, if you are not allowed to touch the heart sometimes in spite of syntax, and are not to be loved until you all know the difference between trimeter and tetrameter, may all Poetry go to the deuce, and every schoolmaster perish miserably!

William Makepeace Thackeray

Vanity Fair

CHAPTER XV

In Which Rebecca's Husband Appears for a Short Time. Every reader of a sentimental turn and we desire no other must have been pleased with the tableau with which the last act of our little drama concluded; for what can be prettier than an image of Love on his knees before Beauty?

But when Love heard that awful confession from Beauty that she was married already, he bounced up from his attitude of humility on the carpet, uttering exclamations which caused poor little Beauty to be more frightened than she was when she made her avowal. "Married; you're joking," the Baronet cried, after the first explosion of rage and wonder. "You're making vun of me, Becky. Who'd ever go to marry you without a shilling to your vortune?"

"Married! married!" Rebecca said, in an agony of tears—her voice choking with emotion, her handkerchief up to her ready eyes, fainting against the mantelpiece a figure of woe fit to melt the most obdurate heart. "O Sir Pitt, dear Sir Pitt, do not think me ungrateful for all your goodness to me. It is only your generosity that has extorted my secret."

"Generosity be hanged!" Sir Pitt roared out. "Who is it tu, then, you're married? Where was it?"

"Let me come back with you to the country, sir! Let me watch over you as faithfully as ever! Don't, don't separate me from dear Queen's Crawley!"

"The feller has left you, has he?" the Baronet said, beginning, as he fancied, to comprehend. "Well, Becky—come back if you like. You can't eat your cake and have it. Any ways I made you a vair offer. Coom back as governess—you shall have it all your own way." She held out one hand. She cried fit to break her heart; her ringlets fell over her face, and over the marble mantelpiece where she laid it.

"So the rascal ran off, eh?" Sir Pitt said, with a hideous attempt at consolation. "Never mind, Becky, I'LL take care of 'ee." "Oh, sir! it would be the pride of my life to go back to Queen's Crawley, and take care of the children, and of you as formerly, when you said you were pleased with the services of your little Rebecca. When I think of what you have just offered me, my heart fills with gratitude indeed it does. I can't be your wife, sir; let me—let me be your daughter." Saying which, Rebecca went down on HER knees in a most tragical way, and, taking Sir Pitt's horny black hand between her own two which were very pretty and white, and as soft as satin, looked up in his face with an expression of exquisite pathos and confidence, when—when the door opened, and Miss Crawley sailed in.

Mrs. Firkin and Miss Briggs, who happened by chance to

be at the parlour door soon after the Baronet and Rebecca entered the apartment, had also seen accidentally, through the keyhole, the old gentleman prostrate before the governess, and had heard the generous proposal which he made her. It was scarcely out of his mouth when Mrs. Firkin and Miss Briggs had streamed up the stairs, had rushed into the drawing-room where Miss Crawley was reading the French novel, and had given that old lady the astounding intelligence that Sir Pitt was on his knees, proposing to Miss Sharp.

And if you calculate the time for the above dialogue to take place—the time for Briggs and Firkin to fly to the drawing-room—the time for Miss Crawley to be astonished, and to drop her volume of Pigault le Brun —and the time for her to come downstairs—you will see how exactly accurate this history is, and how Miss Crawley must have appeared at the very instant when Rebecca had assumed the attitude of humility.

"It is the lady on the ground, and not the gentleman," Miss Crawley said, with a look and voice of great scorn. "They told me that YOU were on your knees, Sir Pitt: do kneel once more, and let me see this pretty couple!"

"I have thanked Sir Pitt Crawley, Ma'am," Rebecca said, rising, "and have told him that—that I never can become Lady Crawley."

"Refused him!" Miss Crawley said, more bewildered than ever. Briggs and Firkin at the door opened the eyes of astonishment and the lips of wonder.

"Yes—refused," Rebecca continued, with a sad, tearful voice.

"And am I to credit my ears that you absolutely proposed to her, Sir Pitt?" the old lady asked.

"Ees," said the Baronet, "I did."

"And she refused you as she says?"

"Ees," Sir Pitt said, his features on a broad grin.

"It does not seem to break your heart at any rate," Miss Crawley remarked.

"Nawt a bit," answered Sir Pitt, with a coolness and good-humour which set Miss Crawley almost mad with bewilderment. That an old gentleman of station should fall on his knees to a penniless governess, and burst out laughing because she refused to marry him— that a penniless governess should refuse a Baronet with four thousand a year—these were mysteries which Miss Crawley could never comprehend. It surpassed any complications of intrigue in her favourite Pigault le Brun.

"I'm glad you think it good sport, brother," she continued, groping wildly through this amazement.

"Vamous," said Sir Pitt. "Who'd ha' thought it! what a sly little devil! what a little fox it waws!" he muttered to himself, chuckling with pleasure.

"Who'd have thought what?" cries Miss Crawley, stamping with her foot. "Pray, Miss Sharp, are you waiting for the Prince Regent's divorce, that you don't think our family good enough for you?"

"My attitude," Rebecca said, "when you came in, ma'am, did not look as if I despised such an honour as this good—this noble man has deigned to offer me. Do you think I have no heart? Have you all loved me, and been so kind to the poor orphan—deserted—girl, and am I to feel nothing? O my friends! O my benefactors! may not my love, my life, my duty, try to repay the confidence you have shown me? Do you grudge me even gratitude, Miss Crawley? It is too much—my heart is too full"; and she sank down in a chair so pathetically, that most of the audience present were perfectly melted with her sadness.

"Whether you marry me or not, you're a good little girl, Becky, and I'm your vriend, mind," said Sir Pitt, and putting on his crape-bound hat, he walked away—greatly to Rebecca's relief; for it was evident that her secret was unrevealed to Miss Crawley, and she had the advantage of a brief reprieve.

Putting her handkerchief to her eyes, and nodding away honest Briggs, who would have followed her upstairs, she went up to her apartment; while Briggs and Miss Crawley, in a high state of excitement, remained to discuss the strange event, and Firkin, not less moved, dived down into the kitchen regions, and talked of it with all the male and female company there. And so impressed was Mrs. Firkin with the news, that she thought proper to write off by that very night's post, "with her humble duty to Mrs. Bute Crawley and the family at the Rectory, and Sir Pitt has been and proposed for to marry Miss Sharp, wherein she has refused him, to the wonder of all."

The two ladies in the dining-room where worthy Miss Briggs was delighted to be admitted once more to confidential conversation with her patroness wondered to their hearts' content at Sir Pitt's offer, and Rebecca's refusal; Briggs very acutely suggesting that there must have been some obstacle in the shape of a previous attachment, otherwise no young woman in her senses would ever have refused so advantageous a proposal.

"You would have accepted it yourself, wouldn't you, Briggs?" Miss Crawley said, kindly.

"Would it not be a privilege to be Miss Crawley's sister?" Briggs replied, with meek evasion.

"Well, Becky would have made a good Lady Crawley, after all," Miss Crawley remarked who was mollified by the girl's refusal, and very liberal and generous now there was no call for her sacrifices. "She has brains in plenty much more wit in her little finger than you have, my poor dear Briggs, in all your head. Her manners are excellent, now I have formed her. She is a Montmorency, Briggs, and blood is something, though I despise it for my part; and she would have held her own amongst those pompous stupid Hampshire people much better than that unfortunate ironmonger's daughter."

Briggs coincided as usual, and the "previous attachment" was then discussed in conjectures. "You poor friendless creatures are always having some foolish tendre," Miss Crawley said. "You yourself, you know, were in love with a writing-master don't cry, Briggs—you're always crying, and it won't bring him to life again, and I suppose this unfortunate Becky has been silly and sentimental too—some apothecary, or house-steward, or painter, or young curate, or something of that sort."

"Poor thing! poor thing!" says Briggs who was thinking of twenty-four years back, and that hectic young writing-master whose lock of yellow hair, and whose letters, beautiful in their illegibility, she cherished in her old desk upstairs. "Poor thing, poor thing!" says Briggs. Once more she was a fresh-cheeked lass of eighteen; she was at evening church, and the hectic writing-master and she were quavering out of the same psalm-book.

"After such conduct on Rebecca's part," Miss Crawley said enthusiastically, "our family should do something. Find out who is the objet, Briggs. I'll set him up in a shop; or order my portrait of him, you know; or speak to my cousin, the Bishop and I'll doter Becky, and we'll have a wedding, Briggs, and you shall make the breakfast, and be a bridesmaid."

Briggs declared that it would be delightful, and vowed that her dear Miss Crawley was always kind and generous, and went up to Rebecca's bedroom to console her and prattle about the offer, and the refusal, and the cause thereof; and to hint at the generous intentions of Miss Crawley, and to find out who was the gentleman that had the mastery of Miss Sharp's heart.

Rebecca was very kind, very affectionate and affected—responded to Briggs's offer of tenderness with grateful fervour—owned there was a secret attachment—a delicious mystery—what a pity Miss Briggs had not remained half a minute longer at the keyhole! Rebecca might, perhaps, have told more: but five minutes after Miss Briggs's arrival in Rebecca's apartment, Miss Crawley actually made her appearance there—an unheard-of honour—her impatience had overcome her; she could not wait for the tardy operations of her ambassadress: so she came in person, and ordered Briggs out of the room. And expressing her approval of Rebecca's conduct, she asked particulars of the interview, and the previous transactions which had brought about the astonishing offer of Sir Pitt.

Rebecca said she had long had some notion of the partiality with which Sir Pitt honoured her for he was in the habit of making his feelings known in a very frank and unreserved manner but, not to mention private reasons with which she would not for the present trouble Miss Crawley, Sir Pitt's age, station, and habits were such as to render a marriage quite impossible; and could a woman with any feeling of self-respect and any decency listen to proposals at such a moment, when the funeral of the lover's deceased wife had not actually taken place?

"Nonsense, my dear, you would never have refused him had there not been some one else in the case," Miss Crawley said, coming to her point at once. "Tell me the private reasons; what are the private reasons? There is some one; who is it that has touched your heart?"

Rebecca cast down her eyes, and owned there was. "You have guessed right, dear lady," she said, with a sweet simple faltering voice. "You wonder at one so poor and friendless having an attachment, don't you? I have never heard that poverty was any safeguard against it. I wish it were."

"My poor dear child," cried Miss Crawley, who was always quite ready to be sentimental, "is our passion unrequited, then? Are we pining in secret? Tell me all, and let me console you."

"I wish you could, dear Madam," Rebecca said in the same tearful tone. "Indeed, indeed, I need it." And she laid her head upon Miss Crawley's shoulder and wept there so naturally that the old lady, surprised into sympathy, embraced her with an almost maternal kindness, uttered many soothing protests of regard and affection for her, vowed that she loved her as a daughter, and would do everything in her power to serve her. "And now who is it, my dear? Is it that pretty Miss Sedley's brother? You said something about an affair with him. I'll ask him here, my dear. And you shall have him: indeed you shall."

"Don't ask me now," Rebecca said. "You shall know all soon. Indeed you shall. Dear kind Miss Crawley—dear friend, may I say so?"

"That you may, my child," the old lady replied, kissing her. "I can't tell you now," sobbed out Rebecca, "I am very miserable. But O! love me always—promise you will love me always." And in the midst of mutual tears—for the emotions of the younger woman had awakened the sympathies of the elder—this promise was solemnly given by Miss Crawley, who left her little protege, blessing and admiring her as a dear, artless, tender-hearted, affectionate, incomprehensible creature. And now she was left alone to think over the sudden and wonderful events of the day, and of what had been and what might have been. What think you were the private feelings of Miss, no begging her pardon of Mrs. Rebecca? If, a few pages back, the present writer claimed the privilege of peeping into Miss Amelia Sedley's bedroom, and understanding with the omniscience of the novelist all the gentle pains and passions which were tossing upon that innocent pillow, why should he not declare himself to be Rebecca's confidante too, master of her secrets, and seal-keeper of that young woman's conscience?

Well, then, in the first place, Rebecca gave way to some very sincere and touching regrets that a piece of marvellous good fortune should have been so near her, and she actually obliged to decline it. In this natural emotion every properly regulated mind will certainly share. What good mother is there that would not commiserate a penniless spinster, who might have been my lady, and have shared four thousand a year? What well-bred young person is there in all Vanity Fair, who will not feel for a hard-working, ingenious, meritorious girl, who gets such an honourable, advantageous, provoking offer, just at the very moment when it is out of her power to accept it? I am sure our friend Becky's disappointment deserves and will command every sympathy.

I remember one night being in the Fair myself, at an evening party. I observed old Miss Toady there also present, single out for her special attentions and flattery little Mrs. Briefless, the barrister's wife, who is of a good family certainly, but, as we all know, is as poor as poor can be.

What, I asked in my own mind, can cause this obsequiousness on the part of Miss Toady; has Briefless got a county court, or has his wife had a fortune left her? Miss Toady explained presently, with that simplicity which distinguishes all her conduct. "You know," she said, "Mrs Briefless is granddaughter of Sir John Redhand, who is so ill at Cheltenham that he can't last six months. Mrs. Briefless's papa succeeds; so you see she will be a baronet's daughter." And

Toady asked Briefless and his wife to dinner the very next week. If the mere chance of becoming a baronet's daughter can procure a lady such homage in the world, surely, surely we may respect the agonies of a young woman who has lost the opportunity of becoming a baronet's wife.

Who would have dreamed of Lady Crawley dying so soon? She was one of those sickly women that might have lasted these ten years—Rebecca thought to herself, in all the woes of repentance—and I might have been my lady! I might have led that old man whither I would. I might have thanked Mrs. Bute for her patronage, and Mr. Pitt for his insufferable condescension. I would have had the town-house newly furnished and decorated. I would have had the handsomest carriage in London, and a box at the opera; and I would have been presented next season. All this might have been; and now—now all was doubt and mystery.

But Rebecca was a young lady of too much resolution and energy of character to permit herself much useless and unseemly sorrow for the irrevocable past; so, having devoted only the proper portion of regret to it, she wisely turned her whole attention towards the future, which was now vastly more important to her. And she surveyed her position, and its hopes, doubts, and chances.

In thc first place, she was MARRIED—that was a great fact. Sir Pitt knew it. She was not so much surprised into the avowal, as induced to make it by a sudden calculation. It must have come some day: and why not now as at a later period? He who would have married her himself must at least be silent with regard to her marriage. How Miss Crawley would bear the news—was the great question.

Misgivings Rebecca had; but she remembered all Miss Crawley had said; the old lady's avowed contempt for birth; her daring liberal opinions; her general romantic propensities; her almost doting attachment to her nephew, and her repeatedly expressed fondness for Rebecca herself. She is so fond of him, Rebecca thought, that she will forgive him anything: she is so used to me that I don't think she could be comfortable without me: when the eclaircissement comes there will be a scene, and hysterics, and a great quarrel, and then a great reconciliation. At all events, what use was there in delaying? the die was thrown, and now or to-morrow the issue must be the same. And so, resolved that Miss Crawley should have the news, the young person debated in her mind as to the best means of conveying it to her; and whether she should face the storm that must come, or fly and avoid it until its first fury was blown over. In this state of meditation she wrote the following letter: Dearest Friend,

The great crisis which we have debated about so often is COME. Half of my secret is known, and I have thought and thought, until I am quite sure that now is the time to reveal THE WHOLE OF THE MYSTERY. Sir Pitt came to me this morning, and made—what do you think?—A DECLARATION IN FORM. Think of that! Poor little me. I might have been Lady Crawley. How pleased Mrs. Bute would have been: and ma tante if I had taken precedence of her! I might have been somebody's mamma, instead of—O, I tremble, I tremble, when I think how soon we must tell all!

Sir Pitt knows I am married, and not knowing to whom, is not very much displeased as yet. Ma tante is ACTUALLY ANGRY that I should have refused him. But she is all kindness and graciousness. She condescends to say I would have made him a good wife; and vows that she will be a mother to your little Rebecca. She will be shaken when she first hears the news. But need we fear anything beyond a momentary anger? I think not: I AM SURE not. She dotes upon you so you naughty, good-for-nothing man, that she would pardon you ANYTHING: and, indeed, I believe, the next place in her heart is mine: and that she would be miserable without me. Dearest! something TELLS ME we shall conquer. You shall leave that odious regiment: quit gaming, racing, and BE A GOOD BOY; and we shall all live in Park Lane, and ma tante shall leave us all her money.

I shall try and walk to-morrow at 3 in the usual place. If Miss B. accompanies me, you must come to dinner, and bring an answer, and put it in the third volume of Porteus's Sermons. But, at all events, come to your own

To Miss Eliza Styles, At Mr. Barnet's, Saddler, Knightsbridge. And I trust there is no reader of this little story who has not discernment enough to perceive that the Miss Eliza Styles an old schoolfellow, Rebecca said, with whom she had resumed an active correspondence of late, and who used to fetch these letters from the saddler's, wore brass spurs, and large curling mustachios, and was indeed no other than Captain Rawdon Crawley.

William Makepeace Thackeray

Vanity Fair

CHAPTER XIX

Miss Crawley at Nurse: We have seen how Mrs. Firkin, the lady's maid, as soon as any event of importance to the Crawley family came to her knowledge, felt bound to communicate it to Mrs. Bute Crawley, at the Rectory; and have before mentioned how particularly kind and attentive that good-natured lady was to Miss Crawley's confidential servant. She had been a gracious friend to Miss Briggs, the companion, also; and had secured the latter's good-will by a number of those attentions and promises, which cost so little in the making, and are yet so valuable and agreeable to the recipient. Indeed every good economist and manager of a household must know how cheap and yet how amiable these professions are, and what a flavour they give to the most homely dish in life.

Who was the blundering idiot who said that "fine words butter no parsnips"? Half the parsnips of society are served and rendered palatable with no other sauce. As the immortal Alexis Soyer can make more delicious soup for a half-penny than an ignorant cook can concoct with pounds of vegetables and meat, so a skilful artist will make a few simple and pleasing phrases go farther than ever so much substantial benefit-stock in the hands of a mere bungler. Nay, we know that substantial benefits often sicken some stomachs; whereas, most will digest any amount of fine words, and be always eager for more of the same food. Mrs. Bute had told Briggs and Firkin so often of the depth of her affection for them; and what she would do, if she had Miss Crawley's fortune, for friends so excellent and attached, that the ladies in question had the deepest regard for her; and felt as much gratitude and confidence as if Mrs. Bute had loaded them with the most expensive favours.

Rawdon Crawley, on the other hand, like a selfish heavy dragoon as he was, never took the least trouble to conciliate his aunt's aides-de-camp, showed his contempt for the pair with entire frankness— made Firkin pull off his boots on one occasion—sent her out in the rain on ignominious messages—and if he gave her a guinea, flung it to her as if it were a box on the ear. As his aunt, too, made a butt of Briggs, the Captain followed the example, and levelled his jokes at her—jokes about as delicate as a kick from his charger. Whereas, Mrs. Bute consulted her in matters of taste or difficulty, admired her poetry, and by a thousand acts of kindness and politeness, showed her appreciation of Briggs; and if she made Firkin a twopenny-halfpenny present, accompanied it with so many compliments, that the twopence-half-penny was transmuted into gold in the heart of the grateful waiting-maid, who, besides, was looking forwards quite contentedly to some prodigious benefit which must happen to her on the day when Mrs. Bute came into her fortune.

The different conduct of these two people is pointed out respectfully to the attention of persons commencing the world. Praise everybody, I say to such: never be squeamish, but speak out your compliment both point-blank in a man's face, and behind his back, when you know there is a reasonable chance of his hearing it again. Never lose a chance of saying a kind word. As Collingwood never saw a vacant place in his estate but he took an acorn out of his pocket and popped it in; so deal with your compliments through life. An acorn costs nothing; but it may sprout into a prodigious bit of timber.

In a word, during Rawdon Crawley's prosperity, he was only obeyed with sulky acquiescence; when his disgrace came, there was nobody to help or pity him. Whereas, when Mrs. Bute took the command at Miss Crawley's house, the garrison there were charmed to act under such a leader, expecting all sorts of promotion from her promises, her generosity, and her kind words. That he would consider himself beaten, after one defeat, and make no attempt to regain the position he had lost, Mrs. Bute Crawley never allowed herself to suppose. She knew Rebecca to be too clever and spirited and desperate a woman to submit without a struggle; and felt that she must prepare for that combat, and be incessantly watchful against assault; or mine, or surprise.

In the first place, though she held the town, was she sure of the principal inhabitant? Would Miss Crawley herself hold out; and had she not a secret longing to welcome back the ousted adversary? The old lady liked Rawdon, and Rebecca, who amused her. Mrs. Bute could not disguise from herself the fact that none of her party could so contribute to the pleasures of the town-bred lady. "My girls' singing, after that little odious governess's, I know is unbearable," the candid Rector's wife owned to herself. "She always used to go to sleep when Martha and Louisa played their duets. Jim's stiff college manners and poor dear Bute's talk about his dogs and horses always annoyed her. If I took her to the Rectory, she would grow angry with us all, and fly, I know she would; and might fall into that horrid Rawdon's clutches again, and be the victim of that little viper of a Sharp. Meanwhile, it is clear to me that she is exceedingly unwell, and cannot move for some weeks, at any rate; during which we must think of some plan to protect her from the arts of those unprincipled people."

In the very best-of moments, if anybody told Miss Crawley that she was, or looked ill, the trembling old lady sent off for her doctor; and I daresay she was very unwell after the sudden family event, which might serve to shake stronger nerves than hers. At least, Mrs. Bute thought it was her duty to inform the physician, and the apothecary, and the dame-de-compagnie, and the domestics, that Miss Crawley was in a most critical state, and that they were to act accordingly. She had the street laid knee-deep with straw; and the knocker put by with Mr. Bowls's plate. She insisted that the Doctor should call twice a day; and deluged her patient with draughts every two hours. When anybody entered the room, she uttered a shshshsh so sibilant and ominous, that it frightened the poor old lady in her bed, from which she could not look without seeing Mrs. Bute's beady eyes eagerly fixed on her, as the latter sate steadfast in the arm-chair by the bedside. They seemed to lighten in the dark for she kept the curtains closed as she moved about the room on velvet paws like a cat.

There Miss Crawley lay for days—ever so many days—Mr. Bute reading books of devotion to her: for nights, long nights, during which she had to hear the watchman sing, the night-light sputter; visited at midnight, the last thing, by the stealthy apothecary; and then left to look at Mrs. Bute's twinkling eyes, or the flicks of yellow that the rushlight threw on the dreary darkened ceiling. Hygeia herself would have fallen sick under such a regimen; and how much more this poor old nervous victim? It has been said that when she was in health and good spirits, this venerable inhabitant of Vanity Fair had as free notions about religion and morals as Monsieur de Voltaire himself could desire, but when illness overtook her, it was aggravated by the most dreadful terrors of death, and an utter cowardice took possession of the prostrate old sinner. Sick-bed homilies and pious reflections are, to be sure, out of place in mere story-books, and we are not going after the fashion of some novelists of the present day to cajole the public into a sermon, when it is only a comedy that the reader pays his money to witness.

But, without preaching, the truth may surely be borne in mind, that the bustle, and triumph, and laughter, and gaiety which Vanity Fair exhibits in public, do not always pursue the performer into private life, and that the most dreary depression of spirits and dismal repentances sometimes overcome him. Recollection of the best ordained banquets will scarcely cheer sick epicures. Reminiscences of the most becoming dresses and brilliant ball triumphs will go very little way to console faded beauties. Perhaps statesmen, at a particular period of existence, are not much gratified at thinking over the most triumphant divisions; and the success or the pleasure of yesterday becomes of very small account when a certain albeit uncertain morrow is in view, about which all of us must some day or other be speculating. O brother wearers of motley! Are there not moments when one grows sick of grinning and tumbling, and the jingling of cap and bells? This, dear friends and companions, is my amiable object—to walk with you through the Fair, to examine the shops and the shows there; and that we should all come home after the flare, and the noise, and the gaiety, and be perfectly miserable in private.

"If that poor man of mine had a head on his shoulders," Mrs. Bute Crawley thought to herself, "how useful he might be, under present circumstances, to this unhappy old lady! He might make her repent of her shocking free-thinking ways; he might urge her to do her duty, and cast off that odious reprobate who has disgraced himself and his family; and he might induce her to do justice to my dear girls and the two boys, who require and deserve, I am sure, every assistance which their relatives can give them."

And, as the hatred of vice is always a progress towards virtue, Mrs. Bute Crawley endeavoured to instil her sister-in-law a proper abhorrence for all Rawdon Crawley's manifold sins: of which his uncle's wife brought forward such a catalogue as indeed would have served to condemn a whole regiment of young officers. If a man has committed wrong in life, I don't know any moralist more anxious to point his errors out to the world than his own relations; so Mrs. Bute showed a perfect family interest and knowledge of Rawdon's history. Shc had all the particulars of that ugly quarrel with Captain Marker, in which Rawdon, wrong from the beginning, ended in shooting the Captain.

She knew how the unhappy Lord Dovedale, whose mamma had taken a house at Oxford, so that he might be educated there, and who had never touched a card in his life till he came to London, was perverted by Rawdon at the Cocoa-Tree, made helplessly tipsy by this abominable seducer and perverter of youth, and fleeced of four thousand pounds. She described with the most vivid minuteness the agonies of the country families whom he had ruined— the sons whom he had plunged into dishonour and poverty—the daughters whom he had inveigled into perdition. She knew the poor tradesmen who were bankrupt by his extravagance—the mean shifts and rogueries with which he had ministered to it—the astounding falsehoods by which he had imposed upon the most generous of aunts, and the ingratitude and ridicule by which he had repaid her sacrifices.

She imparted these stories gradually to Miss Crawley; gave her the whole benefit of them; felt it to be her bounden duty as a Christian woman and mother of a family to do so; had not the smallest remorse or compunction for the victim whom her tongue was immolating; nay, very likely thought her act was quite meritorious, and plumed herself upon her resolute manner of performing it. Yes, if a man's character is to be abused, say what you will, there's nobody like a relation to do the business. And one is bound to own, regarding this unfortunate wretch of a Rawdon Crawley, that the mere truth was enough to condemn him, and that all inventions of scandal were quite superfluous pains on his friends' parts.

Rebecca, too, being now a relative, came in for the fullest share of Mrs. Bute's kind inquiries. This indefatigable pursuer of truth having given strict orders that the door was to be denied to all emissaries or letters from Rawdon, took Miss Crawley's carriage, and drove to her old friend Miss Pinkerton, at Minerva House, Chiswick Mall, to whom she announced the dreadful intelligence of Captain Rawdon's seduction by Miss Sharp, and from whom she got sundry strange particulars regarding the ex-governess's birth and early history. The friend of the Lexicographer had plenty of information to give. Miss Jemima was made to fetch the drawing-master's receipts and letters. This one was from a spunging-house: that entreated an advance: another was full of gratitude for Rebecca's reception by the ladies of Chiswick: and the last document from the unlucky artist's pen was that in which, from his dying bed, he recommended his orphan child to Miss Pinkerton's protection.

There were juvenile letters and petitions from Rebecca, too, in the collection, imploring aid for her father or declaring her own gratitude. Perhaps in Vanity Fair there are no better satires than letters. Take a bundle of your dear friend's of ten years back— your dear friend whom you hate now. Look at a file of your sister's! how you clung to each other till you quarrelled about the twenty-pound legacy! Get down the round-hand scrawls of your son who has half broken your heart with selfish undutifulness since; or a parcel of your own, breathing endless ardour and love eternal, which were sent back by your mistress when she married the Nabob— your mistress for whom you now care no more than for Queen Elizabeth. Vows, love, promises, confidences, gratitude, how queerly they read after a while!

There ought to be a law in Vanity Fair ordering the destruction of every written document except receipted tradesmen's bills after a certain brief and proper interval. Those quacks and misanthropes who advertise indelible Japan ink should be made to perish along with their wicked discoveries. The best ink for Vanity Fair use would be one that faded utterly in a couple of days, and left the paper clean and blank, so that you might write on it to somebody else.

From Miss Pinkerton's the indefatigable Mrs. Bute followed the track of Sharp and his daughter back to the lodgings in Greek Street, which the defunct painter had occupied; and where portraits of the landlady in white satin, and of the husband in brass buttons, done by Sharp in lieu of a quarter's rent, still decorated the parlour walls. Mrs. Stokes was a communicative person, and quickly told all she knew about Mr. Sharp; how dissolute and poor he was; how good-natured and amusing; how he was always hunted by bailiffs and duns; how, to the landlady's horror, though she never could abide the woman, he did not marry his wife till a short time before her death; and what a queer little wild vixen his daughter was; how she kept them all laughing with her fun and mimicry; how she used to fetch the gin from the public-house, and was known in all the studios in the quarter—in brief, Mrs. Bute got such a full account of her new niece's parentage, education, and behaviour as would scarcely have pleased Rebecca, had the latter known that such inquiries were being made concerning her.

Of all these industrious researches Miss Crawley had the full benefit. Mrs. Rawdon Crawley was the daughter of an opera-girl. She had danced herself. She had been a model to the painters. She was brought up as became her mother's daughter. She drank gin with her father, &c. &c. It was a lost woman who was married to a lost man; and the moral to be inferred from Mrs. Bute's tale was, that the knavery of the pair was irremediable, and that no properly conducted person should ever notice them again.

These were the materials which prudent Mrs. Bute gathered together in Park Lane, the provisions and ammunition as it were with which she fortified the house against the siege which she knew that Rawdon and his wife would lay to Miss Crawley.

But if a fault may be found with her arrangements, it is this, that she was too eager: she managed rather too well; undoubtedly she made Miss Crawley more ill than was necessary; and though the old invalid succumbed to her authority, it was so harassing and severe, that the victim would be inclined to escape at the very first chance which fell in her way. Managing women, the ornaments of their sex—women who order everything for everybody, and know so much better than any person concerned what is good for their neighbours, don't sometimes speculate upon the possibility of a domestic revolt, or upon other extreme consequences resulting from their overstrained authority.

Thus, for instance, Mrs. Bute, with the best intentions no doubt in the world, and wearing herself to death as she did by foregoing sleep, dinner, fresh air, for the sake of her invalid sister-in-law, carried her conviction of the old lady's illness so far that she almost managed her into her coffin. She pointed out her sacrifices and their results one day to the constant apothecary, Mr. Clump.

"I am sure, my dear Mr. Clump," she said, "no efforts of mine have been wanting to restore our dear invalid, whom the ingratitude of her nephew has laid on the bed of sickness. I never shrink from personal discomfort: I never refuse to sacrifice myself."

"Your devotion, it must be confessed, is admirable," Mr. Clump says, with a low bow; "but—"

"I have scarcely closed my eyes since my arrival: I give

up sleep, health, every comfort, to my sense of duty. When my poor James was in the smallpox, did I allow any hireling to nurse him? No."

"You did what became an excellent mother, my dear Madam—the best of mothers; but—"

"As the mother of a family and the wife of an English clergyman, I humbly trust that my principles are good," Mrs. Bute said, with a happy solemnity of conviction; "and, as long as Nature supports me, never, never, Mr. Clump, will I desert the post of duty. Others may bring that grey head with sorrow to the bed of sickness here Mrs. Bute, waving her hand, pointed to one of old Miss Crawley's coffee-coloured fronts, which was perched on a stand in the dressing-room, but I will never quit it. Ah, Mr. Clump! I fear, I know, that the couch needs spiritual as well as medical consolation."

"What I was going to observe, my dear Madam,"—here the resolute Clump once more interposed with a bland air—"what I was going to observe when you gave utterance to sentiments which do you so much honour, was that I think you alarm yourself needlessly about our kind friend, and sacrifice your own health too prodigally in her favour."

"I would lay down my life for my duty, or for any member of my husband's family," Mrs. Bute interposed.

"Yes, Madam, if need were; but we don't want Mrs Bute Crawley to be a martyr," Clump said gallantly. "Dr Squills and myself have both considered Miss Crawley's case with every anxiety and care, as you may suppose. We see her low-spirited and nervous; family events have agitated her."

"Her nephew will come to perdition," Mrs. Crawley cried. "Have agitated her: and you arrived like a guardian angel, my dear Madam, a positive guardian angel, I assure you, to soothe her under the pressure of calamity. But Dr. Squills and I were thinking that our amiable friend is not in such a state as renders confinement to her bed necessary. She is depressed, but this confinement perhaps adds to her depression. She should have change, fresh air, gaiety; the most delightful remedies in the pharmacopoeia," Mr. Clump said, grinning and showing his handsome teeth. "Persuade her to rise, dear

Madam; drag her from her couch and her low spirits; insist upon her taking little drives. They will restore the roses too to your cheeks, if I may so speak to Mrs. Bute Crawley."

"The sight of her horrid nephew casually in the Park, where I am told the wretch drives with the brazen partner of his crimes," Mrs. Bute said letting the cat of selfishness out of the bag of secrecy, "would cause her such a shock, that we should have to bring her back to bed again. She must not go out, Mr. Clump. She shall not go out as long as I remain to watch over her; And as for my health, what matters it? I give it cheerfully, sir. I sacrifice it at the altar of my duty."

"Upon my word, Madam," Mr. Clump now said bluntly, "I won't answer for her life if she remains locked up in that dark room. She is so nervous that we may lose her any day; and if you wish Captain Crawley to be her heir, I warn you frankly, Madam, that you are doing your very best to serve him.""Gracious mercy! is her life in danger?" Mrs. Bute cried. "Why, why, Mr. Clump, did you not inform me sooner?"

The night before, Mr. Clump and Dr. Squills had had a consultation over a bottle of wine at the house of Sir Lapin Warren, whose lady was about to present him with a thirteenth blessing, regarding Miss Crawley and her case.

"What a little harpy that woman from Hampshire is, Clump," Squills remarked, "that has seized upon old Tilly Crawley. Devilish good Madeira."

"What a fool Rawdon Crawley has been," Clump replied, "to go and marry a governess! There was something about the girl, too."

"Green eyes, fair skin, pretty figure, famous frontal development," Squills remarked. "There is something about her; and Crawley was a fool, Squills."

"A d—— fool—always was," the apothecary replied.

"Of course the old girl will fling him over," said the physician, and after a pause added, "She'll cut up well, I suppose."

"Cut up," says Clump with a grin; "I wouldn't have her cut up for two hundred a year."

"That Hampshire woman will kill her in two months,

Clump, my boy, if she stops about her," Dr. Squills said. "Old woman; full feeder; nervous subject; palpitation of the heart; pressure on the brain; apoplexy; off she goes. Get her up, Clump; get her out: or I wouldn't give many weeks' purchase for your two hundred a year." And it was acting upon this hint that the worthy apothecary spoke with so much candour to Mrs. Bute Crawley.

Having the old lady under her hand: in bed: with nobody near, Mrs. Bute had made more than one assault upon her, to induce her to alter her will. But Miss Crawley's usual terrors regarding death increased greatly when such dismal propositions were made to her, and Mrs. Bute saw that she must get her patient into cheerful spirits and health before she could hope to attain the pious object which she had in view. Whither to take her was the next puzzle.

The only place where she is not likely to meet those odious Rawdons is at church, and that won't amuse her, Mrs. Bute justly felt. "We must go and visit our beautiful suburbs of London," she then thought. "I hear they are the most picturesque in the world"; and so she had a sudden interest for Hampstead, and Hornsey, and found that Dulwich had great charms for her, and getting her victim into her carriage, drove her to those rustic spots, beguiling the little journeys with conversations about Rawdon and his wife, and telling every story to the old lady which could add to her indignation against this pair of reprobates.

Perhaps Mrs. Bute pulled the string unnecessarily tight. For though she worked up Miss Crawley to a proper dislike of her disobedient nephew, the invalid had a great hatred and secret terror of her victimizer, and panted to escape from her. After a brief space, she rebelled against Highgate and Hornsey utterly. She would go into the Park. Mrs. Bute knew they would meet the abominable Rawdon there, and she was right. One day in the ring, Rawdon's stanhope came in sight; Rebecca was seated by him. In the enemy's equipage Miss Crawley occupied her usual place, with Mrs. Bute on her left, the poodle and Miss Briggs on the back seat. It was a nervous moment, and Rebecca's heart beat quick as she recognized the carriage;

and as the two vehicles crossed each other in a line, she clasped her hands, and looked towards the spinster with a face of agonized attachment and devotion. Rawdon himself trembled, and his face grew purple behind his dyed mustachios. Only old Briggs was moved in the other carriage, and cast her great eyes nervously towards her old friends. Miss Crawley's bonnet was resolutely turned towards the Serpentine. Mrs. Bute happened to be in ecstasies with the poodle, and was calling him a little darling, and a sweet little zoggy, and a pretty pet. The carriages moved on, each in his line.

"Done, by Jove," Rawdon said to his wife.

"Try once more, Rawdon," Rebecca answered. "Could not you lock your wheels into theirs, dearest?"

Rawdon had not the heart for that manoeuvre. When the carriages met again, he stood up in his stanhope; he raised his hand ready to doff his hat; he looked with all his eyes. But this time Miss Crawley's face was not turned away; she and Mrs. Bute looked him full in the face, and cut their nephew pitilessly. He sank back in his seat with an oath, and striking out of the ring, dashed away desperately homewards.

It was a gallant and decided triumph for Mrs. Bute. But she felt the danger of many such meetings, as she saw the evident nervousness of Miss Crawley; and she determined that it was most necessary for her dear friend's health, that they should leave town for a while, and recommended Brighton very strongly.

William Makepeace Thackeray

Vanity Fair

CHAPTER XXVIII

In Which Amelia Invades the Low Countries: The regiment with its officers was to be transported in ships provided by His Majesty's government for the occasion: and in two days after the festive assembly at Mrs. O'Dowd's apartments, in the midst of cheering from all the East India ships in the river, and the military on shore, the band playing "God Save the King," the officers waving their hats, and the crews hurrahing gallantly, the transports went down the river and proceeded under convoy to Ostend. Meanwhile the gallant Jos had agreed to escort his sister and the Major's wife, the bulk of whose goods and chattels, including the famous bird of paradise and turban, were with the regimental baggage: so that our two heroines drove pretty much unencumbered to Ramsgate, where there were plenty of packets plying, in one of which they had a speedy passage to Ostend.

That period of Jos's life which now ensued was so full of incident, that it served him for conversation for many years after, and even the tiger-hunt story was put aside for more stirring narratives which he had to tell about the great campaign of Waterloo. As soon as he had agreed to escort his sister abroad, it was remarked that he ceased shaving his upper lip. At Chatham he followed the parades and drills with great assiduity. He listened with the utmost attention to the conversation of his brother officers as he called them in after days sometimes, and learned as many military names as he could. In these studies the excellent Mrs. O'Dowd was of great assistance to him; and on the day finally when they embarked on board the Lovely Rose, which was to carry them to their destination, he made his appearance in a braided frock-coat and duck trousers, with a foraging cap ornamented with a smart gold band. Having his carriage with him, and informing everybody on board confidentially that he was going to join the Duke of Wellington's army, folks mistook him for a great personage, a commissary-general, or a government courier at the very least.

He suffered hugely on the voyage, during which the ladies were likewise prostrate; but Amelia was brought to life again as the packet made Ostend, by the sight of the transports conveying her regiment, which entered the harbour almost at the same time with the Lovely Rose. Jos went in a collapsed state to an inn, while Captain Dobbin escorted the ladies, and then busied himself in freeing Jos's carriage and luggage from the ship and the custom-house, for Mr. Jos was at present without a servant, Osborne's man and his own pampered menial having conspired together at Chatham, and refused point-blank to cross the water. This revolt, which came very suddenly, and on the last day, so alarmed Mr. Sedley, junior, that he was on the point of giving up the expedition, but Captain Dobbin who made himself immensely officious in the business, Jos said, rated him and laughed at him soundly: the mustachios were grown in advance, and Jos finally was persuaded to embark. In place of the well-bred and well-fed London domestics, who could only speak English, Dobbin procured for Jos's party a swarthy little Belgian servant who could speak no language at all; but who, by his bustling behaviour, and by invariably addressing Mr. Sedley as "My lord," speedily acquired that gentleman's favour. Times are altered at Ostend now; of the Britons who go thither, very few look like lords, or act like those members of our hereditary aristocracy. They seem for the most part shabby in attire, dingy of linen, lovers of billiards and brandy, and cigars and greasy ordinaries.

But it may be said as a rule, that every Englishman in the Duke of Wellington's army paid his way. The remembrance of such a fact surely becomes a nation of shopkeepers. It was a blessing for a commerce-loving country to be overrun by such an army of customers: and to have such creditable warriors to feed. And the country which they came to protect is not military. For a long period of history they have let other people fight there. When the present writer went to survey with eagle glance the field of Waterloo, we asked the conductor of the diligence, a portly warlike-looking veteran, whether he had been at the battle. "Pas si bete"—such an answer and sentiment as no Frenchman would own to—was his reply. But, on the other hand, the postilion who drove us was a Viscount, a son of some bankrupt Imperial General, who accepted a pennyworth of beer on the road. The moral is surely a good one. This flat, flourishing, easy country never could have looked more rich and prosperous than in that opening summer of 1815, when its green fields and quiet cities were enlivened by multiplied red-coats: when its wide chaussees swarmed with brilliant English equipages: when its great canal-boats, gliding by rich pastures and pleasant quaint old villages, by old chateaux lying amongst old trees, were all crowded with well-to-do English travellers: when the soldier who drank at the village inn, not only drank, but paid his score; and Donald, the Highlander, billeted in the Flemish farm-house, rocked the baby's cradle, while Jean and Jeannette were out getting in the hay. As our painters are bent on military subjects just now, I throw out this as a good subject for the pencil, to illustrate the principle of an honest English war. All looked as brilliant and harmless as a Hyde Park review. Meanwhile, Napoleon screened behind his curtain of frontier-fortresses, was preparing for the outbreak which was to drive all these orderly people into fury and blood; and lay so many of them low.

Everybody had such a perfect feeling of confidence in the leader for the resolute faith which the Duke of Wellington had inspired in the whole English nation was as intense as that more frantic enthusiasm with which at one time the French regarded Napoleon, the country seemed in so perfect a state of orderly defence, and the help at hand in case of need so near and overwhelming, that alarm was unknown, and our travellers, among whom two were naturally of a very timid sort, were, like all the other multiplied English tourists, entirely at ease. The famous regiment, with so many of whose officers we have made acquaintance, was drafted in canal boats to Bruges and Ghent, thence to march to Brussels.

Jos accompanied the ladies in the public boats; the which all old travellers in Flanders must remember for the luxury and accommodation they afforded. So prodigiously good was the eating and drinking on board these sluggish but most comfortable vessels, that there are legends extant of an English traveller, who, coming to Belgium for a week, and travelling in one of these boats, was so delighted with the fare there that he went backwards and forwards from Ghent to Bruges perpetually until the railroads were invented, when he drowned himself on the last trip of the passage-boat. Jos's death was not to be of this sort, but his comfort was exceeding, and Mrs. O'Dowd insisted that he only wanted her sister Glorvina to make his happiness complete. He sate on the roof of the cabin all day drinking Flemish beer, shouting for Isidor, his servant, and talking gallantly to the ladies.

His courage was prodigious. "Boney attack us!" he cried.

"My dear creature, my poor Emmy, don't be frightened. There's no danger. The allies will be in Paris in two months, I tell you; when I'll take you to dine in the Palais Royal, by Jove! There are three hundred thousand Rooshians, I tell you, now entering France by Mayence and the Rhine—three hundred thousand under Wittgenstein and Barclay de Tolly, my poor love. You don't know military affairs, my dear. I do, and I tell you there's no infantry in France can stand against Rooshian infantry, and no general of Boney's that's fit to hold a candle to Wittgenstein. Then there are the Austrians, they are five hundred thousand if a man, and they are within ten marches of the frontier by this time, under Schwartzenberg and Prince Charles. Then there are the Prooshians under the gallant Prince Marshal. Show me a cavalry chief like him now that Murat is gone. Hey, Mrs. O'Dowd? Do you think our little girl here need be afraid? Is there any cause for fear, Isidor? Hey, sir? Get some more beer."

Mrs. O'Dowd said that her "Glorvina was not afraid of any man alive, let alone a Frenchman," and tossed off a glass of beer with a wink which expressed her liking for the beverage. Having frequently been in presence of the enemy, or, in other words, faced the ladies at Cheltenham and Bath, our friend, the Collector, had lost a great deal of his pristine timidity, and was now, especially when fortified with liquor, as talkative as might be. He was rather a favourite with the regiment, treating the young officers with sumptuosity, and amusing them by his military airs. And as there is one well-known regiment of the army which travels with a goat heading the column, whilst another is led by a deer, George said with respect to his brother-in-law, that his regiment marched with an elephant.

Since Amelia's introduction to the regiment, George began to be rather ashamed of some of the company to which he had been forced to present her; and determined, as he told Dobbin with what satisfaction to the latter it need not be said, to exchange into some better regiment soon, and to get his wife away from those damned vulgar women. But this vulgarity of being ashamed of one's society is much more common among men than women except very great ladies of fashion, who, to be sure, indulge in it; and Mrs. Amelia, a natural and unaffected person, had none of that artificial shamefacedness which her husband mistook for delicacy on his own part. Thus Mrs. O'Dowd had a cock's plume in her hat, and a very large "repayther" on her stomach, which she used to ring on all occasions, narrating how it had been presented to her by her fawther, as she stipt into the car'ge after her mar'ge; and these ornaments, with other outward peculiarities of the Major's wife, gave excruciating agonies to Captain Osborne, when his wife and the Major's came in contact; whereas Amelia was only amused by the honest lady's eccentricities, and not in the least ashamed of her company.

As they made that well-known journey, which almost every Englishman of middle rank has travelled since, there might have been more instructive, but few more entertaining, companions than Mrs. Major O'Dowd. "Talk about kenal boats; my dear! Ye should see the kenal boats between Dublin and Ballinasloe. It's there the rapid travelling is; and the beautiful cattle. Sure me fawther got a goold medal and his Excellency himself eat a slice of it, and said never was finer mate in his loif for a four-year-old heifer, the like of which ye never saw in this country any day." And Jos owned with a sigh, "that for good streaky beef, really mingled with fat and lean, there was no country like England."

"Except Ireland, where all your best mate comes from," said the Major's lady; proceeding, as is not unusual with patriots of her nation, to make comparisons greatly in favour of her own country. The idea of comparing the market at Bruges with those of Dublin, although she had suggested it herself, caused immense scorn and derision on her part. "I'll thank ye tell me what they mean by that old gazabo on the top of the market-place," said she, in a burst of ridicule fit to have brought the old tower down. The place was full of English soldiery as they passed. English bugles woke them in the morning; at nightfall they went to bed to the note of the British fife and drum: all the country and Europe was in arms, and the greatest event of history pending: and honest Peggy

O'Dowd, whom it concerned as well as another, went on prattling about Ballinafad, and the horses in the stables at Glenmalony, and the clar't drunk there; and Jos Sedley interposed about curry and rice at Dumdum; and Amelia thought about her husband, and how best she should show her love for him; as if these were the great topics of the world.

Those who like to lay down the History-book, and to speculate upon what MIGHT have happened in the world, but for the fatal occurrence of what actually did take place a most puzzling, amusing, ingenious, and profitable kind of meditation, have no doubt often thought to themselves what a specially bad time Napoleon took to come back from Elba, and to let loose his eagle from Gulf San Juan to Notre Dame. The historians on our side tell us that the armies of the allied powers were all providentially on a war-footing, and ready to bear down at a moment's notice upon the Elban Emperor. The august jobbers assembled at Vienna, and carving out the kingdoms of Europe according to their wisdom, had such causes of quarrel among themselves as might have set the armies which had overcome Napoleon to fight against each other, but for the return of the object of unanimous hatred and fear. This monarch had an army in full force because he had jobbed to himself Poland, and was determined to keep it: another had robbed half Saxony, and was bent upon maintaining his acquisition: Italy was the object of a third's solicitude. Each was protesting against the rapacity of the other; and could the Corsican but have waited in prison until all these parties were by the ears, he might have returned and reigned unmolested. But what would have become of our story and all our friends, then? If all the drops in it were dried up, what would become of the sea?

In the meanwhile the business of life and living, and the pursuits of pleasure, especially, went on as if no end were to be expected to them, and no enemy in front. When our travellers arrived at Brussels, in which their regiment was quartered, a great piece of good fortune, as all said, they found themselves in one of the gayest and most brilliant little capitals in Europe, and where all the Vanity Fair booths were laid out with the most tempting liveliness and splendour. Gambling was here in profusion, and dancing in plenty: feasting was there to fill with delight that great gourmand of a Jos: there was a theatre where a miraculous Catalani was delighting all hearers: beautiful rides, all enlivened with martial splendour; a rare old city, with strange costumes and wonderful architecture, to delight the eyes of little Amelia, who had never before seen a foreign country, and fill her with charming surprises: so that now and for a few weeks' space in a fine handsome lodging, whereof the expenses were borne by Jos and Osborne, who was flush of money and full of kind attentions to his wife—for about a fortnight, I say, during which her honeymoon ended, Mrs. Amelia was as pleased and happy as any little bride out of England.

Every day during this happy time there was novelty and amusement for all parties. There was a church to see, or a picture-gallery—there was a ride, or an opera. The bands of the regiments were making music at all hours. The greatest folks of England walked in the Park—there was a perpetual military festival. George, taking out his wife to a new jaunt or junket every night, was quite pleased with himself as usual, and swore he was becoming quite a domestic character. And a jaunt or a junket with HIM! Was it not enough to set this little heart beating with joy? Her letters home to her mother were filled with delight and gratitude at this season. Her husband bade her buy laces, millinery, jewels, and gimcracks of all sorts. Oh, he was the kindest, best, and most generous of men!

The sight of the very great company of lords and ladies and fashionable persons who thronged the town, and appeared in every public place, filled George's truly British soul with intense delight. They flung off that happy frigidity and insolence of demeanour which occasionally characterises the great at home, and appearing in numberless public places, condescended to mingle with the rest of the company whom they met there. One night at a party given by the general of the division to which George's regiment belonged, he had the honour of dancing with Lady Blanche Thistlewood, Lord

Bareacres' daughter; he bustled for ices and refreshments for the two noble ladies; he pushed and squeezed for Lady Bareacres' carriage; he bragged about the Countess when he got home, in a way which his own father could not have surpassed. He called upon the ladies the next day; he rode by their side in the Park; he asked their party to a great dinner at a restaurateur's, and was quite wild with exultation when they agreed to come. Old Bareacres, who had not much pride and a large appetite, would go for a dinner anywhere.

"I hope there will be no women besides our own party," Lady Bareacres said, after reflecting upon the invitation which had been made, and accepted with too much precipitancy.

"Gracious Heaven, Mamma—you don't suppose the man would bring his wife," shrieked Lady Blanche, who had been languishing in George's arms in the newly imported waltz for hours the night before. "The men are bearable, but their women—"

"Wife, just married, dev'lish pretty woman, I hear," the old Earl said.

"Well, my dear Blanche," said the mother, "I suppose, as Papa wants to go, we must go; but we needn't know them in England, you know." And so, determined to cut their new acquaintance in Bond Street, these great folks went to eat his dinner at Brussels, and condescending to make him pay for their pleasure, showed their dignity by making his wife uncomfortable, and carefully excluding her from the conversation. This is a species of dignity in which the high-bred British female reigns supreme. To watch the behaviour of a fine lady to other and humbler women, is a very good sport for a philosophical frequenter of Vanity Fair.

This festival, on which honest George spent a great deal of money, was the very dismallest of all the entertainments which Amelia had in her honeymoon. She wrote the most piteous accounts of the feast home to her mamma: how the Countess of Bareacres would not answer when spoken to; how Lady Blanche stared at her with her eye-glass; and what a rage Captain Dobbin was in at their behaviour; and how my lord, as they came away from the feast, asked to see the bill, and pronounced it a d—— bad dinner, and d—— dear. But though Amelia told all these stories, and wrote home regarding her guests' rudeness, and her own discomfiture, old Mrs. Sedley was mightily pleased nevertheless, and talked about Emmy's friend, the Countess of Bareacres, with such assiduity that the news how his son was entertaining peers and peeresses actually came to Osborne's ears in the City.

Those who know the present Lieutenant-General Sir George Tufto, K.C.B., and have seen him, as they may on most days in the season, padded and in stays, strutting down Pall Mall with a rickety swagger on his high-heeled lacquered boots, leering under the bonnets of passers-by, or riding a showy chestnut, and ogling broughams in the Parks—those who know the present Sir George Tufto would hardly recognise the daring Peninsular and Waterloo officer. He has thick curling brown hair and black eyebrows now, and his whiskers are of the deepest purple. He was light-haired and bald in 1815, and stouter in the person and in the limbs, which especially have shrunk very much of late. When he was about seventy years of age he is now nearly eighty, his hair, which was very scarce and quite white, suddenly grew thick, and brown, and curly, and his whiskers and eyebrows took their present colour. Ill-natured people say that his chest is all wool, and that his hair, because it never grows, is a wig. Tom Tufto, with whose father he quarrelled ever so many years ago, declares that Mademoiselle de Jaisey, of the French theatre, pulled his grandpapa's hair off in the green-room; but Tom is notoriously spiteful and jealous; and the General's wig has nothing to do with our story.

One day, as some of our friends of the —th were sauntering in the flower-market of Brussels, having been to see the Hotel de Ville, which Mrs. Major O'Dowd declared was not near so large or handsome as her fawther's mansion of Glenmalony, an officer of rank, with an orderly behind him, rode up to the market, and descending from his horse, came amongst the flowers, and selected the very finest bouquet which money could buy. The beautiful bundle being tied up in a paper, the officer remounted, giving the nosegay into the charge of his military groom, who carried it with a grin, following his chief, who rode away in great state and self-satisfaction.

Mrs. O'Dowd at the Flower Market

"You should see the flowers at Glenmalony," Mrs. O'Dowd was remarking. "Me fawther has three Scotch garners with nine helpers. We have an acre of hot-houses, and pines as common as pays in the sayson. Our greeps weighs six pounds every bunch of 'em, and upon me honour and conscience I think our magnolias is as big as taykettles."

Dobbin, who never used to "draw out" Mrs. O'Dowd as that wicked Osborne delighted in doing much to Amelia's terror, who implored him to spare her, fell back in the crowd, crowing and sputtering until he reached a safe distance, when he exploded amongst the astonished market-people with shrieks of yelling laughter.

"Hwhat's that gawky guggling about?" said Mrs. O'Dowd. "Is it his nose bleedn? He always used to say 'twas his nose bleedn, till he must have pomped all the blood out of 'um. An't the magnolias at Glenmalony as big as taykettles, O'Dowd?" "'Deed then they are, and bigger, Peggy," the Major said. When the conversation was interrupted in the manner stated by the arrival of the officer who purchased the bouquet.

"Devlish fine horse—who is it?" George asked.

"You should see me brother Molloy Malony's horse, Molasses, that won the cop at the Curragh," the Major's wife was exclaiming, and was continuing the family history, when her husband interrupted her by saying—

"It's General Tufto, who commands the —— cavalry division"; adding quietly, "he and I were both shot in the same leg at Talavera." "Where you got your step," said George with a laugh. "General Tufto! Then, my dear, the Crawleys are come." Amelia's heart fell—she knew not why. The sun did not seem to shine so bright. The tall old roofs and gables looked less picturesque all of a sudden, though it was a brilliant sunset, and one of the brightest and most beautiful days at the end of May.

William Makepeace Thackeray

Vanity Fair

CHAPTER L

Contains a Vulgar Incident: The Muse, whoever she be, who presides over this Comic History must now descend from the genteel heights in which she has been soaring and have the goodness to drop down upon the lowly roof of John Sedley at Brompton, and describe what events are taking place there. Here, too, in this humble tenement, live care, and distrust, and dismay. Mrs. Clapp in the kitchen is grumbling in secret to her husband about the rent, and urging the good fellow to rebel against his old friend and patron and his present lodger. Mrs. Sedley has ceased to visit her landlady in the lower regions now, and indeed is in a position to patronize Mrs. Clapp no longer. How can one be condescending to a lady to whom one owes a matter of forty pounds, and who is perpetually throwing out hints for the money? The Irish maidservant has not altered in the least in her kind and respectful behaviour; but Mrs. Sedley fancies that she is growing insolent and ungrateful, and, as the guilty thief who fears each bush an officer, sees threatening innuendoes and hints of capture in all the girl's speeches and answers.

Miss Clapp, grown quite a young woman now, is declared by the soured old lady to be an unbearable and impudent little minx. Why Amelia can be so fond of her, or have her in her room so much, or walk out with her so constantly, Mrs. Sedley cannot conceive. The bitterness of poverty has poisoned the life of the once cheerful and kindly woman. She is thankless for Amelia's constant and gentle bearing towards her; carps at her for her efforts at kindness or service; rails at her for her silly pride in her child and her neglect of her parents. Georgy's house is not a very lively one since Uncle Jos's annuity has been withdrawn and the little family are almost upon famine diet. Amelia thinks, and thinks, and racks her brain, to find some means of increasing the small pittance upon which the household is starving. Can she give lessons in anything? paint card-racks? do fine work? She finds that women are working hard, and better than she can, for twopence a day. She buys a couple of begilt Bristol boards at the Fancy Stationer's and paints her very best upon them— a shepherd with a red waistcoat on one, and a pink face smiling in the midst of a pencil landscape—a shepherdess on the other, crossing a little bridge, with a little dog, nicely shaded.

The man of the Fancy Repository and Brompton Emporium of Fine Arts of whom she bought the screens, vainly hoping that he would repurchase them when ornamented by her hand can hardly hide the sneer with which he examines these feeble works of art. He looks askance at the lady who waits in the shop, and ties up the cards again in their envelope of whitey-brown paper, and hands them to the poor widow and Miss Clapp, who had never seen such beautiful things in her life, and had been quite confident that the man must give at least two guineas for the screens. They try at other shops in the interior of London, with faint sickening hopes. "Don't want 'em," says one. "Be off," says another fiercely. Three-and-sixpence has been spent in vain— the screens retire to Miss Clapp's bedroom, who persists in thinking them lovely.

She writes out a little card in her neatest hand, and after long thought and labour of composition, in which the public is informed that "A Lady who has some time at her disposal, wishes to undertake the education of some little girls, whom she would instruct in English, in French, in Geography, in History, and in Music—address A. O., at Mr. Brown's"; and she confides the card to the gentleman of the Fine Art Repository, who consents to allow it to lie upon the counter, where it grows dingy and fly-blown. Amelia passes the door wistfully many a time, in hopes that Mr. Brown will have some news to give her, but he never beckons her in. When she goes to make little purchases, there is no news for her. Poor simple lady, tender and weak—how are you to battle with the struggling violent world?

She grows daily more care-worn and sad, fixing upon her child alarmed eyes, whereof the little boy cannot interpret the expression. She starts up of a night and peeps into his room stealthily, to see that he is sleeping and not stolen away. She sleeps but little now. A constant thought and terror is haunting her. How she weeps and prays in the long silent nights—how she tries to hide from herself the thought which will return to her, that she ought to part with the boy, that she is the only barrier between him and prosperity. She can't, she can't. Not now, at least. Some other day. Oh! it is too hard to think of and to bear.

A thought comes over her which makes her blush and turn from herself—her parents might keep the annuity—the curate would marry her and give a home to her and the boy. But George's picture and dearest memory are there to rebuke her. Shame and love say no to the sacrifice. She shrinks from it as from something unholy, and such thoughts never found a resting-place in that pure and gentle bosom.

The combat, which we describe in a sentence or two, lasted for many weeks in poor Amelia's heart, during which she had no confidante; indeed, she could never have one, as she would not allow to herself the possibility of yielding, though she was giving way daily before the enemy with whom she had to battle. One truth after another was marshalling itself silently against her and keeping its ground. Poverty and misery for all, want and degradation for her parents, injustice to the boy—one by one the outworks of the little citadel were taken, in which the poor soul passionately guarded her only love and treasure.

At the beginning of the struggle, she had written off a letter of tender supplication to her brother at Calcutta, imploring him not to withdraw the support which he had granted to their parents and painting in terms of artless pathos their lonely and hapless condition. She did not know the truth of the matter. The payment of Jos's annuity was still regular, but it was a money-lender in the City who was receiving it: old Sedley had sold it for a sum of money wherewith to prosecute his bootless schemes. Emmy was calculating eagerly the time that would elapse before the letter would arrive and be answered. She had written down the date in her pocket-book of the day when she dispatched it. To her son's guardian, the good Major at Madras, she had not communicated any of her griefs and perplexities. She had not written to him since she wrote to congratulate him on his approaching marriage.

She thought with sickening despondency, that that friend—the only one, the one who had felt such a regard for her—was fallen away. One day, when things had come to a very bad pass—when the creditors were pressing, the mother in hysteric grief, the father in more than usual gloom, the inmates of the family avoiding each other, each secretly oppressed with his private unhappiness and notion of wrong —the father and daughter happened to be left alone together, and Amelia thought to comfort her father by telling him what she had done. She had written to Joseph—an answer must come in three or four months. He was always generous, though careless. He could not refuse, when he knew how straitened were the circumstances of his parents.

Then the poor old gentleman revealed the whole truth to her—that his son was still paying the annuity, which his own imprudence had flung away. He had not dared to tell it sooner. He thought Amelia's ghastly and terrified look, when, with a trembling, miserable voice he made the confession, conveyed reproaches to him for his concealment. "Ah!" said he with quivering lips and turning away, "you despise your old father now!"

"Oh, papal it is not that," Amelia cried out, falling on his neck and kissing him many times. "You are always good and kind. You did it for the best. It is not for the money—it is—my God! my God! have mercy upon me, and give me strength to bear this trial"; and she kissed him again wildly and went away.

Still the father did not know what that explanation meant, and the burst of anguish with which the poor girl left him. It was that she was conquered. The sentence was passed. The child must go from her—to others—to forget her. Her heart and her treasure—her joy, hope, love, worship—her God, almost! She must give him up, and then—and then she would go to George, and they would watch over the child and wait for him until he came to them in Heaven.

She put on her bonnet, scarcely knowing what she did, and went out to walk in the lanes by which George used to come back from school, and where she was in the habit of going on his return to meet the boy. It was May, a half-holiday. The leaves were all coming out, the weather was brilliant; the boy came running to her flushed with health, singing, his bundle of school-books hanging by a thong. There he was. Both her arms were round him. No, it was impossible. They could not be going to part. "What is the matter, Mother?" said he; "you look very pale."

"Nothing, my child," she said and stooped down and kissed him.

That night Amelia made the boy read the story of Samuel to her, and how Hannah, his mother, having weaned him, brought him to Eli the High Priest to minister before the Lord. And he read the song of gratitude which Hannah sang, and which says, who it is who maketh poor and maketh rich, and bringeth low and exalteth—how the poor shall be raised up out of the dust, and how, in his own might, no man shall be strong. Then he read how Samuel's mother made him a little coat and brought it to him from year to year when she came up to offer the yearly sacrifice. And then, in her sweet simple way, George's mother made commentaries to the boy upon this affecting story. How Hannah, though she loved her son so much, yet gave him up because of her vow. And how she must always have thought of him as she sat at home, far away, making the little coat; and Samuel, she was sure, never forgot his mother; and how happy she must have been as the time came and the years pass away very quick when she should see her boy and how good and wise he had grown. This little sermon she spoke with a gentle solemn voice, and dry eyes, until she came to the account of their meeting—then the discourse broke off suddenly, the tender heart overflowed, and taking the boy to her breast, she rocked him in her arms and wept silently over him in a sainted agony of tears.

Her mind being made up, the widow began to take such measures as seemed right to her for advancing the end which she proposed. One day, Miss Osborne, in Russell Square Amelia had not written the name or number of the house for ten years—her youth, her early story came back to her as she wrote the superscription one day Miss Osborne got a letter from Amelia which made her blush very much and look towards her father, sitting glooming in his place at the other end of the table.

In simple terms, Amelia told her the reasons which had induced her to change her mind respecting her boy. Her father had met with fresh misfortunes which had entirely ruined him. Her own pittance was so small that it would barely enable her to support her parents and would not suffice to give George the advantages which were his due. Great as her sufferings would be at parting with him she would, by God's help, endure them for the boy's sake. She knew that those to whom he was going would do all in their power to make him happy. She described his disposition, such as she fancied it—quick and impatient of control or harshness, easily to be moved by love and kindness. In a postscript, she stipulated that she should have a written agreement, that she should see the child as often as she wished—she could not part with him under any other terms.

"What? Mrs. Pride has come down, has she?" old Osborne said, when with a tremulous eager voice Miss Osborne read him the letter. "Reg'lar starved out, hey? Ha, ha! I knew she would." He tried to keep his dignity and to read his paper as usual—but he could not follow it. He chuckled and swore to himself behind the sheet.

At last he flung it down and, scowling at his daughter, as his wont was, went out of the room into his study adjoining, from whence he presently returned with a key. He flung it to Miss Osborne.

"Get the room over mine—his room that was—ready," he said. "Yes, sir," his daughter replied in a tremble. It was George's room. It had not been opened for more than ten years. Some of his clothes, papers, handkerchiefs, whips and caps, fishing-rods and sporting gear, were still there. An Army list of 1814, with his name written on the cover; a little dictionary he was wont to use in writing; and the Bible his mother had given him, were on the mantelpiece, with a pair of spurs and a dried inkstand covered with the dust of ten years. Ah! since that ink was wet, what days and people had passed away! The writing-book, still on the table, was blotted with his hand.

Miss Osborne was much affected when she first entered this room with the servants under her. She sank quite pale on the little bed. "This is blessed news, m'am—indeed, m'am," the housekeeper said; "and the good old times is returning, m'am. The dear little feller, to be sure, m'am; how happy he will be! But some folks in May Fair, m'am, will owe him a grudge, m'am"; and she clicked back the bolt which held the window-sash and let the air into the chamber.

"You had better send that woman some money," Mr. Osborne said, before he went out. "She shan't want for nothing. Send her a hundred pound."

"And I'll go and see her to-morrow?" Miss Osborne asked.

"That's your look out. She don't come in here, mind. No, by not for all the money in London. But she mustn't want now. So look out, and get things right." With which brief speeches Mr. Osborne took leave of his daughter and went on his accustomed way into the City.

"Here, Papa, is some money," Amelia said that night, kissing the old man, her father, and putting a bill for a hundred pounds into his hands. "And—and, Mamma, don't be harsh with Georgy. He—he is not going to stop with us long." She could say nothing more, and walked away silently to her room. Let us close it upon her prayers and her sorrow. I think we had best speak little about so much love and grief.

Miss Osborne came the next day, according to the promise contained in her note, and saw Amelia. The meeting between them was friendly. A look and a few words from Miss Osborne showed the poor widow that, with regard to this woman at least, there need be no fear lest she should take the first place in her son's affection. She was cold, sensible, not unkind. The mother had not been so well pleased, perhaps, had the rival been better looking, younger, more affectionate, warmer-hearted. Miss Osborne, on the other hand, thought of old times and memories and could not but be touched with the poor mother's pitiful situation. She was conquered, and laying down her arms, as it were, she humbly submitted. That day they arranged together the preliminaries of the treaty of capitulation. George was kept from school the next day, and saw his aunt. Amelia left them alone together and went to her room. She was trying the separation—as that poor gentle Lady Jane Grey felt the edge of the axe that was to come down and sever her slender life.

Days were passed in parleys, visits, preparations. The widow broke the matter to Georgy with great caution; she looked to see him very much affected by the intelligence. He was rather elated than otherwise, and the poor woman turned sadly away. He bragged about the news that day to the boys at school; told them how he was going to live with his grandpapa his father's father, not the one who comes here sometimes; and that he would be very rich, and have a carriage, and a pony, and go to a much finer school, and when he was rich he would buy Leader's pencil-case and pay the tart-woman. The boy was the image of his father, as his fond mother thought.

Indeed I have no heart, on account of our dear Amelia's sake, to go through the story of George's last days at home.

At last the day came, the carriage drove up, the little humble packets containing tokens of love and remembrance were ready and disposed in the hall long since—George was in his new suit, for which the tailor had come previously to measure him. He had sprung up with the sun and put on the new clothes, his mother hearing him from the room close by, in which she had been lying, in speechless grief and watching. Days before she had been making preparations for the end, purchasing little stores for the boy's use, marking his books and linen, talking with him and preparing him for the change— fondly fancying that he needed preparation.

So that he had change, what cared he? He was longing for it. By a thousand eager declarations as to what he would do, when he went to live with his grandfather, he had shown the poor widow how little the idea of parting had cast him down. "He would come and see his mamma often on the pony," he said. "He would come and fetch her in the carriage; they would drive in the park, and she should have everything she wanted." The poor mother was fain to content herself with these selfish demonstrations of attachment, and tried to convince herself how sincerely her son loved her. He must love her. All children were so: a little anxious for novelty, and—no, not selfish, but self-willed. Her child must have his enjoyments and ambition in the world. She herself, by her own selfishness and imprudent love for him had denied him his just rights and pleasures hitherto.

I know few things more affecting than that timorous debasement and self-humiliation of a woman. How she owns that it is she and not the man who is guilty; how she takes all the faults on her side; how she courts in a manner punishment for the wrongs which she has not committed and persists in shielding the real culprit! It is those who injure women who get the most kindness from them—they are born timid and tyrants and maltreat those who are humblest before them.

So poor Amelia had been getting ready in silent misery for her son's departure, and had passed many and many a long solitary hour in making preparations for the end. George stood by his mother, watching her arrangements without the least concern. Tears had fallen into his boxes; passages had been scored in his favourite books; old toys, relics, treasures had been hoarded away for him, and packed with strange neatness and care—and of all these things the boy took no note. The child goes away smiling as the mother breaks her heart. By heavens it is pitiful, the bootless love of women for children in Vanity Fair.

A few days are past, and the great event of Amelia's life is consummated. No angel has intervened. The child is sacrificed and offered up to fate, and the widow is quite alone.

The boy comes to see her often, to be sure. He rides on a pony with a coachman behind him, to the delight of his old grandfather, Sedley, who walks proudly down the lane by his side. She sees him, but he is not her boy any more. Why, he rides to see the boys at the little school, too, and to show off before them his new wealth and splendour. In two days he has adopted a slightly imperious air and patronizing manner. He was born to command, his mother thinks, as his father was before him. It is fine weather now. Of evenings on the days when he does not come, she takes a long walk into London—yes, as far as Russell Square, and rests on the stone by the railing of the garden opposite Mr. Osborne's house.

It is so pleasant and cool. She can look up and see the drawing-room windows illuminated, and, at about nine o'clock, the chamber in the upper story where Georgy sleeps. She knows—he has told her. She prays there as the light goes out, prays with an humble heart, and walks home shrinking and silent. She is very tired when she comes home. Perhaps she will sleep the better for that long weary walk, and she may dream about Georgy.

Georgie goes to the church genteelly: One Sunday she happened to be walking in Russell Square, at some distance from Mr. Osborne's house she could see it from a distance though when all the bells of Sabbath were ringing, and George and his aunt came out to go to church; a little sweep asked for charity, and the footman, who carried the books, tried to drive him away; but Georgy stopped and gave him money. May God's blessing be on the boy! Emmy ran round the square and, coming up to the sweep, gave him her mite too. All the bells of Sabbath were ringing, and she followed them until she came to the Foundling Church, into which she went. There she sat in a place whence she could see the head of the boy under his father's tombstone. Many hundred fresh children's voices rose up there and sang hymns to the Father Beneficent, and little George's soul thrilled with delight at the burst of glorious psalmody. His mother could not see him for awhile, through the mist that dimmed her eyes.

William Makepeace Thackeray

Vanity Fair

CHAPTER LXVII

Which Contains Births, Marriages and Deaths: Whatever Becky's private plan might be by which Dobbin's true love was to be crowned with success, the little woman thought that the secret might keep, and indeed, being by no means so much interested about anybody's welfare as about her own, she had a great number of things pertaining to herself to consider, and which concerned her a great deal more than Major Dobbin's happiness in this life. She found herself suddenly and unexpectedly in snug comfortable quarters, surrounded by friends, kindness, and good-natured simple people such as she had not met with for many a long day; and, wanderer as she was by force and inclination, there were moments when rest was pleasant to her.

As the most hardened Arab that ever careered across the desert over the hump of a dromedary likes to repose sometimes under the date-trees by the water, or to come into the cities, walk into the bazaars, refresh himself in the baths, and say his prayers in the mosques, before he goes out again marauding, so Jos's tents and pilau were pleasant to this little Ishmaelite. She picketed her steed, hung up her weapons, and warmed herself comfortably by his fire. The halt in that roving, restless life was inexpressibly soothing and pleasant to her.

So, pleased herself, she tried with all her might to please everybody; and we know that she was eminent and successful as a practitioner in the art of giving pleasure. As for Jos, even in that little interview in the garret at the Elephant Inn, she had found means to win back a great deal of his good-will. In the course of a week, the civilian was her sworn slave and frantic admirer. He didn't go to sleep after dinner, as his custom was in the much less lively society of Amelia. He drove out with Becky in his open carriage. He asked little parties and invented festivities to do her honour.

Tapeworm, the Charge d'Affaires, who had abused her so cruelly, came to dine with Jos, and then came every day to pay his respects to Becky. Poor Emmy, who was never very talkative, and more glum and silent than ever after Dobbin's departure, was quite forgotten when this superior genius made her appearance. The French Minister was as much charmed with her as his English rival. The German ladies, never particularly squeamish as regards morals, especially in English people, were delighted with the cleverness and wit of Mrs. Osborne's charming friend, and though she did not ask to go to Court, yet the most august and Transparent Personages there heard of her fascinations and were quite curious to know her. When it became known that she was noble, of an ancient

English family, that her husband was a Colonel of the Guard, Excellenz and Governor of an island, only separated from his lady by one of those trifling differences which are of little account in a country where Werther is still read and the Wahlverwandtschaften of Goethe is considered an edifying moral book, nobody thought of refusing to receive her in the very highest society of the little Duchy; and the ladies were even more ready to call her du and to swear eternal friendship for her than they had been to bestow the same inestimable benefits upon Amelia.

Love and Liberty are interpreted by those simple Germans in a way which honest folks in Yorkshire and Somersetshire little understand, and a lady might, in some philosophic and civilized towns, be divorced ever so many times from her respective husbands and keep her character in society. Jos's house never was so pleasant since he had a house of his own as Rebecca caused it to be. She sang, she played, she laughed, she talked in two or three languages, she brought everybody to the house, and she made Jos believe that it was his own great social talents and wit which gathered the society of the place round about him.

As for Emmy, who found herself not in the least mistress of her own house, except when the bills were to be paid, Becky soon discovered the way to soothe and please her. She talked to her perpetually about Major Dobbin sent about his business, and made no scruple of declaring her admiration for that excellent, high-minded gentleman, and of telling Emmy that she had behaved most cruelly regarding him. Emmy defended her conduct and showed that it was dictated only by the purest religious principles; that a woman once, &c., and to such an angel as him whom she had had the good fortune to marry, was married forever; but she had no objection to hear the Major praised as much as ever Becky chose to praise him, and indeed, brought the conversation round to the Dobbin subject a score of times every day.

Becky's second appearance in the character of Clytemnestra

Means were easily found to win the favour of Georgy and

the servants. Amelia's maid, it has been said, was heart and soul in favour of the generous Major. Having at first disliked Becky for being the means of dismissing him from the presence of her mistress, she was reconciled to Mrs. Crawley subsequently, because the latter became William's most ardent admirer and champion. And in those nightly conclaves in which the two ladies indulged after their parties, and while Miss Payne was "brushing their 'airs," as she called the yellow locks of the one and the soft brown tresses of the other, this girl always put in her word for that dear good gentleman Major Dobbin. Her advocacy did not make Amelia angry any more than Rebecca's admiration of him. She made George write to him constantly and persisted in sending Mamma's kind love in a postscript. And as she looked at her husband's portrait of nights, it no longer reproached her—perhaps she reproached it, now William was gone.

Emmy was not very happy after her heroic sacrifice. She was very distraite, nervous, silent, and ill to please. The family had never known her so peevish. She grew pale and ill. She used to try to sing certain songs "Einsam bin ich nicht alleine," was one of them, that tender love-song of Weber's which in old-fashioned days, young ladies, and when you were scarcely born, showed that those who lived before you knew too how to love and to sing certain songs, I say, to which the Major was partial; and as she warbled them in the twilight in the drawing-room, she would break off in the midst of the song, and walk into her neighbouring apartment, and there, no doubt, take refuge in the miniature of her husband.

Some books still subsisted, after Dobbin's departure, with his name written in them; a German dictionary, for instance, with "William Dobbin, —th Reg.," in the fly-leaf; a guide-book with his initials; and one or two other volumes which belonged to the Major. Emmy cleared these away and put them on the drawers, where she placed her work-box, her desk, her Bible, and prayer-book, under the pictures of the two Georges. And the Major, on going away, having left his gloves behind him, it is a fact that Georgy, rummaging his mother's desk some time afterwards, found the gloves neatly folded up and put away in what they call the secret-drawers of the desk. Not caring for society, and moping there a great deal, Emmy's chief pleasure in the summer evenings was to take long walks with Georgy during which Rebecca was left to the society of Mr. Joseph, and then the mother and son used to talk about the Major in a way which even made the boy smile. She told him that she thought Major William was the best man in all the world—the gentlest and the kindest, the bravest and the humblest. Over and over again she told him how they owed everything which they possessed in the world to that kind friend's benevolent care of them; how he had befriended them all through their poverty and misfortunes; watched over them when nobody cared for them; how all his comrades admired him though he never spoke of his own gallant actions; how Georgy's father trusted him beyond all other men, and had been constantly befriended by the good William. "Why, when your papa was a little boy," she said, "he often told me that it was William who defended him against a tyrant at the school where they were; and their friendship never ceased from that day until the last, when your dear father fell."

"Did Dobbin kill the man who killed Papa?" Georgy said. "I'm sure he did, or he would if he could have caught him, wouldn't he, Mother? When I'm in the Army, won't I hate the French?—that's all."

In such colloquies the mother and the child passed a great deal of their time together. The artless woman had made a confidant of the boy. He was as much William's friend as everybody else who knew him well.

By the way, Mrs. Becky, not to be behind hand in sentiment, had got a miniature too hanging up in her room, to the surprise and amusement of most people, and the delight of the original, who was no other than our friend Jos. On her first coming to favour the Sedleys with a visit, the little woman, who had arrived with a remarkably small shabby kit, was perhaps ashamed of the meanness of her trunks and bandboxes, and often spoke with great respect about her baggage left behind at Leipzig, which she must have from that city. When a traveller talks to you perpetually about the splendour of his luggage, which he does not happen to have with him, my son, beware of that traveller! He is, ten to one, an impostor.

Neither Jos nor Emmy knew this important maxim. It seemed to them of no consequence whether Becky had a quantity of very fine clothes in invisible trunks; but as her present supply was exceedingly shabby, Emmy supplied her out of her own stores, or took her to the best milliner in the town and there fitted her out. It was no more torn collars now, I promise you, and faded silks trailing off at the shoulder. Becky changed her habits with her situation in life—the rouge-pot was suspended—another excitement to which she had accustomed herself was also put aside, or at least only indulged in privacy, as when she was prevailed on by Jos of a summer evening, Emmy and the boy being absent on their walks, to take a little spirit-and-water. But if she did not indulge—the courier did: that rascal Kirsch could not be kept from the bottle, nor could he tell how much he took when he applied to it. He was sometimes surprised himself at the way in which Mr. Sedley's Cognac diminished. Well, well, this is a painful subject. Becky did not very likely indulge so much as she used before she entered a decorous family.

At last the much-bragged-about boxes arrived from Leipzig; three of them not by any means large or splendid; nor did Becky appear to take out any sort of dresses or ornaments from the boxes when they did arrive. But out of one, which contained a mass of her papers it was that very box which Rawdon Crawley had ransacked in his furious hunt for Becky's concealed money, she took a picture with great glee, which she pinned up in her room, and to which she introduced Jos. It was the portrait of a gentleman in pencil, his face having the advantage of being painted up in pink. He was riding on an elephant away from some cocoa-nut trees and a pagoda: it was an Eastern scene.

"God bless my soul, it is my portrait," Jos cried out. It was he indeed, blooming in youth and beauty, in a nankeen jacket of the cut of 1804. It was the old picture that used to hang up in Russell Square. "I bought it," said Becky in a voice trembling with emotion; "I went to see if I could be of any use to my kind friends. I have never parted with that picture—I never will." "Won't you?" Jos cried with a look of unutterable rapture and satisfaction. "Did you really now value it for my sake?" "You know I did, well enough," said Becky; "but why speak—why think—why look back! It is too late now!"

That evening's conversation was delicious for Jos. Emmy only came in to go to bed very tired and unwell. Jos and his fair guest had a charming tete-a-tete, and his sister could hear, as she lay awake in her adjoining chamber, Rebecca singing over to Jos the old songs of 1815. He did not sleep, for a wonder, that night, any more than Amelia.

It was June, and, by consequence, high season in London; Jos, who read the incomparable Galignani the exile's best friend through every day, used to favour the ladies with extracts from his paper during their breakfast. Every week in this paper there is a full account of military movements, in which Jos, as a man who had seen service, was especially interested. On one occasion he read out— "Arrival of the —th regiment. Gravesend, June 20.—The Ramchunder, East Indiaman, came into the river this morning, having on board 14 officers, and 132 rank and file of this gallant corps.

They have been absent from England fourteen years, having been embarked the year after Waterloo, in which glorious conflict they took an active part, and having subsequently distinguished themselves in the Burmese war. The veteran colonel, Sir Michael O'Dowd, K.C.B., with his lady and sister, landed here yesterday, with Captains Posky, Stubble, Macraw, Malony; Lieutenants Smith, Jones, Thompson, F. Thomson; Ensigns Hicks and Grady; the band on the pier playing the national anthem, and the crowd loudly cheering the gallant veterans as they went into Wayte's hotel, where a sumptuous banquet was provided for the defenders of Old England. During the repast, which we need not say was served up in Wayte's best style, the cheering continued so enthusiastically that Lady O'Dowd and the Colonel came forward to the balcony and drank the healths of their fellow-countrymen in a bumper of Wayte's best claret." On a second occasion Jos read a brief announcement—Major Dobbin had joined the —th regiment at Chatham; and subsequently he promulgated accounts of the presentations at the Drawing-room of Colonel Sir Michael O'Dowd, K.C.B., Lady O'Dowd by Mrs. Malloy Malony of Ballymalony, and Miss Glorvina O'Dowd by Lady O'Dowd. Almost directly after this, Dobbin's name appeared among the Lieutenant-Colonels: for old Marshal Tiptoff had died during the passage of the —th from Madras, and the Sovereign was pleased to advance Colonel Sir Michael O'Dowd to the rank of Major-General on his return to England, with an intimation that he should be Colonel of the distinguished regiment which he had so long commanded.

Amelia had been made aware of some of these movements. The correspondence between George and his guardian had not ceased by any means: William had even written once or twice to her since his departure, but in a manner so unconstrainedly cold that the poor woman felt now in her turn that she had lost her power over him and that, as he had said, he was free. He had left her, and she was wretched. The memory of his almost countless services, and lofty and affectionate regard, now presented itself to her and rebuked her day and night. She brooded over those recollections according to her wont, saw the purity and beauty of the affection with which she had trifled, and reproached herself for having flung away such a treasure.

It was gone indeed. William had spent it all out. He loved her no more, he thought, as he had loved her. He never could again. That sort of regard, which he had proffered to her for so many faithful years, can't be flung down and shattered and mended so as to show no scars. The little heedless tyrant had so destroyed it. No, William thought again and again, "It was myself I deluded and persisted in cajoling; had she been worthy of the love I gave her, she would have returned it long ago. It was a fond mistake. Isn't the whole course of life made up of such? And suppose I had won her, should I not have been disenchanted the day after my victory? Why pine, or be ashamed of my defeat?" The more he thought of this long passage of his life, the more clearly he saw his deception. "I'll go into harness again," he said, "and do my duty in that state of life in which it has pleased Heaven to place me. I will see that the buttons of the recruits are properly bright and that the sergeants make no mistakes in their accounts. I will dine at mess and listen to the Scotch surgeon telling his stories. When I am old and broken, I will go on half-pay, and my old sisters shall scold me. I have geliebt und gelebet, as the girl in 'Wallenstein' says. I am done. Pay the bills and get me a cigar: find out what there is at the play to-night, Francis; to-morrow we cross by the Batavier." He made the above speech, whereof Francis only heard the last two lines, pacing up and down the Boompjes at Rotterdam. The Batavier was lying in the basin. He could see the place on the quarter-deck where he and Emmy had sat on the happy voyage out. What had that little Mrs. Crawley to say to him? Psha; to-morrow we will put to sea, and return to England, home, and duty!

After June all the little Court Society of Pumpernickel used to separate, according to the German plan, and make for a hundred watering-places, where they drank at the wells, rode upon donkeys, gambled at the redoutes if they had money and a mind, rushed with hundreds of their kind to gourmandise at the tables d'hote, and idled away the summer. The English diplomatists went off to Teoplitz and Kissingen, their French rivals shut up their chancellerie and whisked away to their darling Boulevard de Gand. The Transparent reigning family took too to the waters, or retired to their hunting lodges. Everybody went away having any pretensions to politeness, and of course, with them, Doctor von Glauber, the Court Doctor, and his Baroness. The seasons for the baths were the most productive periods of the Doctor's practice—he united business with pleasure, and his chief place of resort was Ostend, which is much frequented by Germans, and where the Doctor treated himself and his spouse to what he called a "dib" in the sea.

His interesting patient, Jos, was a regular milch-cow to the Doctor, and he easily persuaded the civilian, both for his own health's sake and that of his charming sister, which was really very much shattered, to pass the summer at that hideous seaport town. Emmy did not care where she went much. Georgy jumped at the idea of a move. As for Becky, she came as a matter of course in the fourth place inside of the fine barouche Mr. Jos had bought, the two domestics being on the box in front. She might have some misgivings about the friends whom she should meet at Ostend, and who might be likely to tell ugly stories—but bah! she was strong enough to hold her own. She had cast such an anchor in Jos now as would require a strong storm to shake.

That incident of the picture had finished him. Becky took down her elephant and put it into the little box which she had had from Amelia ever so many years ago. Emmy also came off with her Lares—her two pictures—and the party, finally, were, lodged in an exceedingly dear and uncomfortable house at Ostend. There Amelia began to take baths and get what good she could from them, and though scores of people of Becky's acquaintance passed her and cut her, yet Mrs. Osborne, who walked about with her, and who knew nobody, was not aware of the treatment experienced by the friend whom she had chosen so judiciously as a companion; indeed, Becky never thought fit to tell her what was passing under her innocent eyes. Some of Mrs. Rawdon Crawley's acquaintances, however, acknowledged her readily enough,—perhaps more readily than she would have desired.

Among those were Major Loder, and Captain Rook late of the Rifles, who might be seen any day on the Dike, smoking and staring at the women, and who speedily got an introduction to the hospitable board and select circle of Mr. Joseph Sedley. In fact they would take no denial; they burst into the house whether Becky was at home or not, walked into Mrs. Osborne's drawing-room, which they perfumed with their coats and mustachios, called Jos "Old buck," and invaded his dinner-table, and laughed and drank for long hours there.

"What can they mean?" asked Georgy, who did not like these gentlemen. "I heard the Major say to Mrs. Crawley yesterday, 'No, no, Becky, you shan't keep the old buck to yourself. We must have the bones in, or, dammy, I'll split.' What could the Major mean, Mamma?" "Major! don't call him

Major!" Emmy said. "I'm sure I can't tell what he meant." His presence and that of his friend inspired the little lady with intolerable terror and aversion. They paid her tipsy compliments; they leered at her over the dinner-table. And the Captain made her advances that filled her with sickening dismay, nor would she ever see him unless she had George by her side.

Rebecca, to do her justice, never would let either of these men remain alone with Amelia; the Major was disengaged too, and swore he would be the winner of her. A couple of ruffians were fighting for this innocent creature, gambling for her at her own table, and though she was not aware of the rascals' designs upon her, yet she felt a horror and uneasiness in their presence and longed to fly. She besought, she entreated Jos to go. Not he. He was slow of movement, tied to his Doctor, and perhaps to some other leading-strings. At least Becky was not anxious to go to England.

At last she took a great resolution—made the great plunge. She wrote off a letter to a friend whom she had on the other side of the water, a letter about which she did not speak a word to anybody, which she carried herself to the post under her shawl; nor was any remark made about it, only that she looked very much flushed and agitated when Georgy met her, and she kissed him, and hung over him a great deal that night. She did not come out of her room after her return from her walk. Becky thought it was Major Loder and the Captain who frightened her.

"She mustn't stop here," Becky reasoned with herself. "She must go away, the silly little fool. She is still whimpering after that gaby of a husband—dead and served right! these fifteen years. She shan't marry either of these men. It's too bad of Loder. No; she shall marry the bamboo cane, I'll settle it this very night." So Becky took a cup of tea to Amelia in her private apartment and found that lady in the company of her miniatures, and in a most melancholy and nervous condition. She laid down the cup of tea."

Thank you," said Amelia: "Listen to me, Amelia," said Becky, marching up and down the room before the other and surveying her with a sort of contemptuous kindness. "I want to talk to you. You must go away from here and from the impertinences of these men. I won't have you harassed by them: and they will insult you if you stay. I tell you they are rascals: men fit to send to the hulks. Never mind how I know them. I know everybody. Jos can't protect you; he is too weak and wants a protector himself. You are no more fit to live in the world than a baby in arms. You must marry, or you and your precious boy will go to ruin. You must have a husband, you fool; and one of the best gentlemen I ever saw has offered you a hundred times, and you have rejected him, you silly, heartless, ungrateful little creature!"

"I tried—I tried my best, indeed I did, Rebecca," said Amelia deprecatingly, "but I couldn't forget—"; and she finished the sentence by looking up at the portrait.

"Couldn't forget HIM!" cried out Becky, "that selfish humbug, that low-bred cockney dandy, that padded booby, who had neither wit, nor manners, nor heart, and was no more to be compared to your friend with the bamboo cane than you are to Queen Elizabeth. Why, the man was weary of you, and would have jilted you, but that Dobbin forced him to keep his word. He owned it to me. He never cared for you. He used to sneer about you to me, time after time, and made love to me the week after he married you."

"It's false! It's false! Rebecca," cried out Amelia, starting up. "Look there, you fool," Becky said, still with provoking good humour, and taking a little paper out of her belt, she opened it and flung it into Emmy's lap. "You know his handwriting. He wrote that to me—wanted me to run away with him—gave it me under your nose, the day before he was shot—and served him right!" Becky repeated.

Emmy did not hear her; she was looking at the letter. It was that which George had put into the bouquet and given to Becky on the night of the Duchess of Richmond's ball. It was as she said: the foolish young man had asked her to fly.

Emmy's head sank down, and for almost the last time in which she shall be called upon to weep in this history, she commenced that work. Her head fell to her bosom, and her hands went up to her eyes; and there for a while, she gave way to her emotions, as Becky stood on and regarded her. Who shall analyse those tears and say whether they were sweet or bitter? Was she most grieved because the idol of her life was tumbled down and shivered at her feet, or indignant that her love had been so despised, or glad because the barrier was removed which modesty had placed between her and a new, a real affection? "There is nothing to forbid me now," she thought. "I may love him with all my heart now. Oh, I will, I will, if he will but let me and forgive me." I believe it was this feeling rushed over all the others which agitated that gentle little bosom.

Indeed, she did not cry so much as Becky expected—the other soothed and kissed her—a rare mark of sympathy with Mrs. Becky. She treated Emmy like a child and patted her head. "And now let us get pen and ink and write to him to come this minute," she said. "I—I wrote to him this morning," Emmy said, blushing exceedingly. Becky screamed with laughter—"Un biglietto," she sang out with Rosina, "eccolo qua!"—the whole house echoed with her shrill singing.

Two mornings after this little scene, although the day was rainy and gusty, and Amelia had had an exceedingly wakeful night, listening to the wind roaring, and pitying all travellers by land and by water, yet she got up early and insisted upon taking a walk on the Dike with Georgy; and there she paced as the rain beat into her face, and she looked out westward across the dark sea line and over the swollen billows which came tumbling and frothing to the shore. Neither spoke much, except now and then, when the boy said a few words to his timid companion, indicative of sympathy and protection.

"I hope he won't cross in such weather," Emmy said.

"I bet ten to one he does," the boy answered. "Look, Mother, there's the smoke of the steamer." It was that signal, sure enough.

But though the steamer was under way, he might not be on board; he might not have got the letter; he might not choose to come. A hundred fears poured one over the other into the little heart, as fast as the waves on to the Dike. The boat followed the smoke into sight. Georgy had a dandy telescope and got the vessel under view in the most skilful manner. And he made appropriate nautical comments upon the manner of the approach of the steamer as she came nearer and nearer, dipping and rising in the water. The signal of an English steamer in sight went fluttering up to the mast on the pier. I daresay Mrs. Amelia's heart was in a similar flutter.

Emmy tried to look through the telescope over George's shoulder, but she could make nothing of it. She only saw a black eclipse bobbing up and down before her eyes.

George took the glass again and raked the vessel. "How she does pitch!" he said. "There goes a wave slap over her bows. There's only two people on deck besides the steersman. There's a man lying down, and a—chap in a—cloak with a—Hooray!—it's Dob, by Jingo!" He clapped to the telescope and flung his arms round his mother. As for that lady, let us say what she did in the words of a favourite poet—"Dakruoen gelasasa." She was sure it was William. It could be no other. What she had said about hoping that he would not come was all hypocrisy. Of course he would come; what could he do else but come? She knew he would come.

The ship came swiftly nearer and nearer. As they went in to meet her at the landing-place at the quay, Emmy's knees trembled so that she scarcely could run. She would have liked to kneel down and say her prayers of thanks there. Oh, she thought, she would be all her life saying them!

It was such a bad day that as the vessel came alongside of the quay there were no idlers abroad, scarcely even a commissioner on the look out for the few passengers in the steamer. That young scapegrace George had fled too, and as the gentleman in the old cloak lined with red stuff stepped on to the shore, there was scarcely any one present to see what took place, which was briefly this:

A lady in a dripping white bonnet and shawl, with her two little hands out before her, went up to him, and in the next minute she had altogether disappeared under the folds of the old cloak, and was kissing one of his hands with all her might; whilst the other, I suppose, was engaged in holding her to his heart which her head just about reached and in preventing her from tumbling down. She was murmuring something about—forgive—dear William—dear, dear, dearest friend—kiss, kiss, kiss, and so forth—and in fact went on under the cloak in an absurd manner.

When Emmy emerged from it, she still kept tight hold of one of William's hands, and looked up in his face. It was full of sadness and tender love and pity. She understood its reproach and hung down her head.

"It was time you sent for me, dear Amelia," he said.

"You will never go again, William?"

"No, never," he answered, and pressed the dear little soul once more to his heart.

As they issued out of the custom-house precincts, Georgy broke out on them, with his telescope up to his eye, and a loud laugh of welcome; he danced round the couple and performed many facetious antics as he led them up to the house. Jos wasn't up yet; Becky not visible though she looked at them through the blinds. Georgy ran off to see about breakfast. Emmy, whose shawl and bonnet were off in the passage in the hands of Mrs. Payne, now went to undo the clasp of William's cloak, and—we will, if you please, go with George, and look after breakfast for the Colonel. The vessel is in port. He has got the prize he has been trying for all his life. The bird has come in at last. There it is with its head on his shoulder, billing and cooing close up to his heart, with soft outstretched fluttering wings. This is what he has asked for every day and hour for eighteen years. This is what he pined after. Here it is—the summit, the end—the last page of the third volume. Good-bye, Colonel—God bless you, honest William!—Farewell, dear Amelia—Grow green again, tender little parasite, round the rugged old oak to which you cling!

Perhaps it was compunction towards the kind and simple creature, who had been the first in life to defend her, perhaps it was a dislike to all such sentimental scenes—but Rebecca, satisfied with her part in the transaction, never presented herself before Colonel Dobbin and the lady whom he married. "Particular business," she said, took her to Bruges, whither she went, and only Georgy and his uncle were present at the marriage ceremony. When it was over, and Georgy had rejoined his parents, Mrs. Becky returned just for a few days to comfort the solitary bachelor, Joseph Sedley. He preferred a continental life, he said, and declined to join in housekeeping with his sister and her husband.

Emmy was very glad in her heart to think that she had written to her husband before she read or knew of that letter of George's. "I knew it all along," William said; "but could I use that weapon against the poor fellow's memory? It was that which made me suffer so when you—"

"Never speak of that day again," Emmy cried out, so contrite and humble that William turned off the conversation by his account of Glorvina and dear old Peggy O'Dowd, with whom he was sitting when the letter of recall reached him. "If you hadn't sent for me," he added with a laugh, "who knows what Glorvina's name might be now?"

At present it is Glorvina Posky now Mrs. Major Posky; she took him on the death of his first wife, having resolved never to marry out of the regiment. Lady O'Dowd is also so attached to it that, she says, if anything were to happen to Mick, bedad she'd come back and marry some of 'em. But the Major-General is quite well and lives in great splendour at O'Dowdstown, with a pack of beagles, and with the exception of perhaps their neighbour, Hoggarty of Castle Hoggarty he is the first man of his county. Her Ladyship still dances jigs, and insisted on standing up with the Master of the Horse at the Lord Lieutenant's last ball. Both she and Glorvina declared that Dobbin had used the latter SHEAMFULLY, but Posky falling in, Glorvina was consoled, and a beautiful turban from Paris appeased the wrath of Lady O'Dowd.

When Colonel Dobbin quitted the service, which he did immediately after his marriage, he rented a pretty little country place in Hampshire, not far from Queen's Crawley, where, after the passing of the Reform Bill, Sir Pitt and his family constantly resided now. All idea of a Peerage was out of the question, the Baronet's two seats in Parliament being lost. He was both out of pocket and out of spirits by that catastrophe, failed in his health, and prophesied the speedy ruin of the Empire.

Lady Jane and Mrs. Dobbin became great friends—there was a perpetual crossing of pony-chaises between the Hall and the Evergreens, the Colonel's place rented of his friend Major Ponto, who was abroad with his family. Her Ladyship was godmother to Mrs. Dobbin's child, which bore her name, and was christened by the Rev. James Crawley, who succeeded his father in the living: and a pretty close friendship subsisted between the two lads, George and Rawdon, who hunted and shot together in the vacations, were both entered of the same college at Cambridge, and quarrelled with each other about Lady Jane's daughter, with whom they were both, of course, in love. A match between George and that young lady was long a favourite scheme of both the matrons, though I have heard that Miss Crawley herself inclined towards her cousin.

Mrs. Rawdon Crawley's name was never mentioned by either family. There were reasons why all should be silent regarding her. For wherever Mr. Joseph Sedley went, she travelled likewise, and that infatuated man seemed to be entirely her slave. The Colonel's lawyers informed him that his brother-in-law had effected a heavy insurance upon his life, whence it was probable that he had been raising money to discharge debts. He procured prolonged leave of absence from the East India House, and indeed, his infirmities were daily increasing.

On hearing the news about the insurance, Amelia, in a good deal of alarm, entreated her husband to go to Brussels, where Jos then was, and inquire into the state of his affairs. The Colonel quitted home with reluctance for he was deeply immersed in his History of the Punjaub which still occupies him, and much alarmed about his little daughter, whom he idolizes, and who was just recovering from the chicken-pox and went to Brussels and found Jos living at one of the enormous hotels in that city. Mrs. Crawley, who had her carriage, gave entertainments, and lived in a very genteel manner, occupied another suite of apartments in the same hotel. The Colonel, of course, did not desire to see that lady, or even think proper to notify his arrival at Brussels, except privately to Jos by a message through his valet. Jos begged the Colonel to come and see him that night, when Mrs. Crawley would be at a soiree, and when they could meet alone. He found his brother-in-law in a condition of pitiable infirmity—and dreadfully afraid of Rebecca, though eager in his praises of her. She tended him through a series of unheard-of illnesses with a fidelity most admirable. She had been a daughter to him. "But—but—oh, for God's sake, do come and live near me, and—and—see me sometimes," whimpered out the unfortunate man.

The Colonel's brow darkened at this. "We can't, Jos," he said. "Considering the circumstances, Amelia can't visit you."

"I swear to you—I swear to you on the Bible," gasped out Joseph, wanting to kiss the book, "that she is as innocent as a child, as spotless as your own wife."

"It may be so," said the Colonel gloomily, "but Emmy can't come to you. Be a man, Jos: break off this disreputable connection. Come home to your family. We hear your affairs are involved."

"Involved!" cried Jos. "Who has told such calumnies? All my money is placed out most advantageously. Mrs. Crawley—that is—I mean— it is laid out to the best interest."

"You are not in debt, then? Why did you insure your life?"

"I thought—a little present to her—in case anything happened; and you know my health is so delicate—common gratitude you know—and I intend to leave all my money to you—and I can spare it out of my income, indeed I can," cried out William's weak brother-in-law.

The Colonel besought Jos to fly at once—to go back to India, whither Mrs. Crawley could not follow him; to do anything to break off a connection which might have the most fatal consequences to him.

Jos clasped his hands and cried, "He would go back to India. He would do anything, only he must have time: they mustn't say anything to Mrs. Crawley—she'd—she'd kill me if she knew it. You don't know what a terrible woman she is," the poor wretch said. "Then, why not come away with me?"

said Dobbin in reply; but Jos had not the courage. "He would see Dobbin again in the morning; he must on no account say that he had been there. He must go now. Becky might come in." And Dobbin quitted him, full of forebodings.

He never saw Jos more. Three months afterwards Joseph Sedley died at Aix-la-Chapelle. It was found that all his property had been muddled away in speculations, and was represented by valueless shares in different bubble companies. All his available assets were the two thousand pounds for which his life was insured, and which were left equally between his beloved "sister Amelia, wife of, &c., and his friend and invaluable attendant during sickness, Rebecca, wife of Lieutenant-Colonel Rawdon Crawley, C.B.," who was appointed administratrix.

The solicitor of the insurance company swore it was the blackest case that ever had come before him, talked of sending a commission to Aix to examine into the death, and the Company refused payment of the policy. But Mrs., or Lady Crawley, as she styled herself, came to town at once attended with her solicitors, Messrs. Burke, Thurtell, and Hayes, of Thavies Inn and dared the Company to refuse the payment. They invited examination, they declared that she was the object of an infamous conspiracy, which had been pursuing her all through life, and triumphed finally. The money was paid, and her character established, but Colonel Dobbin sent back his share of the legacy to the insurance office and rigidly declined to hold any communication with Rebecca.

She never was Lady Crawley, though she continued so to call herself. His Excellency Colonel Rawdon Crawley died of yellow fever at Coventry Island, most deeply beloved and deplored, and six weeks before the demise of his brother, Sir Pitt. The estate consequently devolved upon the present Sir Rawdon Crawley, Bart.

Virtue is rewarded; A booth in Vanity Fair

He, too, has declined to see his mother, to whom he makes a liberal allowance, and who, besides, appears to be very wealthy. The Baronet lives entirely at Queen's Crawley, with Lady Jane and her daughter, whilst Rebecca, Lady Crawley, chiefly hangs about Bath and Cheltenham, where a very strong party of excellent people consider her to be a most injured woman. She has her enemies.

Who has not? Her life is her answer to them. She busies herself in works of piety. She goes to church, and never without a footman. Her name is in all the Charity Lists. The destitute orange-girl, the neglected washerwoman, the distressed muffin-man find in her a fast and generous friend. She is always having stalls at Fancy Fairs for the benefit of these hapless beings. Emmy, her children, and the Colonel, coming to London some time back, found themselves suddenly before her at one of these fairs. She cast down her eyes demurely and smiled as they started away from her; Emmy scurrying off on the arm of George now grown a dashing young gentleman and the Colonel seizing up his little Janey, of whom he is fonder than of anything in the world—fonder even than of his History of the Punjaub.

"Fonder than he is of me," Emmy thinks with a sigh But he never said a word to Amelia that was not kind and gentle, or thought of a want of hers that he did not try to gratify.

Ah! Vanitas Vanitatum! which of us is happy in this world? Which of us has his desire? or, having it, is satisfied?—come, children, let us shut up the box and the puppets, for our play is played out.

Chapter 12

Study Questions

Q Write an Essay on Thackeray's deep and fundamental individual skepticism.

Or

Q. The Shaping Influence of the Marketplace. Discuss.

AMONG THE CONCLUSIONS a study like this one reveals is that books are shaped by the demands they are intended to fulfill. If one is writing for money, as Thackeray quite clearly was, one must write that which will be accepted by publishers. Likewise, this study shows that the production of a book is a multifaceted cooperative affair and that the resulting printed text is not attributable to the author solely. One is led inevitably, then, to a number of fundamental questions concerning literary works: about competing authorities for the verbal content and visual design of the books, about the authenticity of the text in any given book, about the relative claims as "best text" that could be made for competing editions.

Fundamental to any answers is another rather metaphysical question: At what point or points in a continuum from pure, free authorial autonomy to rigid social determinism does the production of literary art take place? If one thinks art is the product of the artist exercising creative freedom to write as he or she pleases, then the answers to the questions about authority, authenticity, and "the best text" will tend to be answered differently from the way they are answered by one who thinks art is the product of social forces fulfilling external demands for a market. These concepts are more easily adjudicated in the abstract than in specific cases; so this chapter is devoted to an effort to understand the consequences of various answers as they relate to a specific work, Thackeray's Henry Esmond. I try to demonstrate that the questions raised here are of crucial importance to any reader of the novel, not just an editor trying to determine the textual details of a new edition.

A brief orientation regarding theories of textual criticism will help establish their importance. The authority of the text, or more accurately, the authority for the text, is the person, persons, or "force" that has the final responsibility for "getting the text right." Among common notions about authority are, first, that of the author, who originated the linguistic text and read proof, giving authorial approval to additions, deletions, and alterations introduced by other hands.

A second centre of authority is the production personnel, for they create the combination of verbal text and visual book that "for the first time really" constitutes the "public work." A third idea is that regardless of romantic ideals, the final object, often referred to reverentially as "the text itself," is its own authority and, regardless of its provenance, must be treated as "the work." And a fourth is that any thinking, careful, sensitive, knowledgeable person can, through close reading and/or research into the developing text, find and correct flaws and improve the work to better represent its potential ideal artistic form. These views are basically incompatible with one another and appeal variously to different people.

Once a notion of the "properly responsible" authority has been settled, questions about the authenticity of the text in any particular copy of the work can be asked. Identifying typographical errors and unauthoritative interpolations starts the effort to authenticate the text. Locating and restoring or incorporating authoritative readings that "belong" in the text complete the authentication.

Some works, however, do not fit easily into the procrustean bed created by the concepts of authority and authenticity. Authors sometimes revise, or the works become significantly altered in other ways, so that alternate authoritative and authentic versions vie for attention. Persons who think a literary work should be one thing usually push for one text. They would like for statements about a work of art to have a stable referent. In the case of Henry Esmond, such a goal is easier to wish for than to have cf. Shillingsburg, Scholarly Editing in the Computer Age, and Scholarly Editing, ed. David Greetham.

There is no one answer to these questions. What needs to be recognized is that every reader answers them, perhaps not explicitly, in the act of reading by placing some credence in the symbols for the text on the page and by formulating some concept of what kind of thing is being read and what source or sources produced it. It has been usual for readers to assume that Thackeray wrote Henry Esmond, that Thackeray wrote what is printed on the pages of the book, and that what the readers understand and experience in reading the book came from Thackeray. Some readers, of course, do not have a very clear notion of Thackeray and may think that the text before them is its own authority. More sophisticated readers may wish to discount Thackeray's authority over meaning and choose instead to read "against the grain" for meanings revealed inadvertently by the text about the author or about his society or about the means of production that created the physical book. All of these are common and legitimate readerly acts, and all require some act of faith regarding the authenticity and authority of the text.

One of the objects of this book is to explore the foundations for such acts of faith, to see more than is normally seen about the processes, aims, and social forces that influence the particular sequence of symbols on the page. The problem with this objective is that any historical construct is just that, a construct. Constructs are influenced not just by the evidence of history put together objectively but by the historian's answers to metaphysical questions like, Are works of art the product of individual artistic talent, or are they social acts? For that reason this chapter does not argue in behalf of one point of view, but rather explores the consequences of adopting two or three different points of view.

A working proposition here is the idea that the persuasiveness of any historical construct and of any accommodation of the questions of authority, authenticity, and authorial autonomy or social determinism depends on the context identified as relevant to the construct. Of course, everything is a context for everything else, but historians, editors, and readers usually focus narrowly on "truly relevant" contexts selected from the narrow range of material that survives as evidence.

It is necessary, therefore, to identify the various contexts in which Henry Esmond has been seen and to show the differing consequences to readers and editors. Implicit in the procedure is the idea that coherent explanations can be attempted within defined contexts. In everyday practice: the meanings of verbal utterances are guided heavily, if not actually established, by contexts. In The History of Henry Esmond, Thackeray, writing in 1851 -52, had a mid-nineteenth-century audience consisting of book reviewers, circulating-library readers, his mother, his publishers, his friends, and his ex-lady love Jane Octavia Brookfield.

These people can be seen as having been addressed by the novel. But Thackeray said not one word in Henry Esmond, for his narrator, the aged Esmond, and the memoir's editors and commentators, Esmond's wife and daughter, do all the writing. The writing is understood to take place in the second and third decades of the eighteenth century and records events said to have occurred between 1670 and 1720. Esmond's memoirs are addressed to his grandsons, but his audience clearly includes his wife, who is thought by most critics to resemble Jane Brookfield. The speakers in the novel, in passages of dialogue, also produce their utterances in contexts that help identify their meanings.

One can ask what the character meant, what Esmond meant by reporting the character's speech, and what Thackeray meant by having Esmond report it. One can ask what the passage may have meant to a Victorian totally ignorant of the author and what it may have meant to Jane Octavia Brookfield. And, of course, modern readers produce their own responses to these meanings by contrasting them with their own sense of acceptable beliefs and behaviors. Thus readers contextualize the text in various specific ways as a means of producing what they think are appropriate understandings of the text.

This is only the tip of an iceberg of contexts within which the novel's words can be set and understood. Each context illuminates the text in a different way. Readers know this and act upon that knowledge almost without reflection-they are that good at using and understanding language. And when a scholar/critic points out to readers an aspect of context they had not considered, they gratefully add it to the mix of factors that influence their understanding of the text. The study of genre, the author's other works, biography, cultural history, the history of ideas, all these are understood to extend the readers' awareness of the contexts within which texts create and convey meaning. Even the physical embodiments of texts, the books themselves as paper, ink, and bindings, influence interpretations.

There is, however, a major flaw in the ordinary idea of authentic texts. If it is assumed that the text of a work is stable, that is, if we work with a text that is thought to have been established, we use the principle of contexts to produce "readings of the text" for contemplation. But if it is recognized that the text itself is not stable, we tend to use the principle of contexts to produce a "reading of the text" that will help establish what the text is by leading us to the right critical choices among variants. That is clearly circular reasoning and leads to predictable texts that best fulfill the editor's particular contextual construct.

But the situation is worse than that. It does not matter that no variant survives at a given point in the text; each word or mark of punctuation is potentially an erroneous witness to the context identified for use in interpreting the text. That may seem good to the editor, for that is what makes emendation of errors possible. Editors tend to think that some errors, like typographical errors and scribal errors, are "demonstrable," and they emend them. But they may be too quick to believe an error to be demonstrable because they are not sufficiently aware of the influence of the contextualization that they are using to determine the meaning which identifies the textual anomaly as a demonstrable error.

To illustrate the consequences of this approach, a useful example is The History of Henry Esmond, which for these purposes will have to be examined in the original edition, published in London by Smith, Elder and Company in 1852 in three volumes. In what follows I speak as an editor of Henry Esmond, but I mean to imply that in order for an editor to know what is being edited and why it is being edited, he or she must first be a reader, must know how to read, and must know what effect the editing is having on reading. Consequently, everything I say about the editor is applicable also to any careful reader.

To do a contextual reading, one must try to draw together the historical details of authorship as a profession and printing and publishing as a complex of economic traditions and interests in a continuous struggle with innovation-both technical and moral-and with attitudes toward gender, family, and moral conventions, particularly as they reflected the audiences for lending libraries in order to see what Henry Esmond was. Then, perhaps, it can demonstrate more clearly what the reader's and editor's task is, or, at least, what purposes modern scholarly editions serve.

While not forgetting that authors attempt to create something original that will fulfill their own purposes including the purpose of making money, we will have to examine bibliography, printing history, papermaking, taxes on books and newspapers, copyright law, labour relations, trade guilds relating to printing, publishing, and bookselling, marketing associations, professional societies, the apprentice system, lending libraries, the three-deckers in relationship to parts publication and magazine serials, the growth of the literate public, the development of authorship as a profession, and the developing division of labour into literary agents, publishers, printers, wholesalers, and booksellers.

Each of these can be thought of as a force field influencing what the work became, limiting what the work could say, shaping the work, and thereby influencing reactions to and understandings of the final product. Incidentally, one of the nice things about scorning historical reconstructions is that there is less work involved.

Now obviously all of that cannot be detailed here, but it has been done, and its salient details can be summarized cf. Feltes; Sutherland, Novelists; Harden, edition of Esmond; Altick; Patten; Nowell-Smith; West, "Book Publishing" and "The Chace Act", which explore the development of literary agents and crosscurrents in book production and author/ publisher relations between England and America. The History of Henry Esmond is Thackeray's only book to appear originally as a three-decker.

It was published by a firm whose head, George Smith, was an executive member of the Bookseller's Association. It was Thackeray's second book with Smith, Elder and Company-his first major book with that publisher-and it represented the first significant step in an attempt by George Smith to make Thackeray one of his authors-an object he accomplished thoroughly mid completely in 1859. Smith descended into publishing from the banking business by way of substantial reference works and scientific publications.

His literature list, his fiction, was respectable, yet he was bold and aggressive. He published Charlotte Brontë's Jane Eyre and later went on to acquire as his authors Anthony Trollope and George Eliot. Esmond, therefore, by virtue of its publishing house belongs to a tradition of book production controlled by establishment wealth and power. To be published by Smith implied certain standards of literary and moral content that Thackeray had never been clearly subject to before, though he was subject in a general way to the Mrs. Grundy censorship affecting all Victorian publications above pulp street literature cf. Louis James.

Thackeray rose to the Smith, Elder house from his major publisher, Bradbury and Evans, which in turn had risen into publishing from bookselling, newspaper publishing, and being proprietor of that low comic magazine, Punch, and other comic and sporting publications. In spite of the firm's industry and success, Bradbury and Evans belonged to a decidedly antiestablishment point of view, and in the 1840s Thackeray was one of its chief writers. Thackeray's sojourn in bohemia as an art student in Paris and as a writing hack in London were social and financial descents from which the economic success of books like Vanity Fair and Pendennis were raising him. Those works and the bulk of his writings in the 1840s The Book of Snobs, Novels by Eminent Hands, Barry Lyndon, Catherine, The Yellowplush Papers, The Reminiscences of Major Gahagan all reflect the satirical, antisnob, antiestablishment attitudes of Punch and Fraser's Magazine, the main outlets for his writings.

Esmond was to be different. The author of Esmond was a man financially and socially restored to the level of his upbringing. He was a popular writer and successful public lecturer, having delivered his urbane lectures on the eighteenth-century English humorists to receptive and aristocratic audiences in London, Edinburgh, Oxford, Cambridge, and the larger industrial cities. Esmond was to be his calling card and proof that he could write a thoroughly good, artistically complete, and serious work of art. By and large, Esmond has been seen, both by his contemporaries and by generations of literary critics up to our own day, as a peak in Thackeray's rising career as a writer and artist.

The book belongs to the establishment in otherways, too. The three-decker was in mid-Victorian England a thoroughly establishment commodity, an expensive book made possible and necessary by circulating libraries whose large guaranteed prepublication purchases made three-decker production a book publisher's staple. It was nearly impossible for a book publisher tc lose money on a three-decker that had been adopted by Mudie's library, but the discounts Mudie demanded and the price regulations that kept most ordinary customers from purchasing their own copies instead of subscribing to Mudie's made it equally difficult for a publisher to make very much money on a three-decker. The price-maintenance system for three-deckers worked to the benefit of publishers and the circulating libraries from the mid-1840s to the mid-1890s by providing stability; no one was making an inordinate amount of money, but the system could be counted on. This stability depended not only on control of prices but also on certain simple controls over the content and size of the books. These constraints imposed by Mudie's are now relatively easy to document; their primary focus was on the length of the book and the moral character of the plot and characterizations. An author and publisher who could work within the library constraints and win selection could count on a sound though not spectacular financial return.

But the respectability of the publisher and the library demands are not the only determining or constraining forces observable. Esmond is a historical novel created within a tradition of historical fiction which Thackeray may be said to have modified but not to have invented. Among these constraints was the demand for historical plausibility and the historical research which that demand entailed cf. "The Esmond Notebook" in Edgar Harden's edition of Esmond, pp.429-34. Plausibility was judged by the depth and breadth and accuracy of the historical detail surrounding the fictional characters and events. It was not necessary, however, to maintain historical perspective in moral and intellectual concerns or issues; Sir Walter Scott had made the historical novel both respectable and relevant to current moral and political concerns. But the freedom offered by historical fiction within the establishment contours of the three-decker published by Smith, Elder was a narrow freedom indeed.

N. N. Feltes, in considering Esmond in its marketplace context, has noted that the Booksellers Association and the circulating libraries were fighting a losing battle against an encroaching democratizing, proletarian invasion of the world of books and literature represented by cheap books, serializations in shilling parts, and shilling magazines. The booksellers' battle was to save the commodity which three-deckers epitomized and thereby save the economic control and stability which they enjoyed primarily through the three-decker. Feltes saw the three-decker as symbolic of the upper-class resistance to progressing economic forces and finds in the three-decker morality and traditional structures a corollary conservatism and reactionary spirit. He found in Esmond, a historical novel redolent with nostalgia for a past age, the same conservatism and establishment resistance to mass values, mass mores, and mass tastes. He found in Esmond's literary reputation a confirmation of conservative tastes and socioeconomic politics. In the social history of the last half of the nineteenth century, on the other hand, Feltes saw the slow but irresistible subversion of the commodity book by the new cheap, democratizing commodity text.

The triumph of this movement was the demise of the three-decker novel in the 1890s. For Feltes, therefore, Esmond represents a reactionary, establishment work. As such it represents a change or an anomaly in Thackeray's role, which for Vanity Fair and the early journalism was that of satirist of the establishment. Feltes posited the explanation that within the constraints of the three-decker, Thackeray was determined by cultural forces greater than himself and that an examination of these cultural contexts proves that the language and the culture speak the author, that the autonomous author is a figment of the romantic imagination; "reality" is the reality of social determinism.

If this discussion were to stop here, the weight of the social contract might seem irresistible; the social theory of texts would convincingly vest authority for the linguistic text and the meaning of the work in the social context. And the editorial solution for Esmond would be to select the first edition as the copy-text, emend nothing, and present the novel as a commodity book with large margins, heavy paper, and expensive packaging, thus perpetuating its role as representative of the establishment, standing as an anomaly in Thackeray's literary corpus. But the author, his text, and his meaning need not disappear behind this sociological arrangement of historical details. It is a significant shortcoming in Feltes's work that he did not apply his critical apparatus to a reading of the text.

Careful rereading of Esmond suggests a conclusion opposite to the one Feltes reached. He skated over the elements in the book that do not confirm his social deterministic theory of book production. The flaw of his approach is the rigidity with which his view of the social contract theory of texts controlled and limited his reading of the work by paralyzing his belief in authorial intentionality.

Social determinism apparently obviates autonomy in Feltes's way of looking. Although all that Feltes pointed out about the cultural milieu surrounding Esmond is true, it is hardly as comprehensive or constraining a view as he suggested. Though the novel was hailed by many of its original readers articularly its better-educated and better-heeled readers as a critical triumph, and though it for many years has been held in high regard even by readers who do not generally admire Thackeray's works, it was and is a profoundly troubling book to many others.

Many of its first readers and reviewers were shaken and angered by the ending, in which Esmond marries the woman he has long treated as his mother. That that denouement was Thackeray's intent from the beginning is perfectly clear on rereading with close attention to Rachel's character-she knew her heart's true relation to Henry well before her husband died and years before naive Esmond himself recognized it. It shows in her nearly hysterical reaction to the news that Henry has exposed himself to smallpox by visiting Nancy Sievewright, the blacksmith's daughter, although a superficial reading allows one to think that she is reacting merely as a social snob and doting mother bk. 1, chap. 8.

It also shows in her behaviour to Henry on his third visit home from college when young Frank reveals that she has been fussing over Henry's room for days, having worked a new counterpane for his bed and put fresh-cut roses in his window in anticipation of his arrival, though she pretends not to know if the housekeeper has prepared his room bk. 1, chap. 11. It shows in her reaction to the news that "Henry" has been killed in a carriage accident, though the Henry involved turned out to be Melton, not Esmond bk. 1, chap. 13. It shows in the nearly psychopathic rejection scene in prison after Lord Castlewood has been killed in a duel bk. 2, chap. 1. And it shows in the news that she has sneaked off to Southampton to watch from hiding as Esmond returns from the Continental wars bk. 2, chap. 7. Rachel clearly believes that God has punished her for her disaffection to her husband and her secret affection for Henry by allowing her husband to be killed.

She tells Esmond years later when they meet again that God has forgiven her sin: "But I would love you still-yes, there is no sin in such a love as mine now; and my dear lord in heaven may see my heart; and knows the tears that have washed my sin away" bk. 2, chap. 6. Rachel's secret love was even more disturbing to the Victorian consciousness than the apparent though not real incest at the end of the book, for it portrays a good woman-the heroine angel in the house-in the grip of a powerful and lifelong illicit passion she must and does suppress with visible effort.

Morally the book's psychological realism, though delicately handled, is profoundly subversive to the establishment. It is a measure of Thackeray's artistry that he portrayed these telling scenes in ways susceptible to more conventional interpretations, though to read them as such is to believe Thackeray has overwritten them cf. Geoffrey Tillotson for a particularly good assessment of Thackeray's "philosophy" and the way it influenced how he write.

But the book is subversive in an even more important way, for Esmond's ostensibly weak character, his apparent vacillation and inability to cast himself passionately and unreservedly behind any cause, religious, political, economic, or amorous-though goodness knows he tries-arguably stems not from a psychological weakness but from a fundamental philosophical uncertainty and humility that is very dangerous to establishment mentality.

The elderly narrator of the book, recounting Esmond's youthful naive enthusiasm for Father Holt's Catholicism, Rachel's Anglicanism, the Dowager Castlewood's Jacobitism, Beatrix's concepts of heroism and honour, constantly reveals Esmond discovering himself in an assumed and uncomfortable role-playing. Esmond spends his life fulfilling or trying to fulfill other people's expectations for himself and repeatedly discovering that the goals were not worth winning. He ends ashamed of himself as a soldier witnessing his fel'ows attack nuns, of Father Holt's tawdry lies and deceptions, of Frank Esmond's subjugation to Clotilde, of Beatrix's head-hunting selfishness as courtesan, and ultimately of his own complicity in these other shames he has participated in as a role player rather than in propia persona.

The measure of Esmond's superiority over other characters is that he recognizes his self-delusions and those of his fellow actors. Esmond's way of thinking and suiting action to thought is antiestablisliment. That is why Beatrix has no permanent use for him. Esmond is constantly giving away the store on the grounds of scruples; he loses ground for honour and principle without any compensating social or economic or political gain. He is ultimately anti-imperialist and antiroyalist, and he rejects the optimism of the intellectual rationality for which his age, the eighteenth century, is known. At the end of the book he retreats happily enough to the margins of the empire, where he establishes a domestic kingdom of his own.

The question about Thackeray's "intentions" with regard to Esmond and its potentially antiestablishment meanings can be pursued a bit further in two directions. They both bring to bear on the reading of Esmond other contexts than the Marxist economic contexts just examined.

The first is the biographical background and in particular the events in the year immediately preceding the writing of Esmond concerning Thackeray's love life cf. Letters and Ray, passim. By 1851 Thackeray's wife had been confined under special care for insanity for seven years, In the three years before the writing of Esmond his love for Jane Octavia Brookfield, the wife of his best friend, the Reverend William Brookfield, had gotten as heated as a platonic relationship can get. Thackeray was clearly in love, though he was fully aware of the impossibility of the situation. He imagined that Jane suffered under a sense of repression and lack of appreciation by her husband, which may have been greater in Thackeray's mind than in reality. Whatever the case, in September 1851

William Brookfield, who had tolerated Thackeray's attentions to Mrs. Brookfield with increasing wariness, put his foot down, banning Thackeray from the society of his home and wife. It is not hard to trace Thackeray's melancholy in the Henry Esmond/ Rachel Castlewood relations in the book he was then commencing,

Though he had not written any part of the book, he signed the contract for Esmond in June 1851. It was a story he claimed was boiling up within him as early as January, though his work on his lectures on eighteenth-century English humorists came first. That the rupture with the Brookfields affected the story there can be no doubt. Thackeray complained to Smith as late as December that he could not get on with the book under the effects of an ailment which time alone could mend. In the book itself there is a romanticized version of what could have been: Lord Castlewood's insensitivity to his wife may be read as William Brookfield's insensitivity to Jane writ large; Rachel's deep love for Esmond, suppressed and denied but tortured and irrepressible, may be Thackeray's portrait of what he saw or wished to see in Jane Brookfield's relation to himself. Thackeray seems to have been much more interested, to judge also from his letters, in assuaging his own sorrow than in upholding establishment social mores.

And in the character of Henry Esmond, Thackeray was able to make Rachel suffer the jealous pangs of seeing her unattainable love object throw himself at the feet of another-Beatrix, who was Rachel's daughter. Nor is it hard to see Thackeray beating his own breast and exploring the ecstasies of rejection while describing the perpetual and nearly unstiflable but unrequited love of Esmond for Beatrix. The psychological realism of a complicated and confusing network of love and jealousy involving mothers and sons and other forbidden attractions is carefully handled, for in Victorian fiction serious and troubling life passages could be explored only in code.

And finally, to focus on the way in which interpretation bears on editing, the rhetorical context of Esmond must be considered. It is a memoir: The History of Henry Esmond, Esq., a Colonel in the Service of Her Majesty Q. Anne. Written by Himself. It has all the rhetorical characteristics of an extended dramatic monologue, addressed by Esmond to his grandsons. Thackeray, the author, said not one word in propia persona in the whole book; even the introduction is written by Esmond's daughter.

As with any first-person narration, the potential for irony and for misapprehending irony is great. Traditionally, critics have read Esmond's narrative as something like the preachments of the author's alter ego. Esmond's opening comments, on the nature of history, strike readers as honest and commonsensical. "Why shall History go on kneeling to the end of Time? I am for having her rise up off her knees, and take a natural posture: not to be for ever performing cringes and corgees like a Court-chamberlain, and shuffling backwards out of doors in the presence of the sovereign. In a word," Esmond writes engagingly, "I would have History familiar rather than heroic." It sounds like the sort of attitude Thackeray would adopt; it is like his reviews of pictures in the Academy, knowledgeable but unimpressed.

Esmond seems to reflect Thackeray's own attitude also by placing himself and his neighbors on the stage of history and comparing them with the figures normally found there: "I have seen too much of success in life to take off my hat and huzza to it, as it passes in its gilt coach: and would do my little part with my neighbours on foot that they should not gape with too much wonder, nor applaud too loudly. Is it the Lord Mayor going in stare to mince-pies and the Mansion House? Is it poor Jack of Newgate's procession, with the sheriff and javelin-men, conducting him on this last journey to Tyburn? I look into my heart and think I am as good as my Lord Mayor, and know I am as bad as Tyburn Jack, " In short, the book abounds with reasons not to draw a sharp distinction between the narrator and the author.

Moreover, Esmond has a basic distrust of absolutes-that is, of other peoples' absolutes-he does not trust the judgment of priests, military leaders, political leaders, or kings. His love and his loyalty are always tinged with sardonic self-detachment. As one critic has noted, "Like Vanity Fair, Henry Esmond is a sustained argument against the reality of moral absolutes. Esmond himself does much of the arguing, for he is proficient at identifying illusory values and beliefs. His sophisticated skepticism, however, is itself founded on a dedication to one surviving absolute: truth." Scarry, p. 3 This personal truth of Esmond's is the foundation of his appeal to the reader in his autobiography.

And, as with most monologists, Henry constantly asks the reader to share in his personal recognition and judgment of the self-deception of others. Furthermore., he seldom expects the reader to take him very seriously, and he appears to be disingenuous when he does. Feltes probably would not rejoice over this coup d'état within the camp of the dying establishment, for the book does not subvert the establishment on behalf of the rising proletariat. Instead, the subversion emanates from the principles of a small intellectual elite, the freethinkers of England's Victorian intellectual class.

Some of those freethinkers were ideologues, but Thackeray's religious and philosophical ideas did not develop in a cell of like-minded philosophers or so-called freethinkers though it was not insignificant that he was a close friend of Edward FitzGerald, the translator of Omar Khayyám's Rubáiyát. Thackeray's philosophy is revealed in his letters and private papers as a deep and fundamental individual skepticism about causes of every sort.

It got him into trouble with many proponents of causes in need of money or moral support who approached Thackeray. If the cause was individual, to honour an admirable writer's family, to provide charity on nonsectarian bases, Thackeray was a patsy. But if it was to establish a guild for literature or to propose an evangelical school or cause, his purse and ear alike were closed. He did not trust institutionalized schemes. Esmond is subversive to the establishment it represents, but not on behalf of emerging socioeconomic ideologies. Even the fact that both Thackeray and his publisher made a good bit of money from Esmond, which was all unusually good seller despite its price, does not indicate that its themes or its production was determined or dominated by either a vested production tradition or an emerging public taste. Both of those "ideologies" claim the book by ignoring its subversive elements.

So much for Feltes's establishment interpretation of Esmond; this "establishment" book has a strikingly antiestablishment text-it is a wolf in sheep's clothing. And this interpretation makes the social contract solution to the editorial problem unacceptable. To take the first edition as copy-text for the linguistic text of all edition would be to accept the work of the minions of the establishment. Now, it so happens that in 1852, George Smith did not own his own printing establishment, so he sent Thackeray's manuscript to Bradbury and Evans to be typeset and printed. There may be comfort to be found, then, in the fact that the compositors of Thackeray's "proletarian serial novels" also typeset his "establishment commodity book," but the principle of authorial autonomy which the antiestablishment interpretation tends to support leads one to question the whole production process. That is to say, belief in the possibility of authorial autonomy, even of a limited sort, requires the rejection of any blanket rules for editing.

Rejecting Feltes's conclusions about the meaning of Henry Esmond in three volumes and rejecting the conclusion that a social contract requires special respect from an editorial view I do not mean that the three-volume format and the production process are unimportant. Quite the contrary. The book could not be a wolf in sheep's clothing without the sheep's clothing, and such a wolf means far different things from regular wolves or regular sheep. The novel is quite definitely a collaboration, or at least a joint venture between the author and the social institutions of book production and marketing. And that identifies serious editorial problems.

A close look at Esmond reveals an extensive network of evidence suggesting an intentional subversion of the narrator by the author. Thackeray seems not to have trusted Esmond's foundation rock of personal truth, Elaine Scarry in a 1975 article compiled an extensive list of errors in the book. These she invariably attributed to Esmond, claiming that Thackeray put them there on purpose. Scarry was not the first to notice that Esmond occasionally contradicts himself or forgets what he has said earlier in the narrative, but she was the first to attribute these errors to Esmond instead of to Thackeray or to the publishers. John Sutherland's Penguin edition annotations, for example, point out scores of historical and plotting errors, but Sutherland encouraged the readers to ignore them as understandable though regrettable characteristics of Thackeray's fiction.

Scarry identified an astonishing array of errors and anomalies, including an undermining of the rhetorical force of Esmond's own protestations-as when, having renounced the doctrine of divine right of kings and declared himself a republican, he nevertheless couches his adoration for Beatrix in the language of subjugation to royalty-and other more direct contradictions-as when he declares that an event so impressed him that memory would never fail him, whereupon he recounts the event in such a way as to contradict or distort his own earlier account of it. I believe Scarry is right to say that Esmond, "who has taken truth for his motto," was ironically undercut by Thackeray, "who has taken the absence of truth for his theme."

J. Hillis Miller, following a different line of reasoning altogether, arrived temporarily at the same conclusion Scarry reached. Miller brilliantly revealed the older Henry's ironic stance with respect to the younger Henry and then showed the ironic self-destruction of the self that Henry Esmond the narrator has constructed. Miller saw Thackeray's presence behind the narrator undercutting his claims to memory's sovereignty and the basis upon which Esmond allows himself to become "king" of the Virginia Castlewood and to accept the "worship" of Rachel and his daughter. Miller did not use any references to the "narrative errors" in the book to detect this irony. But his view of Thackeray undercutting the narrator was a temporary stop an Miller's deconstructive way through the novel, for he then undercut or deconstructed this third level of irony by arguing that Thackeray was trying to "understand

and control his life by taking ironic authority over that assumed role and by showing the imagined person to have made a false interpretation of himself." Miller, p. 106.

Miller was more interested in his theory of irony as "infinite absolute negativity" than he was in the meaning of Henry Esmond, the book being in the final analysis only an illustration for what Miller had to say about irony. Furthermore, his conclusion about the novel could not stop with resolution, for it is the nature of deconstructive criticism to deconstruct the deconstruction. Resolution would put an end to the fun and games. However, Miller's point is not without seriousness.

Resolution-say, the conclusion Miller considered at one point, that Thackeray undercut the narrator through telling references to Oedipus Rex and Hamlet which the reader with the help of Freud's Interpretation of Dreams can use to see Thackeray's ironic distance from his narrator-cannot be reached with any conviction if one is fully cognizant of the slippery ground such a resolution must take for its base. Miller implied that Thackeray, like his narrator, revealed himself rather than justified himself in the endless cycle of ironic undercuttings. This view makes Henry Esmond "one of the best texts in English fiction by means of which to explore the workings of irony in narrative."

But in order to get boxed up, as Miller wanted the reader to be, one must agree that Thackeray was seeking "authority over his own life by way of a detour representing that life in ironically displaced form in a fiction." Miller's conclusion that Beatrix is a sad mirror image of Esmond, revealing unconsciously the "corrosive power" of both characters and of their author, was based on the idea that Thackeray was seriously trying to present a "Pretense of mastery." Miller, pp. 106, 114 It would be possible-in fact, preferable-to conclude that Thackeray was not trying any such thing. Instead, he was demonstrating the inability to exercise any such mastery. Beatrix, in her cold-blooded, calculating attempts, which from the cynic's point of view should succeed, fails just as truly as does Esmond, whose machinations the reader is led to believe are wholly unconscious. The melancholy nihilism of the book can and has been seen as Thackeray's cynicism. But it is one thing to recognize the lack of control implied by nihilism and quite another to give in to it. Beatrix recognizes it and gives in to it. Henry Esmond recognizes it up to a point; that is, he recognizes it for others but not for himself, and the sensitive reader of his memoirs is bruised by Esmond's lack of self-awareness, revealed, for example, in the way he punishes Rachel for "unfaithfulness" to him in the prison while excusing his own blatant and egregious "unfaithfulness" to her during the years of his infatuation with Beatrix.

It is inconceivable that Thackeray failed to see Esmond's self-deception or the dual view of nihilism implied by Beatrix's and Esmond's stories. Thackeray did not give in to it, as the cynical view would have it, nor did he close his eyes to it, reverting blindly to an assertion of good that would be no more than a repetition of Esmond's quest for something worth believing in at one further level of self-deception. Anyone who has read Thackeray's own story-in the Letters and Gordon Ray's two-volume biography-can see the melancholy acceptance of uncertainty, as opposed to mastery, that characterized his mature years.

But two things mitigate against Miller's reading of Esmond, which was after all based on a reading of the text alone. One is Thackeray's determination expressed in conversation to John Chapman in 1851, thirteen days before he signed the contract to write Henry Esmond, that he did not feel "called upon to martyrise himself for the sake of his views" by expressing them too clearly to his reading public Chapman's MS diary, Beinecke. The second is, that Thackeray's personal reaction to his nihilistic ideas was to resist the temptation to give in. His personal intense desire not to hurt anyone, not to take advantage of anyone, not to manipulate others out of a sense that his version of "the truth" was the right version of it all reveals the light in which he created in Esmond the views Miller has described.

That is to say, in view of the emptiness of institutionalized values such as royalty, inherited rank, honour, party and country loyalty, marriage, and institutional religion, Thackeray chose not to sneer and not to pontificate, but to assert a sardonic kindliness and gentleness that are as far from sentimentality as those qualities can get. Nihilism in Thackeray bred humility about his politics, religion, and responsibilities. It did not, of course, keep him from reacting rather dangerously when his dignity was bruised by Edmund Yates's caricature of him in 1858. That episode may appear to give the lie to the portrait sketched here, but in spite of what the episode ultimately turned into, Thackeray's actions began as self-defence against what he saw as unprovoked attack. That, at least, is not antithetical to the view that Thackeray in Henry Esmond, was giving up mastery over his life rather than desperately trying to gain control of it.

The Force of Chosen Contexts: Now the point of all that is this: The contexts we identify as relevant to the text we read determines our interpretation, and the interpretation that is adopted determines the text we establish or edit. If N. N. Feltes's interpretation is adopted, one chooses the first edition as copy-text and makes the reading text ape the result of the social contract that originally produced it. The emendations policy will be documentary and conservative. If, however, John Sutherland's interpretation is adopted, one selects the manuscript or possibly the first edition and emends the text to conform as closely as possible to one's notion of Thackeray's intentions by correcting as many errors as possible and writing notes for all the rest to explain them away or de-emphasize any damage they might do to the reader's enjoyment of Thackeray's tour de force historical pastiche. And if Elaine Scarry's interpretation is adopted, one chooses the manuscript as copy-text and emends the text so that it effectively undermines the narrator's credibility, thus emphasizing Thackeray's rejection even of Esmond's attachment to personal truth.

But if J. Hillis Miller's interpretation is adopted, there is no need to edit the text since his reading is untrammeled by information of any sort from Thackeray's life, the period in which he lived, the production institutions which enabled the book to become a book, or the genesis of the text. If our goal is to read the text as a finished product, edited according to a "better way," then we must take a stand or abide by the editor's stand on answers to the following questions: To what extent was the author aware of and in control of the book's potential ironies? Did Thackeray intend to undermine Esmond's trust in personal truth, or did he share Esmond's view? Did Thackeray deliberately undercut Esmond's credibility by introducing obvious errors and memory lapses into Esmond's memoirs, or are the errors those of the novelist, Thackeray? To what extent did the production crew understand the author's intention and enhance or inhibit it? These questions are to be answered by critical inquiry, not by ascertaining discoverable facts.

This situation illustrates well what is critical about critical editing. But it also illustrates the way any single text edition of the book is capable of distorting it and hiding its possible meanings by privileging one context over others as the determiner of meaning. It does not take genius to see that an editorial approach to Esmond which sets about correcting errors may well be thwarting the author's intentional and meaningful introduction of those errors. On the other hand, not to correct the errors also may thwart authorial intention. Only persons who regard their personal solutions to these imponderables as universally acceptable would say that editing can be done by anyone correctly.

The economic, biographical, and rhetorical contexts in the cultural envelope where Esmond became a three-decker historical novel all influenced what that book became; but it is a gross oversimplification to conclude that the book became inevitably what it is through determining forces over which the author had no control. A concept of the editorial task is not helped by the glittering generalities that suggest "the language speaks the artist" or "the social complex employs authors to produce books" or "the author is dead." These conclusions are half-truths. Likewise, it does not help one to understand the business of editing if one concludes that the author is autonomous, the sole authority over text. That view tends to cast the editor in the role of rescuer and restorer. But the illustration just detailed demonstrates that it is impossible to say with any certainty what Thackeray is to be rescued from or what needs to be restored.

This brief survey of the complexities of *Esmond's* text seems to indicate that the author's communication to the reader is not only individual and free but constrained and directed by external forces. That is not a contradiction, nor is it a tragedy. It is a fact. Nothing understandable can be said or thought without the contextual frame of language and society and genre and custom and economic realities. But all establishments and power structures have within them the capacity to be satirized, subverted, criticized, and amended-that is to say, the author is free within the limits allowed by the medium. The power of some texts is that their subsurface purposefully subverts the surface meanings. The question about the reader's and editor's dual responsibility to authorial intention and the social contract can be answered by saying they are both operative. It follows that a critical theory that ignores either is a lopsided theory, and it also follows that an editorial practice that edits away the evidence of either is equally lopsided.

The concept of editions which emphasize the importance of process and avoid extravagant claims for the correctness of the product is gaining ground, but not without resistance-resistance stemming from editors who are reluctant to give up power over the texts, from critics who want a stable text, and from publishers who, market driven, wish to save expense. Editions such as Hans Gabler's of *Ulysses*, Michael Warren's of *King Lear*, and the Garland Thackeray edition are attempts in different ways to emphasize alternative texts, or multiple texts, or indeterminate texts, but all these editions are controversial.

Resistance to them in preference for editions with supposedly unproblematic, stabilized texts accounts for the polemics of textual theory. Any single solution requires commitment to one of several orientations toward texts which are mutually exclusive. At that level there is considerable debate among editors about the right way to edit or the right goal or end product to present as the established text. The alternative to a single text solution represents not an extension of polemic but a resolution. It represents a more comprehensive view of textual criticism, which, though probably not stable, at least does not stagger distractedly from one polemic to another.

What then is the function of a scholarly edition? In the Garland edition of Vanity Fair, the famous last paragraph of chapter 32, in which Jos takes flight and the war is brought to a close, reads: "No more firing was heard at Brussels-the pursuit rolled miles away. The darkness came down on the field and city, and Amelia was praying for George, who was lying on his face, dead, with a bullet through his heart."

The effect is both thrilling and chilling, and even first readers of this passage as it appears here can feel the tear of opposing passions as the pleasure of seeing George dead combats the sorrow for sudden death and for poor Amelia, while at the same time the reader feels she is a sap for turning on the ever-ready waterworks for what one already knows is a "selfish humbug", a "low-bred cockney-dandy," and "padded booby," though Becky does not provide these words to describe George till chapter 67. First-time readers will also, no doubt, sense the clean, crisp, efficient, and flat i.e., nonpejorative, nonheroic diction which gives the account its force and gives free play to the reader's conflicting feelings.

If readers were inclined to contemplate the passage, they might note that the phrase "The darkness came down" probably means primarily that night fell, but it allows the potential reverberations of the thought that "the darkness" has ominous symbolic overtones. There is little to encourage such a speculation, however, except the juxtaposition of Amelia's own sorrow-which one can only partially share-and perhaps a twentieth-century propensity to see symbols everywhere. Should these readers turn to the "Record of Composition and Revision" in the Garland edition, they will find that the printed text reflects the reading of the first edition and that in 1853 someone it is not entirely definite that it was Thackeray revised the phrase to "Darkness came down." Now, if the revised reading had been in the text in the first place, the sense of potential ominous symbolic overtones to the descent of "Darkness" now fortuitously capitalized might have struck readers more forcibly. Some might say, because this reading is "stronger," it should have been chosen for the Garland edition. It was not chosen because such aesthetic judgments were not part of the editorial strategy. To choose readings that correspond with the historical integrity of Thackeray's text at the time of first publication is not to reject the 1853 revisions. The point is not which of these readings is the correct one. The fact is that no one knows if either is correct or if both are correct.

The point is that in a scholarly edition both are available and have their various effects on the reading of Vanity Fair. Having read "The darkness came down," readers then find that a change was made to "Darkness came down." Either reading, by itself, conveys the fall of night, and both reveal the potential for a symbolic reading, the revised reading perhaps more so. But discovering that the reading was revised is the strongest indication that something was being attempted here beyond indication that night fell. The changing itself is a stronger indication of meaning than either phrase is alone.

That is a crucial point in understanding the importance of a scholarly edition. The aim of the editorial work should not be to produce a pristine, correct, reliable text, a product. It should instead be to trace the growth and development of the work and to place the reading text in its developing context, a process. The effect is lost on readers who insist on reading the text as product, but the potential is there for serious, sensitive reading directed in part by reaction to what the author did-as opposed just to what the author said.

This paragraph from Vanity Fair reveals a flaw in the Garland edition. The edition fails to include a parallel account of George's death from a letter Thackeray wrote to his mother who had complained about Amelia s selfishness. Thackeray's response is pretty well known, but it all should have been quoted in the edition, including his anticipation of the time two months ahead when Amelia's "scoundrel of a husband is well dead with a ball in his odious bowels" Letters 2:309. With that highly inflammatory and emotionally laden phrase ringing in one's ears, one cannot read the printed passage in the book without trying to account for the clean, flat, efficient diction found there in terms of Thackeray's narrative strategies and, perhaps, the demands of serial publication.

Scholarly editions should encourage and make possible such intertextual readings. The richness and satisfaction of such reading complexities go up when the countertexts are understood for what they are: parallel texts in letters, revisions in manuscripts, or alternative printed texts emanating either from revision or from compositorial or editorial intervention. The sources and relative dates of countertexts have a great deal to do with a reader's assessment of their significance. It seems, then, that the duty of a scholarly edition is not arbitrarily and stealthily to reduce the complexity and richness of a work of art to one correct and established standard text, but rather to lay out the materials as clearly and usefully as possible.

Q. Discuss Marriage in Vanity Fair.

or

Q. Many of the characters in "Vanity Fair" are married from the start of the novel, or are betrothed during the novel. Explain.

Many of the characters in "Vanity Fair" are married from the start of the novel, or are betrothed during the novel. The reasons behind the marriage vary from character to character- even within relationships. While some may have love in mind, it is the temptation of money and social status that encourages others to walk down the aisle. The perspectives on marriage also depend on the position in the relationship. Mothers and fathers sometimes have more economic ideals while their children are in love, or even have no regard for each another at all. The protagonist of the novel, Becky Sharp, laments not having a mother to whom she could leave the arduous task of finding a fiancé.

Little is said of the relationship between Becky's parents. Her father was an artist and her mother a French opera dancer. It is unlikely that, as she was orphaned at a young age, Becky was greatly affected in any way by her parents' relationship. Perhaps indirectly, she felt that because she was an orphan, her impact on society had to be all the more memorable and successful.

Before so much as being introduced to a portrait of her friend Amelia's brother, Becky is reasoning with herself, "If Mr. Joseph Sedley is rich and unmarried, why should I not marry him?" Although Becky sees an opportunity to join the Sedley family, initially of some standing in society, Jos's behaviour is not exemplary for a young gentlemen. Before his drunken behaviour at Vauxhall, he allows Becky to eat a hot chili; an example of how he does not see the pursuit of matrimony as a worthwhile occupation; not a pastime that concerns him, although he appreciates the attention that Miss Sharp pays him.

Sir Pitt Crawley has a similar lack of appreciation for the attention of women that Jos holds. However, Sir Pitt is a little more extreme in both his views and actions. He brands his first wife as a "confounded quarrelsome high bred jade". He treats his second wife no better, evidently seeing marriage as something that has to be done, rather than an institution to join a man and a woman together in a loving relationship. However, Thackeray comments that "a title and a coach and four are more precious than happiness in Vanity Fair." As a narrator, Thackeray also sees marriage as an institution to be used to one's own advantage.

When Sir Pitt's second wife dies, he loses no time before proposing to Becky Sharp, although Miss Crawley hopes that he will have the "decency" not to marry again.. In her he sees a young, stimulating life. She is not someone to be beaten and left alone as his second wife seemed to be. She had "more brains in little finger than any baronet's wife in the country." The offer of marriage was made almost as a way in which to tempt Becky back to Queen's Crawley, where she was needed by Sir Pitt as a backbone to the household.

Becky's revelation that she is married to Sir Pitt's son, Rawdon, was a disappointment not only for Sir Pitt, but for Becky too. She sincerely regretted "that a piece of marvellous good fortune should have been so near her, and she actually obliged to decline it." This readiness to take the hand of the father or the son is similar to the thoughts of Maria Osborne, who would have married her wealthy fiancé's father, "only the old gentleman was married already; so she bestowed her young affections on the junior partner". Maria's fiancé, Frederick Bullock has to be persuaded to go forth with the marriage with the promise of estate when Maria's father died. However, when the charming and valuable Miss Swartz makes her entrance, Frederick "would have liked to make a bid for her himself". It is his use of business like terms that shows how he regards marriage. It is a business transaction that is won by the highest bidder-the man with the most material possessions to offer.

While Becky may outwardly regret not having a mother to arrange a marriage for emotional reasons, she shuns the idea of love secretly as she marries Rawdon Crawley in the belief that he will inherit Miss Crawley's money. Paradoxically, Rawdon is full of love and admiration for his wife. Although there is a problem in that the marriage is displeasing to Miss Crawley, Becky seems content as Rawdon is someone over whom she can exert control and with whom she can enter society.

Rawdon does not have the education that his wife has and the "dragoon" is easily manipulated as Becky sees the best ways in which to work their relationship. Becky has great entrepreneurial skills to bring to the marriage and it is these that seem to be initially most valuable to Rawdon. She is able to fend off creditors and the like and her "husband found the immense value of such a wife." On losing her husband, Becky mourns only the loss of his money and her time that now seems to have been wasted in climbing up in society. When parting at Waterloo, she simply turned off her emotions to save problems, there were no emotional ties and support on her side. However, the adulation of her husband is not enough to keep Becky's attention and she flirts with George Osborne at Brussels, despite the fact that he is married to her friend, Amelia. George told Dobbin before he was married that "there's no fun in winning a thing unless you play for it. It become apparent that George wants to elope. His ideas of marriage are now somewhat different as he is fired by the liveliness and danger of the affair. While George previously stood up for Amelia, her passive uselessness offers no competition for Becky.

Another character longs for what he cannot have. William Dobbin is in love with Amelia, but she is so committed to her hero, George, she only sees Dobbin as a friend. Dobbin is responsible for persuading George to marry Amelia as it is the right thing to do. The job also falls to him to inform Mr Osborne that George has married. In some ways, Dobbin uses the marriage of George and Amelia to further his own interests. He persuades Mr Osborne not to disinherit George and he also buys the piano for Amelia-but this act remains anonymous.

When Dobbin and Amelia eventually marry, their romantic sensibilities appear to have been lost to a great degree and Dobbin's passionate feelings for Amelia no longer exist. He possibly thinks more of their child than of his wife, but "he never said a word to Amelia that was not kind and gentle".

As the couple are finally brought together, Amelia is described as a "tender little parasite" around Dobbin's "rugged old oak". From this kind of comparison, Amelia can be considered to be dependent on a partner and dependent on marriage. Someone as weak as Amelia requires a protector in marriage. Having lost the memory of her late husband, albeit false, she can cling to Dobbin.

However, the female is not necessarily the parasite of the relationship. As has been shown previously, Rawdon is the parasite and Becky is the oak. It becomes clearer that many relationships in "Vanity Fair" have oaks and parasites, but the older, more matured relationships have more equal partnerships, such as that of Major and Mrs O'Dowd. It could be inferred that in the past years when these marriages first took place, marriage was not of such economical, social and material use as it is at the time of Becky Sharp's exploits.

Amelia's original ideas about marriage and love were somewhat more romantic and rose-tinted. The man to whom she had been expected to be married since childhood, was built up as a hero in her mind as time progressed. When George dies, Amelia's idea of a committed marriage to one person does not allow her to see past the memory of George to new love. Whenever he began to think about Dobbin's friendship and more, "George's picture and dearest memory were there to rebuke her." When George was alive, her wish to remain happily married to him prevented her from following her gut feelings about George's infidelity. While she could see his flirtations and behaviour with Becky, she dismissed her ideas. George's first ideas about his marriage to Amelia differed from his wife's. He felt that he "was one of the generousest creatures alive" as he sacrificed the life of a bachelor for married life.

More business like language is used in association with George and Amelia's relationship. The business relationship between Mr Sedley and Mr Osborne also greatly affected their children's relationship as once Mr Sedley lost money, Mr Osborne forbade the marriage, saying to his son, "unless I see Amelia's ten thousand down, you don't marry her." Mr Osborne's sights are set on the more profitable Miss Swartz. It becomes clearer and clearer how he perceives marriage. It is not a question of love, it is to do with the advancement of individual, but more gratifyingly-the advancement of families if at all possible. "I ain't going to have any of this dam sentimental nonsense and humbug" he declares as George attempts to defend Amelia.

While the parent's desire for advancement in society and wealth attempts to start that relationship, it is Becky's similar motivations that are responsible for her relationship with Lord Steyne. She considers him to simply be another step up the ladder of society. However, he is inadvertently a clue to what else Becky expects from a relationship. when Rawdon attacks Steyne on his arrival back home, Becky admires Rawdon's physical strength. Again, this is a more material aspect of a relationship.

The ideals behind marriage differ, often between generations. While parents can see economic and social gain, a situation such as with George and Amelia causes problems when the parents' meddling results in the children falling in love. Becky Sharp's use for marriage seems only to be self-advancement. When a relationship ends, her regrets are based on what she has lost, rather than who.

Q. Write a Brief Passage on Glare of Fashion in Vanity Fair.

Or

Q. How does Thackeray Create an appropriate Backdrop for the Humurously Satirical Novel Vanity Fair.

I fancy the doors to society guarded by grooms of the chamber with flaming silver forks with which they prong all those who have not the right of the entrée...the honest newspaper fellow....dies after a little time. He can't survive the glare of fashion long. It scorches him up, as the presence of Jupiter in full dress wasted that poor imprudent Semele&emdash;a giddy moth of a creature who ruined herself by venturing out of her natural atmosphere.

With this sentiment in mind, Thackeray expresses his conception of the danger present when one attempts to step outside of their inherent social strata. Through depicting a world devoted to upholding the inflexible codes of society, Thackeray creates an appropriate backdrop for his humorously satirical novel Vanity Fair. At the heart of this work, the avaricious Becky Sharp, born of common blood, fights against traditional precincts by "venturing" outside of her proper environs and entering into an elevated climate where the credulous yield unquestioningly to her will and the skeptics scorn her with cold indifference. Determined to secure a place in genteel society, Rebecca, disregarding the standards of society, manipulates the naive by engaging in hypocrisy and subterfuge while blinding those who doubt her with an unconquerable charm.

Clearly a perfectionist in the art of deception, Becky Sharp, a young woman with serpentine sentiments, slithers her way into the aristocratic society that composes the hollow cortex of Vanity Fair. With unremitting cupidity, Becky exploits all those she encounters for the sole purpose of ameliorating her own situation, both financially and socially. Commencing her mission for status as a mere governess at the Crawley household, the fortune seeking Becky marries Rawdon Crawley, "a heavy dragoon with strong desires and simple brains," and then continues to entice members of his social sphere in a perpetual pursuit of a position among England's nobility. Attempting to break into the highest ranks of Vanity Fair, Becky indifferently uses countless innocent souls and then disposes of them after she's reeped the benefits, until she eventually loses her husband, child, and friends. Through his sarcastic humour, witty dialogue, and amusing irony, Thackeray exhibits how Becky squirms her way to the top of 19th century, class conscious English society where she ultimately finds herself rebuffed as well as alone with impassive opulence.

However, this final state of Becky's existence results from her endeavors to defect from her appropriate sphere and join a class of people who shun her because of her lack of wealth and genteel blood. During this time the common folk, who have no influence in government, obediently accept their subservient station while the aristocrats possess all the power and wealth of the nation, viewing those beneath them with severe contempt. Families with a coat of arms, maids, a plot of land, footmen, and a seat in Parliament reign supreme and carefully guard their territory from intruders with insufficient bank accounts.

Infatuated with the idea of their own importance these vain aristocrats, who tend to overlook their own foibles, "guard the portals" to their class with "flaming silver forks" with which they "prong" status seekers such as Becky who "don't have the right of the entrée". Common citizens prove insignificant and vulgar to this proud group of English elites who barricade the poor from even peeping their heads into the exclusive circle of Baronets, Dukes, and Earls.

While striving to override these long held social attitudes, Becky confronts the sneers and disregard of those with whom she intends to consort. However, she ignores the pompous snubs of the rich and employs her irresistible charm as a method of ingratiating herself to the affluent. In addition, Rebecca takes advantage of those who naively oblige her in order to move closer to the door leading to the world of the wealthy. When Becky first arrives in Russell Square with her "dearest, sweetest friend" Amelia Sedley, she immediately designs to marry Joseph, Amelia's narcissistic and ungainly brother, because "all nabobs are enormously rich...and he has a very large income".

Yet when George Osborne, the cavalier, ego-centric fiancèe of Amelia, hears of this scheme he advises Jos to leave the country and thus prevents the connection, saying, "Hang it, the family's low enough without her...I'm a liberal man; but I've proper pride, and know my station: let her know hers". In her first attempt at breaking past the impenetrable barriers of society, Rebecca finds herself sorely beaten. Learning from this failure, Becky's knavery deepens as she prepares to feast on her next victim.

While feigning friendship to Amelia in order to extort fine clothing and jewels for herself, the "poor, friendless orphan," adopts a more intensive tactic of ingratiating herself to all influential persons. When she arrives at the prominent Crawley household, Rebecca conceals her disdainful, self-seeking motives behind a facade of beguiling beauty and boundless benevolence. At the same time, she repeatedly refers to her supposed ancestral connection with the illustrious Montmorency family. While still playing confidant to Amelia, Becky also captures the attention and favour of the lofty Sir Pitt Crawley by lauding his intelligence and eliciting his confidence, thus working her way closer to the portal of prosperity.

After Rebecca marries Rawdon Crawley&emdash;her only motive again the acquisition of wealth&emdash;she continues to squeeze her way into the ranks of the rich. With unsurpassable wit, Rebecca entices and cajoles the men of high society, and her efforts seem quite successful. One look at "her green eyes, fair skin, pretty figure, famous frontal development" sends hoards of men flocking to her side. Shamelessly flirting with these admirers, Becky triumphs in making each one feel as though he alone is special to her, yet she never commits to a single one of these dandies and so keeps them all dangling like puppets from her fortune seeking hands. Money, jewels, and other fineries from her enthusiasts facilitate her move into aristocratic society. In addition, Rebecca throws countless extravagant parties in order to augment her popularity and establish her name. As she increases her display of wealth, she slowly lifts the latch of the door that separates her from the nation's dignitaries.

At the threshold of entering this room filled with the most prosperous denizens of England, Becky finds herself engaged in an affair with the prodigiously wealthy Lord Steyne&emdash;her key to a spot in Vanity Fair. Thus far, Becky prevails with her insincere behaviour, for if one person of esteemed society falls subject to her enticements and accepts her, others unquestioningly follow. Yet her greatest challenge from society occurs when she faces the family and friends of Lord Steyne. Warning Becky of the rebuffs that await her, Lord Steyne says, "You've got no money, and you want to compete with those who have.

You poor little earthenware pipkin, you want to swim down the stream along with the great copper kettles...lookout and hold your own! How the women will bully you!" Substantiating Lord Steyne's foreboding, with frigid indifference the ladies at his soirée slight Becky, thus proving that she can never fully advance into their milieu. In view of this, Becky, one step away from pushing open the doors to social dominance, fails. Charms and beauty only carry the unwealthy so far in the world of Vanity Fair, thus Becky remains locked out of the room to which she dedicated her life to gaining entrance. Outstripped by the pretentious peerage, Becky's quest for status reiterates the insuperable fact that one without fortune or noble ancestry "can't survive the glare of fashion long".

Q. Discuss the Structure of Vanity Fair.

Structure of Vanity Fair

Thackeray's original title, Pen and Pencil Sketches of English Society, indicates his intention to describe a succession of social situations. As he was writing his novel, the idea of society as a Vanity Fair came to him, and he changed both his plan for the novel and the title. Though the name Vanity Fair comes from John Bunyan's Pilgrim's Progress, Thackeray uses the concept in a very different way from Bunyan. For Bunyan, Vanity Fair comprises all the worldly activities which distract the Christian from salvation and lead to damnation; they are vanities for this reason. At risk is the Christian's immortal soul.

The phrase "vanity fair" came to mean "a place where all is frivolity and empty show; the world or a section of it as a scene of idle amusement and unsubstantial display" the Oxford English Dictionary or OED. For Thackeray, everyone lives in Vanity Fair or society; vanity has become the desire for society's approval and rewards; the individual seeks, not spiritual salvation, but the rewards of this world–success, status, and wealth.

The change from sketches about society to society as a vanity fair raises a major critical question; is the novel rambling and formless? To paraphrase the subtitle, is it a novel without a structure? This issue was raised by contemporary reviewers. Robert Rintoul, who praised Thackeray's realism, saw the novel as episodic: "if putting Vanity Fair aside as a fiction of high art, we look at it as a series of bits from life, it is entitled to the first ranks as a set of sketches lifelike and natural". Supporting this view is the time difference in the first half and the second half of the novel; the first half covers two years before Waterloo and is compact while the second half sprawls over the next twenty-five years. Even if the novel lacks form, is that necessarily a serious flaw? The Victorians did not perceive structure and unity in a novel the same way as modern readers, who have been raised on James and Conrad and critical theories focusing on structure.

But is the perception that the novel lacks unity accurate?

Do major themes, like selfishness, give it form?

Do the parallel lives of Becky and Amelia structure the novel? They leave school together, to enter the world; their subsequent careers, which include marriage, motherhood, and financial struggles, intersect several times; the tender, loving, and passive Amelia contrasts with the ruthless, ambitious, and active Becky. Is his portrayal of society, with its crippling, perverted values and its lovelessness, the centre which holds the novel together? Does the narrator hold the novel together and structure it?

Is Vanity Fair a panoramic novel, i.e., a novel which presents a broad view of a society? Percy Lubbock uses Vanity Fair as an illustration of the panoramic novel; he says that Thackeray creates the impression of a world, a society, a time–certain manners of life within a few square miles of London, a hundred years ago. Thackeray flings together a crowd of the people he knows so well, and it matters not at all if the tie that holds them to each other is of the slightest... The light link is enough for the unity of his tale, for that unity does not depend on an intricately woven intrigue. It depends in truth upon one fact only, the fact that all his throng of men and women are strongly, picturesquely typical of the world from which they are taken–that in all their different ways can add to the force of its effect. The book is not the story of any of them, it is a story which they unite to tell, a chapter in the notorious career of well-to-do London. Exactly how the various "plots" evolve is not the main matter; behind them is the presence and the pressure of a greater interest, the mass of life which Thackeray packs into his novel.

Q. Discuss the Plot of Vanity Fair

or

Q. Is it true that casual reader loses thread of the story in Vanity Fair. Discuss.

The plot appears complex because of the multitude of characters and because the stated motives are seldom the true ones. Moreover, the author digresses so often in essays on related subjects that the casual reader may lose the thread of the story.

The story, however, is as modern as tomorrow—the struggle to establish oneself in society. Whereas the tale seems disjointed and diverse, it is held together by the one theme: the foibles and deceptions of the inhabitants of Vanity Fair. No matter how minor a character, Thackeray identifies that person—perhaps by the significance of his name only—as living or not living in Vanity Fair. This continuous focus on human nature in all aspects from motherhood to death, from poverty to prosperity, makes the plot both probable and unified. The conflict is always man against man for the joys and advantages of Vanity Fair. There is little soul-searching. The reader does not often enter the minds of the characters. He watches what they do, he hears what the author tells about them, and then with some direct prompting from the author, judges them. Any conflict with nature is conflict with human nature.

Thackeray wishes to impress on the reader the futility of Vanity Fair but he does not underestimate its values either. He admits that roast beef is good, although it vanishes like all pleasures of Vanity Fair. He points out the duplicity, the dishonesty, the double crossing of human beings all under the guise of doing good, being neighborly, or saving souls; but actually the purpose is to get money or position or advantage.

Most of the characters bow down to wealth and position regardless of the persons who have them. This worship of false values makes it possible for Rebecca to climb to the top, and if she had possessed sufficient money she would not have fallen on account of the discovery of her affair with Lord Steyne. For, although citizens of Vanity Fair may have a low opinion of the morals of their leading personages, this scruple will not deter them from attending balls, dinners, or any affair where one may get a free meal or sit beside nobility.

Q. Write down the Characterization in Vanity Fair.

Or

Q. Discuss the role of Society, The Hero, Amelia and Becky in Vanity Fair.

Characterization

Society

Like Austen in Emma, Thackeray identifies the place or status characters have in society and the nature of their relationship to society in Vanity Fair. Unlike Austen, who portrays the limited world of Highbury, Thackeray fills his novel with people, places, and travel. Almost all his characters are individualized, no matter how briefly they appear. We know their attitudes, their values, their hypocrisies and pettiness, their class, their desires and feelings. Taken together they make up the society that Thackeray calls Vanity Fair.

His characters also satirize the institutions they serve or represent: Lord Steyne and Sir Pitt Crawley both the father and the son show up Parliament, the rotten election system, and the aristocracy; religion is satirized with the Rev. Bute Crawley the Church of England and Mr. Pitt Crawley and Lady Southdown; the army leadership is satirized with General Tufto; the Colonial and foreign service, with Joseph Sedley, Rawdon Crawley, Mr. Pitt Crawley, and Tapeworm; the financial system, with Osborne senior. One class, however, is excluded, the poor.

In view of his characters' vitality and their representing major institutions, is it tenable to suggest that society is the real protagonist of Vanity Fair?

The Hero

Even though Thackeray subtitles his novel A Novel Without a Hero, readers in Thackeray's day and in ours want a hero, and many assign the role to Dobbin. Does Thackeray in fact regard him as the hero of the novel or even as a hero? If you see Dobbin as the hero, then the subtitle and the narrator's references to the novel's having no hero are part of Thackeray's satire of novelistic conventions and manipulation of the unthinking or careless reader. Is there any doubt that George Osborne is used to satirize the conventional hero?

Amelia

The question of whether the novel has a heroine is more complex. Amelia seems to be the conventional heroine–sweet, passive, self-sacrificing, gentle, tender, and loving. And Thackeray calls her a heroine–at times, but he contradicts himself at other times and says she is not a heroine he also refers to Becky as a heroine and not a heroine. In addition, he repeatedly calls Amelia "weak" and "selfish." Of Dobbin's faithful love and decades-long submission to her, Thackeray wrote to a friend that finally "he will find her not worth having." Thackeray wrote his mother that

My object is not to make a perfect character or anything like it. Don't you see how odious all the people are in the book with the exception of Dobbin–behind whom all there lies a dark moral I hope. What I want is to make a set of people living without God in the world only that is a cant phrase greedy pompous mean perfectly self-satisfied for the most part and at ease about their superior virtue.

Does this judgment apply to Amelia? Does Thackeray admire her wholeheartedly or admire some of her traits and behaviour but not others? If she is not the heroine, is Thackeray using her to expose the selfishness of the conventional heroine?

Becky

Becky has much more appeal than Amelia for most readers, as Thackeray acknowledged: The famous little Becky Puppet has been pronounced to be uncommonly flexible in the joints, and lively on the wire; the Amelia Doll, though it has had a smaller circle of admirers, has yet been carved and dressed with the greatest care by the artist....

Born with no advantages, in a society that values rank and wealth, Becky makes her way to the highest levels of society through her own resources, with determination, intelligence, hard work, and talent. She is resourceful and bounces back from every reversal. At the same time, her behaviour and character are morally indefensible; she constantly manipulates others, she lies, she cheats, she steals, she betrays Amelia, and perhaps she even commits a murder.

As the novel progresses, some readers feel that she becomes more dangerous and villainous. If so, was Thackeray upset that so many readers found her attractive? Does the change in her portrayal reflect ambivalence toward Becky? was he both attracted to her energy and courage and repelled by some of her actions, for instance? Or is the perception that her characterization changes false?

Dyson explains Becky's appeal in terms of the corrupt

nature of society and her role in that society: surely we do admire Becky, and legitimately, however glad we are to be outside the range of her wiles? The fact is that she belongs to Vanity Fair, both as its true reflection, and as its victim; for both of which reasons, she very resoundingly serves it right. Like Jonson's Volpone, she is a fitting scourge for the world which created her–fitting aesthetically, in the way of poetic justice, and fittingly moral, in that much of her evil is effective only against those who share her taint.

Dobbins is largely immune to her, since he is neither a trifler, a hypocrite nor a snob. The other characters are all vulnerable in one or other of these ways, and we notice that those who judge her most harshly are frequently the ones who have least earned such a right. A question arises about Becky's innocence in the last portion of the novel.

Specifically, is she innocent of adultery? and/or of murder? Thackeray offers a variety of opinions from self-interested and self-righteous observers, who range from the servants to the highest levels of fashionable society; the narrator's opinion remains ambiguous. It is important to keep in mind that though what characters say about one another is significant, their judgments may reveal more about the speaker or society's values than about the person being discussed; the opinion offered may not be trustworthy. The question of Becky's personal innocence raises a larger question; how important or meaningful is the question of her innocence, in view of how universally corrupt society is and how selfish the people judging her are? Who in this society is innocent?

Character Development

Do the characters change or develop in any significant way? or do we merely come to know them better as Thackeray reveals more details about them? Edwin Muir describes Thackeray's presentation of his characters as a gradual "unfolding in a continuously widening present"; the characters have the same weaknesses, vanities and foibles throughout, the only change being "our knowledge of them." The character who seems to change most is Rawdon Crawley, but how great is his change actually? If he does change significantly, are his love for Becky and his love for his son a sufficient, convincing reason for his change?

Q. Discuss the Significance of Illustrations in Vanity Fair.

Or

Q. Thackeray's illustrations for vanity fair

Thackeray, who intended his illustrations to be an integral part of the novel, filled it with drawings. The first letter of every chapter is incorporated into a drawing; almost every chapter includes a full-page drawing with an inscription at the bottom and one or more drawings of various sizes.The drawings supplement or complement the text in various ways. He was not entirely pleased with the final result in print. Firstly, he regarded them as "tenth or twentieth rate performances having a meaning perhaps but a ludicrous bad news of execution." Secondly, the methods of reproducing graphics in the nineteenth century tended to produce less accurate renderings than modern methods. I have included several drawings to illustrate some of the ways that they contribute to the meaning of the novel.

Example 1

Thackeray's drawing of himself holding a mask and a fool's scepter is relevant to the discussion of the narrator: is Thackeray to be equated with the narrator and the narrator's views, or is Thackeray the deliberate creator of a persona whom we call the narrator? Does the mask suggest the possibility of changing guises or identities? A poor copy of this drawing appears on the title page of your text.

Example 2

The meaning of the initial drawing for Chapter 4 is obvious; Becky is angling for a fat fish, Jos. There is irony in the fact that Jos, who distinguishes himself by how much he eats and drinks, is himself in danger of being caught and eaten by Becky. Continuing the fish metaphor, Mr. Sedley tells his wife, "But mark my words, the first woman who fishes for him, hooks him". Besides flattering Jos with references to his knowledge of foods, Becky lures Jos by knitting a green purse, the purse symbolizing money and the green perhaps suggesting Becky's envy of the Sedley's affluence; she shyly implies that she is making it for him. Though Becky is in a natural setting in the drawing, Thackeray's emphasis on society is maintained by the buildings in the background.

Example 3

The initial drawing for Chapter 5 deflates the "epic" fight between Cuff and Dobbin. The boys carry wooden swords, wear paper hats, and Cuff rides a rocking horse. Interestingly, in a novel which deals with the Battle of Waterloo, a watershed in European history, their fight is one of the most violent actions presented.

Example 4

Some drawings are less flattering to Becky than the text is. The drawing which most affects our view of Becky represents Becky as Clytemnestra at the end of the book. I will discuss it after you have finished the novel. The point I am making can readily be seen in the drawing of Becky using the dolls as puppets to mimic Miss Pinkerton and her sister. Note Becky's malicious expression. The posture and dress of the men is somewhat disreputable. Does the picture also suggest why, as an adult, she gets along so well with men? why the Bohemian life appeals to her? and why she enjoys being with people?

Example 5

Thackeray uses a drawing to support the reason he offers for using contemporary dress for his characters, even though the novel is set a generation earlier, when styles were quite different:

It was the author's intention, faithful to history, to depict all the characters of this tale in their proper costume, as they wore them at the commencement of this century. But when I remember the appearance of people in those days, and that an officer and lady were actually habited like this– I have not the heart to disfigure my heroes and heroines by costumes so hideous; and have, on the contrary, engaged a model of rank dressed according to the present fashion.

Q. Discuss the role of women in Vanity Fair

or

Q. Thackeray's attitude toward women

I have listed a number of passages about the role of women in Vanity Fair, for you to consider in deciding what Thackeray's attitude is, toward women in general and toward Amelia in particular, who fits the stereotypical image of woman and of the Angel in the House.

Passage 1

The narrator is discussing the jealousy and condescending attitude of women toward Amelia, who is greatly admired by men. He also discusses the intimidating treatment she receives from the Miss Osbournes and their governess Miss Wirt, who wonder what George sees in her.

How is this? some carping reader exclaims. How is it that Amelia, who had such a number of friends at school, and was so beloved there, comes out into the world and is spurned by her discriminating sex. My dear sir, there were no men at Miss Pinkerton's establishment except the old dancing-master; and you would not have had the girls fall out about him? When George, their handsome brother, ran off directly after breakfast, and drifted from home half-a-dozen times a week, no wonder the neglected sisters felt a little vexation. When young Bullock of the firm Hulker, Bullock & Co., Bankers, Lombard Street, who had been making up to Miss Maria the last two season, actually asked Amelia to dance the cotillion, could you expect that the former young lady should be pleased? Chapter XII, page 130.

Passage 2

The narrator is describing the early days of Becky's marriage and her successful efforts in pleasing Rawdon and hiding her opinion of his abilities. What is Thackeray's attitude toward the women's hypocrisy? How does this passage apply to Becky and to Amelia as wives? The best of women I have heard my grandmother say are hypocrites. We don't know how much they hide from us: how watchful they are when they seem most artless and confidential: how often those frank smiles which they wear so easily, are traps to cajole or elude or disarm–I don't mean in your mere coquettes, but your domestic models, and paragons of female virtue.

Who has not seen a woman hide the dulness of a stupid husband, or coax the fury of a savage one? We accept this amiable slavishness, and praise a woman for it: we call this pretty treachery truth. A good housewife is of necessity a humbug; and Cornelia's husband was hoodwinked, as Potiphar was–only in a different way Chapter XVII, page 197.

Passage 3

The narrator is referring to Miss Briggs and Miss Crawley's abusive treatment of her, all which attacks the poor companion bore with meekness, with cowardice, with a resignation that was half generous and half hypocritical–with the slaving submission, in a word, that women of her disposition and station are compelled to show. Who has not seen how women bully women? What tortures have men to endure, comparable to those daily repeated shafts of scorn and cruelty with which poor women are riddled by the tyrants of their sex? Poor victims! ChapterXXXIII, page 354-5.

Passage 4

Amelia has been blaming herself for selfishness in not giving up Georgy to his grandfather and thereby denying him an education, pleasures, and luxuries. The narrator comments:

I know few things more affecting than that timorous debasement and self-humiliation of a woman. How she owns that it is she and not the man who is guilty; how she takes all the faults on her side; how she courts in a manner punishment for the wrongs which she has not committed and persists in shielding the real culprit. It is those who injure women who get the most kindness from them–they are born timid and tyrants and maltreat those who are humblest before them Chapter L, pages 590-1

Passage 5

Amelia's grief is submerged or lessened by her nursing her dying mother. The illness of that old lady had been the occupation and perhaps the safeguard of Amelia. What do men know about women's martyrdoms? We should go mad had we to endure the hundredth part of those daily pains which are meekly borne by many women. Ceaseless slavery meeting with no reward; constant gentleness and kindness met by cruelty as constant; love, labour, patience, watchfulness, without even so much as the acknowledgment of a good word; all this, how many of them have to bear in quiet, and appear abroad with cheerful faces as if they felt nothing. Tender slaves that they are, they must needs be hypocrites and weak Chapter LVI, page 674.

Passage 6

Amelia accepts money from Osbourne, after giving up Georgy to his wealth. The narrator comments on her lack of pride, which stems from her being naturally simple and needing protection, her suffering, poverty, humility and privations since her marriage. Many women similarly sacrifice themselves.

O you poor secret martyrs and victims, whose life is a torture, who are stretched on racks in your bedrooms, and who lay your heads down on the block daily at the drawing-room table; every man who watches your pains, or peers into those dark places where the torture is administered to you, must pity you–and–and thank God that he has a beard.... if you properly tyrannize over a woman, you will find a h'p'orth of kindness act upon her and bring tears into her eyes, as though you were an angel benefiting her Chapter LVII, pages 678-9.

Passage 7

The narrator describes Amelia's routine of watching for Georgy and tending the sickbed, to suffer the harassment and tyranny of querulous disappointed old age. How many thousands of people are there, women for the most part, who are doomed to endure this long slavery?–who are hospital nurses without wages–sisters of Charity, if you like, without the romance and the sentiment of sacrifice–who strive, fast, watch, and suffer, unpitied, and fade away ignobly and unknown.

The hidden and awful Wisdom which apportions the destinies of mankind is pleased so to humiliate and cast down the gender, good, and wise, and to set up the selfish, the foolish, or the wicked. Oh, be humble, my brother, in your prosperity! Be gentle with those who are less lucky, if not more deserving. Think, what right have you to be scornful, whose virtue is a deficiency of temptation, whose success may be a mere change, whose rank may be an ancestor's accident, whose prosperity is very likely a satire Chapter LVII, pages 679-80.

Passage 8

The narrator describes Amelia's kindness to her father, her taking care of him, and her listening to the same stories over and over as "affectionate hypocrisy".

Q. Discuss the innocence of Becky in Vanity Fair.

Becky's Innocence

Intelligent and outrageous, self-reliant and alone, resourceful and courageous, meeting the world on its own terms and succeeding time and again, refusing to be defeated–Becky engages us with her vitality and aliveness and arouses our admiration for her resilience. An unscrupulous trickster, a liar and a cheat, a schemer and manipulator, a swindler, a hypocrite, a betraying wife and friend, a callous mother, a gambler, and possibly a murderer–Becky has her dark side which we and Thackeray? have to come to terms with. Who is Becky Sharp? How finally are we to feel about her and to think about her? If our feelings and our reason produce contradictory responses, how do we reconcile them?

Becky and Lord Steyne

Becky's innocence becomes a major issue in the novel when Rawdon discovers her alone with Lord Steyne. A great deal of planning goes into making Steyne's tete-a-tete with

Becky possible; her son is placed in a boarding school, Miss Briggs is sent to Steyne's country house, and Rawdon is arrested for debt. Her indifference to his welfare becomes clear to Rawdon when he receives her letter–beautiful in appearance ink paper, light green seal, highly scented, heartless and superficial in content. Rawdon's suspicions of Becky are reawakened and he is desperate to be released.

His suspicions are confirmed when he finds Steyne and Becky alone. Becky, frightened, cries, "I am innocent, Rawdon". Is it significant that the snake image appears at this point, her hands being covered with "serpents, and rings, and baubles"? Rawdon strikes Steyne twice, throwing him to the ground. Becky sees her husband in a new light: "She admired her husband, strong, brave, and victorious". Thackeray was enormously proud of this detail: "When I wrote the sentence, I slapped my fist on the table, and said, 'that is a touch of genius!'" Why does she have this response when all her plans and her success are destroyed at the moment of achievement? Does she perhaps get some satisfaction in seeing the powerful, wealthy Steyne humiliated, in seeing the man who repeatedly sneered at her and held the power to fulfill her social ambitions powerless? Or is Thackeray being ironic?

Steyne vehemently denies her innocence; he has spent thousands of pounds on her. Does this necessarily mean they have slept together? Would Steyne have waited years and spent thousands of pounds without some sexual return from Becky? Did he enjoy her company enough, did she interest him enough and was she clever enough so that he waited? If they have been lovers, why go to all the bother of setting up this evening for them to be alone and to get her son and Miss Briggs out of the house? Is Steyne's word about her guilt necessarily accurate? He erroneously accuses Rawdon of being part of a scheme to shake him down. And does Steyne live in a world and have a view of life in which innocence is possible?

Even if she has not physically betrayed Rawdon, are there other kinds of betrayal that she might be guilty of?

Did she intend to sleep with Steyne? Would an unfulfilled intention make her guilty? Christ taught that a man who lusts in his heart after a woman is guilty of adultery. Does this moral principle apply to Becky? A similar question arises in her flirtation with George at Brussels. When Amelia accuses Becky of trying to take George away from her and of being a false friend, Becky protests, "I have done my husband no wrong". So far as physical infidelity goes, Becky is accurate; that she intends to run off with George, who is poor and whom she holds in contempt, is unlikely. Is she stringing him along so that Rawdon can fleece him gambling? Amelia raises a different offense, betrayal of friendship, "Have you done me no wrong, Rebecca? You did not succeed, but you tried. Ask your heart if you did not". Is Rebecca guilty of this offense? If so, is it serious moral and/or emotional offense?

Has she betrayed Rawdon's trust and love? When he discovers the money she has squirreled away in the desk Amelia gave her in friendship, he says, "You might have spared me a hundred pounds, Becky, out of all this–I have always shared with you".

Rawdon refuses a reconciliation, "If she's not guilty, Pitt, she's as bad as guilty, and I'll never see her again–never". How can Becky be not guilty but "as good as guilty"? Is Rawdon judging morally or emotionally? Is Rawdon qualified to cast moral stones at Becky, in view of his accepting the governorship which Steyne got him because of Becky?

Thackeray leaves the question the question of her innocence open:

What had happened? Was she guilty or not? She said not, but who could tell what was truth which came from those lips, or if that corrupt heart was in this case pure? All her lies and her schemes, all her selfishness and her wiles, all her wit and genius had come to this bankruptcy.

Society's judgment of her guilt is unreliable, because it is not based on the facts or concern for the truth but on rumor, a priori assumptions, and corrupt values: "Was she guilty or not? We all know how charitable the world is, and how the verdict for Vanity Fair goes when there is a doubt".

Should much meaning be attached to a comment Thackeray dryly makes when Becky sees Steyne and other people she remembered from "happier days, when she was not innocent but not found out".

Becky's Innocenceand the Servants

Previous to Rawdon's confrontation with Steyne, the servants had judged her guilty, "the awful kitchen inquisition which sits in judgment in every house and knows everything". Later in this passage, Thackeray explains that Lord Steyne's visits reassured the servants and Raffles into giving Becky credit.

Are servants in a position to know what is happening in a household? are they likely to know their employer's secrets? The reliability of their knowledge is called into question. The narrator warns employers, "If you are not guilty, have a care of appearances, which are as ruinous as guilt". Of Becky specifically, he comments that she was "guiltless very likely".

Chapter 13

Critical Essays

The Gentleman and the Lady

A concern in Thackeray's writing, as in the writing of many other middle-class Victorian novelists, is the question of who and what a gentleman is. The traditional concept of a gentleman is a man of family and fortune who does not work; it is a class-based concept which excluded most middle class men. Having in mind this definition, Thackeray said that it took three generations to make a gentleman. The middle classes, which were growing in number, wealth, and power, did not want to wait to be accepted as gentlemen. To make the concept of the gentleman more inclusive, writers identified character and moral values as the criteria for recognizing a gentleman. Thackeray uses both concepts of the gentleman in Vanity Fair. He uses the older definition ironically in connection with characters like Lord Steyne and Sir Pitt Crawley, the father; the new definition is applied to the honorable–and honest–William Dobbin.

The Gentleman as Man of Family and Wealth

Fashionable society accepts Lord Steyne as indisputably a gentleman even though his immoral lifestyle is notorious. Despite his open womanizing and other vices, his "distinguished courtesy" toward his wife in public "caused the severest critics to admit how perfect a gentleman he was, and to own that his Lordship's heart at least was in the right place". Appearance and status are what matter in determining who is a gentleman, not character or virtue or the whole life of a man. In private, where society cannot see or hear his treatment of his wife or other female dependents, Steyne is heartless or ungentlemanly.

He savagely abuses his wife, Lady Steyne, and daughter-in-law, Lady Gaunt, verbally to force them to invite Becky to their home. Moreover, "To see his wife and daughter suffering always put his Lordship into a good humour". To emphasize the irony, Thackeray uses Steyne's title, "his lordship." When Lady Gaunt defies him to strike her, he replies, "I am a gentleman, and never lay my hand upon a woman, save in the way of kindness". He is brutal in his advice to Becky, when she reveals that she has cheated Miss Briggs out of her money and ruined her financially: "'Ruined her? Then why don't you turn her out?' the gentleman asked". In both of these incidents, the term "gentleman" is used ironically for satiric purpose; Steyne is simultaneousl—and ironically—a sadistic brute and a perfect gentleman. This concept of the gentleman contrasts with the newer one Thackeray espouses.

The Gentleman as Man of Character and Virtue

Thackeray explicitly identifies what the true gentleman is and who of his characters is a true gentleman. On the one hand, his concept democratizes the concept of the gentleman because a man of any class who has the requisite character and integrity could be a gentleman. On the other hand, Thackeray sets such a high standard for the gentleman that very few men actually fit his definition of a true gentlemen, though there are many who regard themselves and are regarded as gentlemen using the standards of Vanity Fair. Thackeray distinguishes between the few true gentlemen and the more numerous group whose claim to being gentlemen is based on externals, not ideals:

Perhaps these are rarer personages than some of us think for. Which of us can point out many such in his circle–men whose aims are generous, whose truth is constant, and not only constant in its kind but elevated in its degree; whose want of meanness makes them simple; who can look the world honestly in the face with an equal manly sympathy for the great and the small? We all know a hundred whose coats are very well made, and a score who have excellent manners, and one or two happy beings who are what they call in the inner circles and have shot into the very centre and bull's-eye of the fashion; but of gentlemen how many? Let us take a little scrap of paper and each make out his list.

My friend the Major I write, without any doubt, in mine. He had very long legs, a yellow face, and a slight lisp, which at first was rather ridiculous. But his thoughts were just, his brains were fairly good, his life was honest and pure, and his heart warm and humble.

The New Concept of the Gentleman Corrupted

The new concept of the gentleman can degenerate into the recognition of appearance, position, wealth, and a conformity to decorum. Sir Pitt Crawley, the son, is the model of the prig who places money and advancement before generosity, honour, and kindness. He is able to listen to Rawdon's request for help and sympathize with him after Rawdon assures him he is not asking for money. On this occasion, Thackeray describes Sir Pitt, ironically, as "a real old English gentleman, in a word–a model of neatness and every propriety". He is wearing a starched cravat with his dressing gown!

Mr. Osborne, made brutal and self-righteous by egotism and pride of success, represents the middle class capitalist who sees the world in terms of money, judges people by their wealth, and uses his children to fulfill his social ambitions and enhance his sense of self-worth. He raises his son to be a gentleman and not surprisingly turns out a self-centered, self-satisfied, superficial snob. He is in the process of ruining his grandson with extravagant indulgence. Ironically the chapter which describes Georgy's life in the Osborne mansion is titled "Georgy is Made a Gentleman"; in reality, his crass, ignorant grandfather is making Georgy less of a gentleman than he starts out as by encouraging his self-importance and by not providing boundaries to guide him. Fortunately Georgy is redeemable. It is true that he has been indulged by his mother, that his egotism has been fostered by her idolizing him, and that he is being turned into his father even by her. Nevertheless he has benefitted morally and emotionally by being raised by a true lady who has many excellent qualities; he is, after all, the recipient of her love, kindness, humility, selflessness, and tenderness. Obnoxious as Georgy can be, he nevertheless has sterling qualities, as shown by his generosity to and tender feeling for the beggar boy whom he gives money to–before his attendant can chase the boy away. Circumstance favors his being saved from his father's character with the elder Osborne's death and the guidance of Dobbin, whose sterling nature George is gentleman enough to perceive.

The Lady Redefined

Redefining the gentleman requires redefining the lady, so that the lady, too, is no longer a class-based concept. Like the gentleman, the lady must have character and be virtuous, though the nature of her character and her specific virtues differ from those of the gentleman. Amelia exemplifies the true lady for Thackeray, in a passage discussing her raising Georgy::

He had been brought up by a kind, weak, and tender woman, who had no pride about anything but about him, and whose heart was so pure and whose bearing so meek and humble that she could not but needs be a true lady. She busied herself in gentle offices and quiet duties; if she never said brilliant things, she never spoke or thought unkind ones; guileless and artless, loving and pure, indeed how could our poor little Amelia be other than a real gentlewoman!". Lady Steyne, suffering, pure, and passive, is a true lady; Lady Jane Sheepshanks, who develops more depth and character as the novel progresses, comes to be another true lady.

The New Concept the Traditional Concept of a of the Lady Corrupted

The new concept of the lady, like that of the gentleman, can degenerate into the recognition of appearance, position, wealth, and a conformity to decorum. As Amelia exemplifies the new true lady, so Becky expresses the corrupted concept of a lady, a concept whose criteria would be easier to meet and would undoubtedly be more widely acceptable:

"It isn't difficult to be a country gentleman's wife," Rebecca thought. "I think I could be a good woman if I had five thousand a year. I could dawdle about in the nursery and count the apricots on the wall. I could water plants in a green-house and pick off dead leaves from the geraniums. I could ask old women about their rheumatisms and order half-a-crown's worth of soup for the poor. I shouldn't miss it much, out of five thousand a year. I could even drive out ten miles to dine at a neighbor's, and dress in the fashions of the year before last. I could go to church and keep awake in the great family pew, or go to sleep behind the curtains, with my veil down, if I only had practice. I could pay everybody, if I had but the money. This is what the conjurors here pride themselves upon doing. They look down with pity upon us miserable sinners who have none. They think themselves generous if they give our children a five-pound note, and us contemptible if we are without one".

Becky's idea of a lady is based on externals–money, clothes, and socially-acceptable behaviour, without the virtues and character which should motivate that behaviour. The satire is clear. But Thackeray introduces ambiguity by wondering in the rest of this paragraph whether Becky is right:

And who knows but Rebecca was right in her speculations–and that it was only a question of money and fortune which made the difference between her and an honest woman? If you take temptations into account, who is to say that he is better than his neighbour? A comfortable career of prosperity, if it does not make people honest, at least keeps them so. An alderman coming from a turtle feast will not step out of his carriage to steal a leg of mutton; but put him to starve, and see if he will not purloin a loaf ages 499-500.

Is this Thackeray speaking or a narrator, a persona who is not expressing Thackeray's view? Is Thackeray expressing a pessimistic view about human nature and our capacity for goodness and honesty? The small number of gentlemen would be explained by such a view.Or is he challenging the smug, reasuring belief his readers may hold of their own righteousness? This passage upset many contemporaries, because it assumes that honesty comes from self-interest and sufficient wealth not to be tempted rather than innate goodness. Thackeray justified this passage to G.H. Lewes, who was offended by it:

I am quite aware of the dismal roguery wh goes all through the Vanity Fair story–and God forbid that the world should be like it altogether: though I fear it is more like it than we like to own. But my object is to make every body engaged, engaged in the pursuit of Vanity and I must carry my story through in this dreary minor key, with only occasional hints here & there of better things–of better things wh it does not become me to preach. Thackeray felt some unease with the role of moralist and preacher because he seldom lost sight of his own flawed nature and regrettable past actions. He had personally experienced Becky's view and feelings. In 1839, when he was facing poverty after the loss of his inheritance, he wrote his mother about a wealthy "good, sobre, and religious" friend, "a fine English squire"; he added that "if I had 3,000 a year I think I'd be so too."

The Narrator, the Reader, and Ambiguity in Vanity Fair

Thackeray's contemporaries equated Thackeray with the narrator, whom they saw as omniscient; as a result, they often missed the irony, read Thackeray's satire as his actual beliefs, and attacked him for cynicism and worse. A more careful reading of the novel indicates that the narrator is not consistently or even mainly omniscient. His character constantly shifts to fallibility, to ignorance, and even to incomprehension. His identity changes too. He is the stage manager, introduced in "Before the Curtain"; even in this guise, his role shifts from directing the performance, to controlling the actions of the characters or puppets, as he calls them, to helplessly watching them do as they wish. So, even when Thackeray adopts the guise of the stage manager, questions arise; is he the creator of the story, the teller, or a hapless observer? He metamorphoses into critic, clown, satirist, commentator, preacher, reporter, and participant. His situation changes, for example, from being married to being single, from having no children to having children. His relationsnip to the characters shifts from being a friend to being a hostile judge. His attitude too undergoes breathtaking transformations, being by turns wise, sentimental, worldly, cynical, amused, sad, inane, smug, and pleased at showing the characters up.

This shifting in the narrator has led some readers to accuse Thackeray of being inconsistent. This is a serious charge and would be a major flaw in any novel. The charge implies that Thackeray lacked the skill to create a consistent narrator, that he was too careless to create a consistent narrator, or that he was too intellectually lacking to be aware of the narrator's inconsistency Thomas Carlyle, for instance, questioned Thackeray's capacity for serious thought. The charge of inconsistency is particularly serious because of the pervasive presence of the narrator; he is everywhere with his comments and his reactions and even appears as a character who has met Amelia and Dobbin. We see the characters through his eyes and know them through his words, though Thackeray also presents myriad other voices and views. For these reasons, the narrator is a major source of the ambiguity—or difficulty in determining Thackeray's intention and meaning–throughout the novel. When are the narrator's comments and attitudes ironic? when are they to be taken literally? and when or how often do they express Thackeray's attitudes and values?

Not everyone concedes that Thackeray is unintentionally inconsistent. If the narrator is seen as a fictional persona, then he does not necessarily speak for or as Thackeray. He becomes one more character, different in kind and in function from the other characters, certainly, but a character nonetheless. Therefore, Thackeray is free to manipulate him to achieve particular effects at different points in the novel. Viewing the narrator as a persona raises another set of considerations and assessments. Are the narrator's shifts justified by achieving special effects, or are they confusing? Do they, in other words, add to or detract from the novel? The views of critics differ significantly on these issues, as the following sampling of opinions suggests: Are the shifts in the narrator a flaw in the novel?

E.D.H. Johnson attributes the shifts in the narrator to Thackeray's ambiguous relationship to his world. Johnson believes that Thackeray had difficulty in combining his satiric bent and his moral purpose, a difficulty which resulted in confused aims:

> The curious alternations of attraction and repulsion manifest in Thackeray's handling of Becky and Amelia characterize his attitude towards the entire world of the novel. As a satirist, he castigates the manners and morals of that world; as a moralist, he is more taken in by its standards than he is presumably aware. Unlike Fielding, he was never able artistically to harmonize his twin purposes, because again unlike Fielding he lacked any compelling vision of forces making for unity and poise within the social organism.

Johnson explains that the eighteenth-century Henry Fielding lived in a stable society with intact institutions underpinned by a robust religious faith. But in Thackeray's society, religion was losing its authority. In Johnson's view, one result of this loss was that love as a generalized form of brotherhood and charity no longer held society together but existed only as a bond between individuals.

Arnold Kettle, on the other hand, attributes the difficulty in determining Thackeray's intention and views to his cowardice, "from a desire to expose illusions and yet keep them."

Are there positive ways to view the narrator's shifts?

Harold Bloom calls Thackeray's narrator "that supreme fiction" and sees the point of view as one of the strengths of the novel. Many readers see the narrative shifts as part of Thackeray's subtlety, a device whereby he indicates the difficulty, if not the impossibility of arriving at the whole truth. If determining the truth is problematic, then making judgments becomes an issue; in this view, the narrator's shifts challenge our right to judge since we are all corrupted, in some way and to some degree. Kathleen Tillotson believes that the narrator's commentary serves other purposes. It bridges past and present. Furthermore, Without Thackeray's own voice, the melancholy and the compassion of his attitude to Vanity Fair might escape us. It is needed merely as relief, from a spectacle that might otherwise be unbearably painful.

And not only morally painful, but mentally impoverished. The characters, the best as well as the worst, are almost without ideas; the intellectual atmosphere of the novel is provided by the commentary. By presenting the narrator's comments and reactions as well as the characters' feelings and reactions, Thackeray gives the novel a richer, more complex, and subtle texture. Juliet McMaster believes that the narrator's commentary, which she calls alternately inane, snug, cloying, or cynical, forces the reader to react, thereby giving the characters a kind of life and making them feel like autonomous beings. You will have to decide these issues for yourself based on your reading and understanding of the novel.

The Narrator and the Reader in Vanity Fair

Just as the narrator's identity shifts, so does the reader's identity. The narrator addresses a succession of different readers–e.g., a supercilious clubman, a lady, women in general, "you"–to whom he attributes specific attitudes and whom he characterizes as behaving in certain ways. Behind these fictional readers there are the actual readers of the novel. What do you see as the functions of the fictional readers addressed by the narrator?

And what is the relationship between the fictional readers and the actual readers, that is, between them and you? For example, do they create a bond between you, the actual reader, and the narrator? or a bond between you, the actual reader, and the characters? Are your feelings and your judgment about the characters, their actions, and their world affected by Thackeray's use of fictional readers? When Thackeray addresses "you," is he addressing the actual reader, or is the "you" a fictional persona? or is the identity of "you" sometimes the actual reader and sometimes a fictional persona?

Discuss the Technique and Style in Vanity Fair

The story is presented by summarized narrative, bits of drama, interpolated essays, without much recourse to the minds of the characters. If there is any doubt as to how the reader should judge an individual, the author steps in and makes appropriate comment. For example, when the Sedleys lose their money, the chief critic and enemy is old Osborne, whom Sedley has started in business. Thackeray comments on the psychology of old Osborne's attitude:

When one man has been under very remarkable obligations to another, with whom he subsequently quarrels, a common sense of decency, as it were, makes of the former a much severer enemy than a mere stranger would be... a persecutor is bound to show that the fallen man is a villain—otherwise he, the persecutor, is a wretch himself.

Here is an example of dramatic presentation. Amelia visits Becky to find out if she can help her. Becky has hidden her brandy bottle in the bed, and is putting forth every effort to engage Amelia's sympathy by way of little Rawdon:

"My agonies," Becky continued, "were terrible I hope she won't sit down on the bottle when they took him away from me I thought I should die; but I fortunately had a brain fever, during which my doctor gave me up, and—and I recovered, and—and—here I am, poor and friendless."

"How old is he?" Emmy asked.

"Eleven," said Becky.

"Eleven!" cried the other. "Why, he was born the same year with George who is—"

"I know, I know," Becky cried out, who had in fact quite forgotten all about little Rawdon's age. "Grief has made me forget so many things, dearest Amelia. I am very much changed: half wild some times. He was eleven when they took him away from me. Bless his sweet face, I have never seen it again."

"Was he fair or dark?" went on that absurd little Emmy. "Show me his hair."

Becky almost laughed at her simplicity...

Usually Thackeray just describes what happens. George

and Becky are talking about how Becky can get next to Briggs, Miss Crawley's maid, and thereby see Miss Crawley and regain her favour for Rawdon. Becky says she will find out when Briggs goes to bathe; she will dive in under Briggs' awning and "insist on a reconciliation".

The idea amuses George, who bursts out laughing, whereat Rawdon shouts at them to ask what the joke is. Thackeray does not say Amelia is jealous, he shows the reader what she does: "Amelia was making a fool of herself in an absurd hysterical manner, and retired to her own room to whimper in private."

Instead of showing, sometimes the author tells what the situation is. Of Sir Pitt's second wife, he says, "Her heart was dead long before her body. She had sold it to become Sir Pitt Crawley's wife. Mothers and daughters are making the same bargain every day in Vanity Fair." Although Thackeray claims to write about real people, at the close of the book, he says, "Come, children, let us shut up the box and the puppets, for our play is played out." Thackeray does write about real people; Amelia is drawn from Mrs. Thackeray. However, in the writing of a story, there is a transformation and adaptation which justifies also the figure of the manipulation of puppets.

The author calls his characters ironic or patronizing names such as "Our poor Emmy," or "Our darling Rebecca." The modern reader may think his writings full of clichés. One must remember, however, that Thackeray makes fun of just such patronizing expressions, and one cannot be sure that he uses such expressions seriously.

Thackeray likes certain words such as "killing." Sometimes his punctuation seems old-fashioned, like his use of the colon instead of a period in sentences like: "William knew her feelings: had he not passed his whole life in divining them?"

Sentence structure ranges from a few words to a whole paragraph. The variety tends to make the story readable, slows the pace or quickens it; variation may come in the form of a question or direct address. Essay or narration alternates with dialogue and dramatic action.

Because the story was written as a serial, Thackeray didn't have the whole manuscript in hand for completion and correction. As a result the story rambles; essays have been inserted as padding; there is a certain amount of confusion in regard to names, places, and time. For example, Mrs. Bute Crawley is sometimes Martha, sometimes Barbara. Georgy sees Dobbin in London at a time when he is in Madras.

The reader has a complete picture of Joseph's visit with his father and Amelia, his reassurance as to their welfare. Then Amelia gets a letter from Jos saying he will be delayed—he hasn't yet left Southampton.

Whatever his faults in producing a sprawling, sometimes inaccurate manuscript, Thackeray has never missed a chance to point out the futility, the snobbery of Vanity Fair.

Vanity Fair, by William Makepeace Thackeray

A review by Edwin Percy Whipple: In the novels of Thackeray, essay is so much mixed up with narrative, and comment with characterization, that they can hardly be thoroughly appreciated in poor editions. The temptation to skip is almost irresistible, when wisdom can be purchased only at the expense of eyesight. We are therefore glad to welcome the commencement of a new edition of his writings, over whose pages the reader can linger at his pleasure, and quietly enjoy the subtleties of humour and observation which in previous perusals he overlooked. The present volumes, published by the Harpers, are among the most tasteful and comely products of the Cambridge University Press.

Printed in large type of tinted paper, elegantly bound in green cloth and with a fac-simile of the author's autograph on the cover, every copy has the appearance of being a presentation copy. No English edition of Vanity Fair is equal to this American one in respect either to convenience of form or beauty of mechanical execution. The illustrations are numerous, well engraved, and embody the writer's own conceptions of his scenes and characters, and are often deliciously humorous.

Vanity Fair, though it does not include the whole extent

of Thackeray's genius, is the most vigorous exhibition of its leading characteristics. In freshness of feeling, elasticity of movement, and unity of aim, it is favorably distinguished from its successors, which too often give the impression of being composed of successive accumulations of incidents and persons, that drift into the story on no principle of artistic selection and combination. The style, while it has the raciness of individual peculiarity and the careless case of familiar gossip, is as clear, pure, and flexible as if its sentences had been subjected to repeated revision, and every pebble which obstructed its lucid and limpid flow had been laboriously removed. The characterization is almost perfect of its kind. Becky Sharp, the Marquis of Steyne, Sir Pitt Crawley and the whole Crawley family, Amelia, the Osbornes, Major Dobbin, not to mention others, are as well known to most cultivated people as their most intimate acquaintances in the Vanity Fair of the actual world.

It has always seemed to us that Mr. Osborne, the father of George, a representation of the most hateful phase of English character, is one of the most vividly true and life-like of all the delineations in the book, and more of a typical personage than even Becky or the Marquis of Steyne. Thackeray's theory of characterization proceeds generally on the assumption that the acts of men and women are directed not by principle, but by instincts, selfish or amiable—that toleration of human weakness is possible only by lowering the standard of human capacity and obligation—and that the preliminary condition of an accurate knowledge of human character is distrust of ideals and repudiation of patterns.

This view is narrow, and by no means covers all the facts of history and human life, but what relative truth it has is splendidly illustrated in Vanity Fair. There is not a person in the book who excites the reader's respect, and not one who fails to excite his interest. The morbid quickness of the author's perceptions of the selfish element, even in his few amiable characters, is a constant source of surprise. The novel not only has no hero, but implies the non-existence of heroism. Yet the fascination of the book is indisputable, and it is due to a variety of causes besides its mere exhibition of the worldly side of life. Among these, the perfect intellectual honesty of the writer, the sad or satirical sincerity with which he gives in his evidence against human nature, is the most prominent.

With all his lightness of manner, he is essentially a witness under oath, and testifies only to what he is confident he knows. Perhaps this quality, rare not only in novel writing, but in all writing, would not compensate for the limitation of his perceptions and the repulsiveness of much that he perceives, were it not for the peculiar charm of his representation. It is here that the individuality of the man appears, and it presents a combination of sentiments and powers more original perhaps than the matter of his works. Take from Vanity Fair that special element of interest which comes from Thackeray's own nature, and it would lose the greater portion of its fascination. It is not so much what is done, as the way in which is is done, that surprises and delights; and the manner is always inimitable, even when the matter is common.

Discuss the Various Aspects of W M Thackeray's Vanity Fair

Setting

The setting so far as physical place is concerned, moves from London to Brighton, to the Continent including Paris, Rome, Brussels, and "Pumpernickel," a small German principality. The reader moves from city house to country estate, from private academy to the sponging house, or debtors' jail.

But there is also a social setting. The story unfolds against the back ground of the estates and attitudes of the landed aristocracy such as the Lord Steynes and the Crawleys; the houses of the city merchants such as the Sedleys, the Osbornes, and the Dobbins the colonial order and money of Miss Swartz and Joseph Sedley, the collector of Boggley Wollab; the military protocol in Brussels before Waterloo and in India; the Anglo-Irish in the persons and prejudices of the O'Dowds and the lesser fringes of Vanity Fair embodied in the Clapps, Raggles,

Briggs, and others. The book, then, has not only a setting as to place but also, and more important, as to position and power. It emerges as a social document, accurate in terms of history, sociology, and psychology.

The highest point in the social strata is the Court, where Becky finally is presented. The lowest is the Fleet prison, where fate sends poor Raggles. The two characters more concerned with human relationships than with position or power are Amelia and Dobbin. Vanity Fair, then, is not so much a story told against a setting, as a state of mind, a state of mind still prevalent in the twentieth century.

Idea

The title suggests the idea: Vanity Fair. The treasures of Vanity Fair, that is, money and position, are desirable but transient. The gaiety, the mask of the ball, do not stay with the person when he faces death. Thackeray does not underestimate the importance of having a home, clothes and food; but he does expose the cruelty, the deception, the futility of making possessions and power the only aim in life.

The book is so saturated with the vanity of Vanity Fair, the duplicity of social climbers, and the weakness of human nature, that it would be impossible to separate idea from plot or plot from characters. If the book appears to ramble, it never strays from the focus of attention on the foibles of human nature in its struggle to reach the highest strata of Vanity Fair.

The setting could be changed to modern times and the observations would be true today. The vanity of man is universal and ever present. Women still berate and betray women; relatives still fight over money; mothers still sell their daughters for popularity, money, or position. Yet, there are some people, the reader hopes and Thackeray indicates, who do not bow down to the idols of Vanity Fair.

The winners at the end of the story are those who cherished human relationships first: Amelia, Dobbin, and Lady Jane, with the children Georgy and little Rawdon. Thackeray's idea, then, is that although one may live in Vanity Fair, one need not be a slave to its values, which in the final analysis turn into futility and emptiness. The reader feels that Georgy and little Rawdon will be better men than their grandfathers.

Symbolism

Thackeray takes symbols from everyday life, from the classics, and from the Bible. He shows Rebecca ensnaring Joseph in a tangle of green silk, at their first acquaintance. As Becky climbs the social stairway, she is likened to a spider. At the close of the book, she has literally entangled and destroyed Joseph just as a spider would its victim. She sucked his money, his vitality, his personality from him. She did not reduce Rawdon to such a shell, but she played Delilah to his Samson.

At the charade party Rebecca plays Clytemnestra, symbolic of her destruction first of Rawdon, second of Joseph. Clytemnestra killed her husband, Agamemnon, when her lover's courage failed. Rebecca is also called Circe, the siren who lured men to their death. Sir Pitt refers to the Bute Crawleys as Beauty and the Beast, a symbolic hint that Bute has married a battle-axe, which he has.

The Osborne household keeps time by a clock representing the sacrifice of Iphigenia. Iphigenia, daughter of Clytemnestra and Agamemnon, was sacrificed by her father for success in war, another route to power and position. Old Osborne tries to sacrifice George to a marriage for money; he destroys Miss Jane's one romance for his own selfish convenience. The Iphigenia clock, then, symbolizes the complete subordination of the Osbornes to money and social success. Amelia's giving up Georgy is compared to Hannah's giving up Samuel. The Bible story has religious significance; Hannah gives up her son to the Lord. In Vanity Fair, Amelia, though she is not of Vanity Fair, surrenders her son to advantages that money and position can provide. The symbol here may be ironic.

Imagery

The symbolism described in the foregoing paragraphs constitutes one form of imagery. To continue with similar figures which may not be considered broadly symbolic, one reads of Miss Pinkerton, "the Semiramis of Hammersmith." Sermiramis was an Assyrian queen noted for beauty, wisdom, and voluptuousness. Hammersmith was a metropolitan borough of London. Obviously the figure is ironic. When Pitt lures James into trouble by urging him to drink and smoke in Miss Crawley's house, Thackeray calls Pitt, Machiavel, a name synonymous with political cunning, duplicity, and bad faith.

Old Sir Pitt, called Silenus, leers at Becky like a satyr. In mythology Silenus is a fat old man, jolly, intoxicated, an attendant of Bacchus. Satyrs are goat-like men, attendants of Bacchus, the god of wine.

Men and women are compared to trees and birds: "While Becky Sharp was on her own wing in the country, hopping on all sorts of twigs and amid a multiplicity of traps, and pecking up her food quite harmless and successful, Amelia lay snug in her home..." He compares George to a tree where Amelia can built her nest but says it is not safe. When Dobbin has at last won Amelia, the author says, "The bird has come in at last. There it is with its head on his shoulder, billing and cooing close up to his heart with soft outstretched fluttering wings..." He calls Dobbin the "rugged old oak to which you cling."

Dobbin, the "uproused British lion," tells his sisters they "hiss and shriek and cackle... don't begin to cry. I only said you were a couple of geese." Thackeray compares Amelia to a violet, speaks of her nursing the corpse of Love, after George seems to have abandoned her In caring for her father, she appears to Dobbin to walk "into the room as silently as a sunbeam."

Pitt Crawley is "pompous as an undertaker." Lady Crawley is a "mere machine in her husband's house." Amelia is a "poor little white-robed angel," who fortunately can't hear George and his fellows roaring over their whiskey-punch.

When the ladies cry, the author says, "The waterworks again began to play." Miss Swartz, in fancy garments, is dressed "about as elegantly... as a she chimney-sweep on May Day." Dobbin, on contemplating Becky's flirtation, has "a countenance as glum as an undertaker's." When Amelia comes out, just before George's departure for battle, holding his sash against her bosom, Thackeray says "the heavy net of crimson dropped like a large stain of blood," a possible symbol of George's fate.

The note George gives Becky asking her to run away with him, lies "coiled like a snake among the flowers." When Becky exploits her fellow men, she is like the mermaid feeding below the surface of the water on the pickled victims. The "sheep-dog," or female companion necessary to the vivacious social climber in Vanity Fair, reminds Thackeray of "the death's head which figured in the repasts of Egyptian bon-vivants..."

Mrs. Bowls, formerly Firkin, maid to Miss Crawley, extends her hand to Becky and "her fingers were like so many sausages, cold and lifeless." Mrs. Frederick Bullock's kiss is "like the contact of an oyster."

One of the most humorous comparisons is that of cleaning a woman's reputation by presenting her at Court as one would clean dirty linen by putting it through the laundry. A countess of sixty is compared with faded street lights. She has "chinks and crannies" in her face. The calling cards from the ladies of Lord Steyne's family are "the trumps of Becky's hand." But Steyne says, "You poor little earthenware pipkin, you want to swim down the stream along with the great copper kettles."

When Georgy's nose is hurt, one does not see blood, but "the claret drawn from his own little nose." Becky calls herself a mouse, perhaps able to help the lion, the second Sir Pitt. To indicate that the servants are gossiping about Becky, Thackeray personifies Discovery and Calumny as the waiters who serve the food and drink.

When Dobbin comes home, the English landscape "seems to shake hands" with him. Dobbin's desire is a "bread-and-butter paradise." Becky is a hardened Ishmaelite who halts at Jos' tents and rests.

Satire

Samuel Chew notes that Thackeray spent much of his time "parodying and satirizing romantic sentiment" and that he "possessed a terrible power to detect and expose men's self-deceptions, shams, pretenses and unworthy aspirations." Also,

Thrall and Hibbard in the section on satire in their Handbook refer to Thackeray as one of the "later satirists," along with Byron, following in the great tradition of the "golden age of satire" characterized by the writings of Dryden, Swift, Addison, Steele, Pope, and Fielding. Thackeray as satirist, then, should not be overlooked even in a cursory review of Vanity Fair. Considered standard among a good many students and teachers of literature is the Thrall and Hibbard definition of satire—"A literary manner which blends a critical attitude with humour and wit to the end that human institutions may be improved." Accepting this definition the student of Thackeray would do well to examine some of the ways Thackeray employs satire—mainly by the use of names, irony, and humorous situations.

The Use of Names

Some of the names have symbolic significance and some apparently are used for humour or irony's sake. For certain occupations the author chooses "killing" names: Lance, the surgeon; Mrs. Briefless, the barrister's wife; Sir Thomas Coffin, the celebrated hanging judge; Dr. Ramshorn, the preacher; Mr. Bawler, minister of the Darbyites. The Miss Scratchleys fight; Mary Box is always thumping her small brother; Mr. Hammerdown is the auctioneer; Quill is a cashier; Dipley is a candlemaker; Miss Grains is the brewer's daughter; Pestler is an apothecary; Mr. Quadroon writes on the slave question.

To portray characteristics there are names such as Mr. Smirk, Miss Toady, the Reverend Mr. Crisp, and the Reverend Mr. Flowerdew. Mrs. Flamingo dresses in a crimson silk gown. Lord Methuselah is an old man, and Mrs. Highflyer is a social climber. Lady Slingstone is a notorious gossip. Madame de St. Amour would be affectionate, while Madame de Belladonna might be quite deadly. Becky outwits the brilliant Lady Stunnington and the witty Mr. Wagg.

The situation, at the time the name is mentioned, frequently augments the satire. Becky is riding with Sir Pitt to Queen's Crawley. Rain is pouring. The towns along the way are Leakington, Mudbury and Squashmore. Lord Steyne stain is the symbolic meaning lives in Gaunt House. Wealthy, honored, and bored, he fills his life with sensuous pleasure, but actually his existence is empty, as Gaunt indicates. Becky Sharp is not named Sharp by accident. Neither are the Crawleys, who use every means to crawl up the social and monetary ladder.

Some names are apparently just for fun: Lord Heehaw, Mrs. Hook Eagles, Swanky, Trotter, Lady Vere Vane, Mrs. Rougemont, Miss Hawky. Bowls is the butler; Heavytop, is the colonel; Knuckles is the private; Cackle is the assistant surgeon; Ensigns Spooney and Stubble are young officers; Mr. Chopper bandies the Osbornes' money; Deuceace is a gambler

Irony

Thackeray's irony takes a wide range—sometimes biting, sometimes playful, but always pertinent. A sample of comment on money follows: "I for my part, have known a five-pound note to interpose and knock up a half-century's attachment between two brethren; and can't but admire, as I think what a fine and durable thing Love is among worldly people." "What a charming reconciler and peacemaker money is!" "The good quality of this old lady has been mentioned... She had a balance at her banker's which would have made her beloved anywhere."

When Becky and Rawdon look for George in order for Rawdon to gamble with him, the author remarks, "I hope the reader has much too good an opinion of Captain and Mrs. Crawley to suppose that they ever would have dreamed of paying a visit to so remote a district as Bloomsbury, if they thought the family whom they proposed to honour with a visit were not merely out of fashion, but out of money, and could be serviceable to them in no possible manner."

Women come in for a good share of Thackeray's sarcasm. He has his tongue-in-cheek as he describes Becky's need of a mother. "All she wanted was the proposal, and ah! how Rebecca now felt the want of a mother!—a dear, tender mother, who would have managed the business in ten minutes..."—"All old women were beauties once, we very well know." Miss

Pinkerton writes Mrs. Bute that Miss Tuffin is sweet, young, eighteen, and therefore, probably not suitable. She illustrates Thackeray's idea that "natural jealousy... is one of the main principles of every honest woman." Mrs. Bute is reluctant to forgive the begging Miss Horrocks. "But those who know a really good woman are aware that she is not in a hurry to forgive, and that the humiliation of an enemy is a triumph to her soul." Mrs. Bute, in her treatment of Miss Crawley "... ground down the old lady in her convalescence in such a way as only belongs to your proper-managing, motherly, moral woman."

Becky's friendship with Lady Jane is such that "... these two ladies did not see much of each other except upon those occasions when the younger brother's wife, having an object to gain from the other, frequented her. They my-loved and my-deared each other assiduously, but kept apart generally..."

In ironical comments on society and life in general, Thackeray lets the reader know that even those in modest circumstances love their children. Dobbin writes his mother "... who was fond of him, although she was a grocer's wife and lived in a back parlour in Thames St."

Captain Dobbin makes conversation "... like a consummate man of the world... some topic of general interest such as the opera... or the weather—that blessing to society."

Gossips have not changed since Vanity Fair—"The tartwoman hints to somebody, who took an affidavit of the fact to somebody else, that there was a great deal more than was made public regarding Mr. Crisp and Miss Sharp..."

Of deaths and funerals, Thackery comments, "Could the best and kindest of us who depart from the earth, have an opportunity of revisiting it, I suppose he or she... would have a pang of mortification at finding how soon our survivors were consoled..."

Of weddings, he says, "After three or four ceremonies, you get accustomed to it, no doubt; but the first dip, everybody allows, is awful." And of the fighting in Belgium, he says, "For a long period of history they have let other people fight there."

Thackeray's characterizations are often ironic. The rich

Miss Crawley says of herself, Rebecca, and Rawdon: "'We're the only three Christians in the county my love,' in which case it must be confessed that religion was at a very low ebb in the county of Hants." George broke up Becky's marriage to Joseph and "she loved George Osborne accordingly." Miss Crawley "showed her friendship by abusing all her intimate acquaintances to her new confidante than which there can't be a more touching proof of regard."

Joseph's eating is "the delightful exercise of gobbling." As an invalid, he takes two-thirds of the bottle of champagne. Mr. Sedley says that if Joseph should receive word of the death of the rest of the family, he would say "Good Gad!" and go on with his dinner.

Mr. Osborne's disposition has suffered because "... he has not been allowed to have his own way. To be thwarted in this reasonable desire was always very injurious to the old gentleman... " Maria Osborne Bullock "... felt it her duty to see her father and sister as little as possible."

Mr. Osborne called kicking a footman downstairs a "hint" to leave. Lord Steyne says his wife is as gay as Lady Macbeth and calls his home a "temple of virtue." Lady Fits-Willis is of the "best people." Her patronage helps Becky. The lady "asked her to her own mansion, and spoke to her twice in the most public and condescending manner... The important fact was known all over London that night..." At Vauxhall "our young people made the most solemn promises to keep together... and separated in ten minutes afterwards."

Humorous Situations

Joseph, embarrassed when he first meets Rebecca, turns red, can't talk, and yanks the bell rope loose. Sir Pitt is a stingy, dirty, disreputable boor who can't spell, doesn't read, eats boiled mutton, and has but one candle in the house; but it stands in an ornate silver candlestick, and three footmen serve the boiled mutton. Old Sir Pitt proposes marriage to Becky:

"I'm an old man, but a good'n. I'm good for twenty years. I'll make you happy, see if I don't. You shall do what you like; spend what you like; and 'av it all your own way. I'll make you a settlement. I'll do everything reglar. Look year!" and the old man fell down on his knees and leered at her like a satyr. Rebecca started back a picture of consternation. In the course of this history we have never seen her lose her presence of mind; but she did now, and wept some of the most genuine tears that ever fell from her eyes.

"Oh, Sir Pitt!" she said. "Oh, sir—I—I'm married already."

When the party gets ready to leave Brighton, Amelia rises to pack, while her husband lies in bed "deploring that she had not a maid to help her." When Becky wants to impress someone with her domesticity and her love for her child, she pulls out a little shirt that she is sewing for little Rawdon, but he outgrows it long before it is finished.

Jos calls on Becky in her room at the "Elephant." She has to do some quick house cleaning: In that instant she put a rouge-pot, a brandy-bottle, and a plate of broken meat into the bed... she placed herself on the bed—not on the bottle and plate, you may be sure... she put her hand to her heart with a passionate gesture of despair, burying her face for a moment on the bed.

The brandy-bottle inside clinked up against the plate which held the cold sausage. Both were moved, no doubt, by the exhibition of so much grief... that spotless being—that miserable unsullied martyr—was present on the bed before Jos—on the bed, sitting on the brandy-bottle.

Money and Matrimony in Vanity Fair

In his novel Vanity Fair, William Thackeray exposes and examines the vanities of 19th century England. His characters pursue wealth, power, and social standing, often through marriage or matrimony. The present essay looks at Thackeray's use of the institution of marriage in Vanity Fair to comment on how these vanities often come at the expense of the true emotions of passion, devotion, and love. Parental Ambitions

In Vanity Fair, money is central to nearly all of the characters' relationships. Thackeray connects England's merchant families, the lesser nobility, and the high aristocracy through money and matrimony, and parents are frequently the chief negotiators in these business transactions. Mr. Osborne is perhaps the novel's most avaricious parent; money and social eminence are all-important to Mr. Osborne, and he is willing to sacrifice his children's happiness to connect his family name with these vanities.

He forbids his daughter Jane to marry an artist with whom she has fallen in love with, swearing to her "that she should not have a shilling of his money if she made a match without his concurrence". For Mr. Osborne love has little to do with matrimony, and marriage is simply a transaction that should increase family wealth and prestige. This concept was by no means uncommon during the 19th century: the rise of industrialism and colonialism meant an influx of wealth into England, and marriage was seen by many as a way of either rising in station or cementing business ties. This latter theme is seen in Mr. Osborne's interference in his son George's relationship with Amelia.

Their courtship is arranged, the "two young people been bred up by their parents" for love and marriage. George and Amelia's relationship is encouraged because of the business connection between Mr. Sedley and Mr. Osborne, and their feelings are not really an issue to be considered. As Mr. Sedley's fortunes fall, Mr. Osborne questions George if the match is not now beneath the Osborne family's station: "Why shouldn't you marry higher than a stockbroker's daughter, George, that's what I want to know?". George replies that it is a "family business," and that "you and Mrs. Sedley made the match a hundred years ago".

The terminology of business is frequent in discussions of marriage in Vanity Fair, and money, not love, is the motive for matrimony. Mr. Osborne states these feelings very clearly to his son: "Unless I see Amelia's ten thousand down you don't marry her". Mr. Sedley's misfortunes are a convenient way for Mr. Osborne to force the cancellation of the engagement, for he sees an opportunity to marry his wealth which was only acquired through Mr. Sedley's facilitation through George to Miss Swartz, a young heiress with connections to the aristocracy. It is important to notice that these aspirations are

Mr. Osborne's and not George's, for George ignores his father's order to marry Miss Swartz, believing that he is in love with Amelia. Thackeray's characterization of Mr. Osborne shows us how love can be subverted by parental aspirations for the many vanities that exist. The Economics of Matrimony

Parental scheming for wealth and power is of course only one side of the issue of marriage for money. Thackeray's characters are often only too willing to forsake true love for money and social eminence. The arrangement between Mr. Osborne's daughter Maria and Fredrick Bullock centers on this theme, with the author noting that in such a marriage whom you marry is quite irrelevant. Maria would just as equally marry Frederick's father: "...She would have taken Bullock Senior, just the same, her mind being fixed as that of a well-bred young woman should be, — upon a house in Park Lane, a country house at Wimbledon, a handsome chariot, and two prodigious tall horses and footmen, and a fourth of the annual profits of the eminent firm of Hulker and Bullock...". Again, love is unimportant, and money is the issue upon which such engagements revolve. Frederick, too, is more concerned with the "economics" of matrimony:

George being dead and cut out of his father's will, Frederick insisted that the half of the old gentleman's property should be settled on his Maria, and indeed, for a long time, refused "to come to the scratch" it was Mr. Frederick's own expression on any other terms. Osborne said Fred had agreed to take his daughter with twenty thousand, and he should bind himself to no more.... thought himself infamously swindled by the old merchant, and for some time made as if he would break off the match altogether.

Fred consents to marry Maria only after his business partners have persuaded him of "the chances of the further division of property" at the death of Mr. Osborne. Theirs is certainly not a match based on love, but it is perhaps a perfect match, for both Maria and Frederick are willing to sell the ideal of true or romantic love for money. Love has no place in the business of marriage, but as we shall see, Thackeray is very clear in pointing out that happiness is frequently sacrificed in the transaction. The Pursuit of the Vanities The relationship of Sir Pitt Crawley and Lady Crawley is another based on the pursuit of the vanities. There is certainly little happiness in their marriage: Sir Pitt is generally rude to Rose, he often leaves her completely alone, and he frequently hits her. Thackeray contrasts their relationship with what might have been had Rose given her hand in youth to a truer, purer love:

O Vanity Fair — Vanity Fair! This might have been, but for you, a cheery lass; Peter Butt and Rose a happy man and wife, in a snug farm, with a hearty family, and an honest portion of pleasures, cares, hopes, and struggles: — but a title and a coach and four are more precious than happiness in Vanity Fair.....

Here Thackeray hints that the lower classes, far less concerned with social standing, perhaps are happier than those with wealth and power. The people of the Fair are willing to sell their happiness for social prestige. The author returns to this idea upon the death of Lady Crawley: "Her heart was dead long before her body. She had sold it to become Sir Pitt Crawley's wife. Mothers and daughters are making the same bargain every day in Vanity Fair". While this commentary seems to be provided in a matter-of-fact tone, there can be little doubt that it is a stark condemnation of the "business" of marriage. Becky Sharp: Advancement Through Matrimony

Perhaps the most interesting character in Vanity Fair engaged in the transactions of matrimony is Rebecca Sharp. Thackeray's anti-heroine is continuously scheming to advance her position in life through marriage. She laments at the outset of the novel that she has no mother to arrange an engagement for her, "a dear, tender mother who would have managed the business in ten minutes, and, in the course of a little delicate confidential conversation, would have extracted the interesting avowal...". Rebecca's own considerable wits and schemes, however, are more than enough to captivate several men. Her first attempt at advancing in society through marriage centers on Joseph Sedley. Even before she has met him, Rebecca decides that she will attempt to wed him: "If Mr. Joseph Sedley is rich and unmarried, why should I not marry him? I have only a fortnight, to be sure, but there is no harm in trying". Becky doesn't even hesitate to consider that there might be something more to marriage than money, and her artifices in attempting to win Jos. are worthy of the most skilled business negotiator. She cares little for him, quietly laughing at his pompousness and inflated airs behind his back. For Becky marriage is simply a way to rise to a new station in life, and when Jos. suddenly takes leave after his embarrassing drunkenness at Vauxhall, she is forced to begin her artful negotiations anew.

By involving herself in the intricacies of Sir Pitt Crawley's affairs, Rebecca manages to become indispensable to him. Upon the day of the death of his wife, Sir Pitt proposes to Becky. She is somewhat devastated by this, of course, because she is already married to his son, Rawdon Crawley. Like Maria Osborne, we see that Rebecca would have married the father just as quickly as the son; she is only interested in the wealth and access to society that either man can offer. She marries Rawdon only because she believes that he will inherit his aunt's money upon her death.

Rawdon, on the other hand, loves his wife: "the admiration, the delight, the passion, the wonder, the unbound confidence, and frantic adoration with which...he got to regard the little Rebecca, were feelings which...were not altogether discreditable to him". Rawdon's emotions would seem to be of the type found in the happiest of marriages, but they are unfortunately not returned. The difference between the two in their emotions for each other is seen as Rawdon is off to battle. He takes inventory of what Becky will be left with should he die, showing love and concern for his wife. Rebecca, too, takes a similar inventory, but she displays little emotion for the possibility that her husband may be killed:

Every calculation made of these valuables Mrs. Rebecca found, not without a pungent feeling of triumph and self-satisfaction, that should circumstances occur, she might reckon on six or seven hundred pounds at the very least, to begin the world with; and she passed the morning disposing, ordering, looking out, and locking up her properties in the most agreeable manner. Becky shows little emotion for her husband except contempt, and her implied affair with Lord Steyne exposes her lack of devotion.

When Rawdon leaves her, she sheds no tears but instead contemplates the lack of return on her investment in the relationship: "He was gone for ever.... She thought of her long past life, and all the dismal incidents of it. Ah, how dreary it seemed, how miserable, lonely, and profitless!...All her lies and her schemes, all her selfishness and her wiles, all her wit and genius had come to this bankruptcy". Thackeray hints at the unhappiness inherent in relationships based on the pursuit of vanities, but Becky ignores the lesson and continues to scheme until the novel's end, "writhing and pushing onward towards what they call 'a position in society'". The novelist comments on how Becky could have been happy:

It may perhaps have struck her that to have been honest and humble, to have done her duty, and to have marched straightforward on her way, would have brought her as near happiness as that path by which she was striving to attain it. But...if ever Becky had these thoughts, she was accustomed to walk round them, and not look in. She eluded them, and despised them — or at least she was committed to the other path from which retreat was now impossible.

Thackeray points out that Becky could have led a simple, happy life, but for her relentless desire to achieve wealth and social status. She never comes to this realization, however, and through Rebecca the author shows us how our desires for the vanities can blind us to more truer, simpler emotions.

Conclusion

The marriages and mésalliances of the characters in Vanity Fair show us the folly and futility of chasing wealth, power, and social eminence at the expense of love and passion. Thackeray's novel reminds us that there are frequently hidden costs when we make such a bargain, and the true expense is often more than we can afford

In his novel Vanity Fair, William Thackeray exposes and examines the vanities of 19th century England. His characters pursue wealth, power, and social standing, often through marriage or matrimony. The present essay looks at Thackeray's use of the institution of marriage in Vanity Fair to comment on how these vanities often come at the expense of the true emotions of passion, devotion, and love. Parental Ambitions

In Vanity Fair, money is central to nearly all of the characters' relationships. Thackeray connects England's merchant families, the lesser nobility, and the high aristocracy through money and matrimony, and parents are frequently the chief negotiators in these business transactions. Mr. Osborne is perhaps the novel's most avaricious parent; money and social eminence are all-important to Mr. Osborne, and he is willing to sacrifice his children's happiness to connect his family name with these vanities.

He forbids his daughter Jane to marry an artist with whom she has fallen in love with, swearing to her "that she should not have a shilling of his money if she made a match without his concurrence". For Mr. Osborne love has little to do with matrimony, and marriage is simply a transaction that should increase family wealth and prestige. This concept was by no means uncommon during the 19th century: the rise of industrialism and colonialism meant an influx of wealth into England, and marriage was seen by many as a way of either rising in station or cementing business ties. This latter theme is seen in Mr. Osborne's interference in his son George's relationship with Amelia.

Their courtship is arranged, the "two young people been bred up by their parents" for love and marriage. George and Amelia's relationship is encouraged because of the business connection between Mr. Sedley and Mr. Osborne, and their feelings are not really an issue to be considered. As Mr. Sedley's fortunes fall, Mr. Osborne questions George if the match is not now beneath the Osborne family's station: "Why shouldn't you marry higher than a stockbroker's daughter, George, that's what I want to know?". George replies that it is a "family business," and that "you and Mrs. Sedley made the match a hundred years ago". The terminology of business is frequent in discussions of marriage in Vanity Fair, and money, not love, is the motive for matrimony. Mr. Osborne states these feelings very clearly to his son: "Unless I see Amelia's ten thousand down you don't marry her". Mr. Sedley's misfortunes are a convenient way for Mr. Osborne to force the cancellation of the engagement, for he sees an opportunity to marry his wealth which was only acquired through Mr. Sedley's facilitation through George to Miss Swartz, a young heiress with connections to the aristocracy. It is important to notice that these aspirations are Mr. Osborne's and not George's, for George ignores his father's order to marry Miss Swartz, believing that he is in love with Amelia. Thackeray's characterization of Mr. Osborne shows us how love can be subverted by parental aspirations for the many vanities that exist. The Economics of Matrimony

Parental scheming for wealth and power is of course only one side of the issue of marriage for money. Thackeray's characters are often only too willing to forsake true love for money and social eminence. The arrangement between Mr. Osborne's daughter Maria and Fredrick Bullock centers on this theme, with the author noting that in such a marriage whom you marry is quite irrelevant. Maria would just as equally marry Frederick's father: "...She would have taken Bullock Senior, just the same, her mind being fixed as that of a well-bred young woman should be, — upon a house in Park Lane, a country house at Wimbledon, a handsome chariot, and two prodigious tall horses and footmen, and a fourth of the annual profits of the eminent firm of Hulker and Bullock...". Again, love is unimportant, and money is the issue upon which such engagements revolve. Frederick, too, is more concerned with the "economics" of matrimony:

George being dead and cut out of his father's will, Frederick insisted that the half of the old gentleman's property should be settled on his Maria, and indeed, for a long time, refused "to come to the scratch" it was Mr. Frederick's own expression on any other terms. Osborne said Fred had agreed to take his daughter with twenty thousand, and he should bind himself to no more.... thought himself infamously swindled by the old merchant, and for some time made as if he would break off the match altogether. Fred consents to marry Maria only after his business partners have persuaded him of "the chances of the further division of property" at the death of Mr. Osborne. Theirs is certainly not a match based on love, but it is perhaps a perfect match, for both Maria and Frederick are willing to sell the ideal of true or romantic love for money. Love has no place in the business of marriage, but as we shall see, Thackeray is very clear in pointing out that happiness is frequently sacrificed in the transaction. The Pursuit of the Vanities The relationship of Sir Pitt Crawley and Lady Crawley is another based on the pursuit of the vanities. There is certainly little happiness in their marriage: Sir Pitt is generally rude to Rose, he often leaves her completely alone, and he frequently hits her. Thackeray contrasts their relationship with what might have been had Rose given her hand in youth to a truer, purer love:

O Vanity Fair—Vanity Fair! This might have been, but for you, a cheery lass; Peter Butt and Rose a happy man and wife, in a snug farm, with a hearty family, and an honest portion of pleasures, cares, hopes, and struggles: — but a title and a coach and four are more precious than happiness in Vanity Fair.....

Here Thackeray hints that the lower classes, far less concerned with social standing, perhaps are happier than those with wealth and power. The people of the Fair are willing to sell their happiness for social prestige. The author returns to this idea upon the death of Lady Crawley: "Her heart was dead long before her body. She had sold it to become Sir Pitt Crawley's wife. Mothers and daughters are making the same bargain every day in Vanity Fair". While this commentary seems to be provided in a matter-of-fact tone, there can be little doubt that it is a stark condemnation of the "business" of marriage. Becky Sharp: Advancement Through Matrimony

Perhaps the most interesting character in Vanity Fair engaged in the transactions of matrimony is Rebecca Sharp. Thackeray's anti-heroine is continuously scheming to advance her position in life through marriage. She laments at the outset of the novel that she has no mother to arrange an engagement for her, "a dear, tender mother who would have managed the business in ten minutes, and, in the course of a little delicate confidential conversation, would have extracted the interesting avowal...". Rebecca's own considerable wits and schemes, however, are more than enough to captivate several men. Her first attempt at advancing in society through marriage centers on Joseph Sedley.

Even before she has met him, Rebecca decides that she will attempt to wed him: "If Mr. Joseph Sedley is rich and unmarried, why should I not marry him? I have only a fortnight, to be sure, but there is no harm in trying". Becky doesn't even hesitate to consider that there might be something more to marriage than money, and her artifices in attempting to win Jos. are worthy of the most skilled business negotiator. She cares little for him, quietly laughing at his pompousness and inflated airs behind his back. For Becky marriage is simply a way to rise to a new station in life, and when Jos. suddenly takes leave after his embarrassing drunkenness at Vauxhall, she is forced to begin her artful negotiations anew.

By involving herself in the intricacies of Sir Pitt Crawley's affairs, Rebecca manages to become indispensable to him. Upon the day of the death of his wife, Sir Pitt proposes to Becky. She is somewhat devastated by this, of course, because she is already married to his son, Rawdon Crawley. Like Maria Osborne, we see that Rebecca would have married the father just as quickly as the son; she is only interested in the wealth and access to society that either man can offer. She marries Rawdon only because she believes that he will inherit his aunt's money upon her death.

Rawdon, on the other hand, loves his wife: "the admiration, the delight, the passion, the wonder, the unbound confidence, and frantic adoration with which...he got to regard the little Rebecca, were feelings which...were not altogether discreditable to him". Rawdon's emotions would seem to be of the type found in the happiest of marriages, but they are unfortunately not returned. The difference between the two in their emotions for each other is seen as Rawdon is off to battle. He takes inventory of what Becky will be left with should he die, showing love and concern for his wife. Rebecca, too, takes a similar inventory, but she displays little emotion for the possibility that her husband may be killed: Every calculation made of these valuables Mrs. Rebecca found, not without a pungent feeling of triumph and self-satisfaction, that should circumstances occur, she might reckon on six or seven hundred pounds at the very least, to begin the world with; and she passed the morning disposing, ordering, looking out, and locking up her properties in the most agreeable manner.

Becky shows little emotion for her husband except contempt, and her implied affair with Lord Steyne exposes her lack of devotion. When Rawdon leaves her, she sheds no tears but instead contemplates the lack of return on her investment in the relationship: "He was gone for ever.... She thought of her long past life, and all the dismal incidents of it. Ah, how dreary it seemed, how miserable, lonely, and profitless!...All her lies and her schemes, all her selfishness and her wiles, all her wit and genius had come to this bankruptcy". Thackeray hints at the unhappiness inherent in relationships based on the pursuit of vanities, but Becky ignores the lesson and continues to scheme until the novel's end, "writhing and pushing onward towards what they call 'a position in society'". The novelist comments on how Becky could have been happy:

It may perhaps have struck her that to have been honest and humble, to have done her duty, and to have marched straightforward on her way, would have brought her as near happiness as that path by which she was striving to attain it. But...if ever Becky had these thoughts, she was accustomed to walk round them, and not look in. She eluded them, and despised them — or at least she was committed to the other path from which retreat was now impossible.

Thackeray points out that Becky could have led a simple, happy life, but for her relentless desire to achieve wealth and social status. She never comes to this realization, however, and through Rebecca the author shows us how our desires for the vanities can blind us to more truer, simpler emotions.

Conclusion

The marriages and mésalliances of the characters in Vanity Fair show us the folly and futility of chasing wealth, power, and social eminence at the expense of love and passion.

Thackeray's novel reminds us that there are frequently hidden costs when we make such a bargain, and the trûe expense is often more than we can afford

A Man of Experience

It is perhaps easy to make too much of the tone with which stray remarks are written in casual correspondence, but it is interesting to note an apparent shift in Thackeray's self-portrayal in his letters to Chapman and Hall and Bradbury and Evans in the months following the appearance of The Irish Sketch-Book, on 15 May 1843, from Brighton, he wrote the former, "I came down here to be alone, & avoid good dinners and do some magazine work".

The letter is otherwise about reviews of, and advertisements for, the Irish book, In August, just before setting out on a tour of the Low Countries, he wrote Chapman and Hall again, lamenting briefly that an article he wrote for the Foreign Quarterly Review did not appear, asking for any money due to him, and devoting the bulk of his letter to proposing a German sketchbook:

I wish I could persuade you to think that Titmarsh in Germany devoting himself to the consideration of the fine arts there, and with a score or two of ballads to decorate the volumes, and plenty, of etchings and a great deal of fantastical humour and much nurture of the poetical and the ludicrous-I say I wish you would think such a book popular, and offer me the same terms for it as the Irish book. People as I hope and trust have only to become better acquainted with Titmarsh to like him more and the success of a German Sketch Book would help off very likely the few remaining copies of the Irish one. I am also in "the interesting situation" with respect to a novel: but I want to produce a very good one and a good work of art, and such a w demands a deal of time and thinking. original in possession of Peter Rhodes, Esq.; transcript supplied by Nicholas Pickwoad.

To Bradbury and Evans he wrote in February 1844: I do not know whether you pay anything extra for great services as all wise persons do but I should not be surprised at hearing that any sum of money had been paid to my bankers as a reward for the astonishing late enclosed. If you publish it again in a little book there will be a deal of extra profit for all of us. In short, Thackeray now fancied himself primarily an author of books who also wrote for the magazines, and he now often thought of the potential book version of his magazine contributions.

Though nothing ever came of the German sketchbook, it is interesting to note Thackeray's warning to the publisher that "such a work demands a deal of time and thinking"-this from the man who on 10 September 1841 signed a contract to deliver by the end of December a two-volume work which he had not even started. The professional author had learned some things from the fact that serious work on the Irish book took four months of touring and writing in Ireland and four more months of writing, illustrating, and proofreading.

His expenses from July 1842 to March 1843 estimated by himself for an account to his mother and therefore, like Pendennis's accounts of college expenses, probably conservative were £370, including £110 spent in Ireland. His income, not counting the £120 advance that had long since been spent, came to £110 for magazine work and under £200 for the book, which seems to have sold fairly well. Although for the purpose of the account to his mother Thackeray counted the £120 advance and figured his income on the book to be near £300, he did have to admit that the "childrens' nest egg is broken in upon as you say" Letters 2: 100. The pressure was clearly still on; and while a visible property was accumulating, Thackeray's fortune was still largely in the inkwell.

Another indication that Thackeray's sense of his profession and of his own position in it had come to a turning point after The Irish Sketch-Book and after agreeing with Fraser's for twelve installments of Barry Lyndon comes in a December 1843 letter of advice to his cousin Richard Bedingfield, who recently had published a book called The Miser's Son. It was advice which Thackeray clearly drew from his own experience and which was given as from one "old in the trade now."

I sent on Tuesday week last a very pressing note to Jerdan regarding the "Miser's Son," with a little notice which I myself had written so as to save him trouble. It was, I need not tell you a favourable one as the story deserved; it has a great deal of talent of a great number of kinds, and many a man has made a fortune with a tithe of the merit.

But in spite of this, Jerdan has not inserted my article. Have you ever advertised in his paper or elsewhere? A laudatory paragraph here and there will do you no earthly good, unless the name of your book is perpetually before the public. The best book I ever wrote I published with an unknown publisher, and we got off two hundred and fifty copies of it, and this was after the success of the Paris book, with some thirty pounds of advertisements, and hugely laudatory notices in a score of journals. Shakespeare himself would not get a hearing in Gray's Inn Lane.

Unless your publisher actually offers you money for a future work, I beg you to have nothing to do with him. Write short tales. Make a dash at all the magazines; and at one or two of them I can promise you, as I have said, not an acceptance of your articles, but a favourable hearing. It is, however, a bad trade at the best. The prizes in it are fewer and worse than in any other professional lottery; but I know it's useless damping a man who will be an author whether or no-men are doomed, as it were, to the calling.

Make up your mind to this, my dear fellow, that the "Miser's Son" will never succeed-not from want of merit, but from want of a publisher. Shut it up without delay, and turn to some work that will pay you. Eschew poetry above all you've had too much of it, and read all the history you can. Don't mind this patriarchal tone from me. I'm old in the trade now, and have lived so much with all sorts of people in the world that I plume myself on my experience.

Bedingfield followed Thackeray's advice, but a new work eighteen months later fared no better than the first with Thackeray, who wrote, "I can suit the magazines but I can't hit the public, be hanged to them, and, from my knowledge of the former, I should say you will never get a good sale for commodities like these... your system may be the right one and mine wrong, but I'm sure I'm right as to the state of the market" Letters 2: 193.

In mid-1843 Thackeray's literary accounts stood thus: two substantial travel books the Paris and Irish sketchbooks-the second an actual success; one collection of novellas and short stories Comic Tales-not a success; three ephemeral pamphlets Fiore et Zéphyr, An Essay on the Genius of George Cruikshank, and The Second Funeral of Napoleon-all of greater critical than financial note. Catherine and The History of Samuel Titmarsh had been written with book publication in mind, but the former never got beyond magazine publication, and the latter was not published at all until after Vanity Fair. The odious magazine work was still the mainstay of his professional income.

Within three years he would be the author of Vanity Fair; but for the present art criticism, travel, and observations on manners, dished out periodically, seemed his forte. The latter two veins of his genius would be extended in From Cornhill to Grand Cairo and "The Snobs of England". But at the same time Thackeray was gearing up for greater things. Catherine and Barry Lyndon develop the satiric fiction; A Shabby Genteel Story, Samuel Titmarsh, and A Legend of the Rhine develop the sentimental pathetic line. All these elements would find their way into Vanity Fair.

Though Thackeray had not produced a best-seller, he was steadily gaining attention. The Irish Sketch-Book was reprinted in America, the pirate being J. Winchester of New York. It became, in 1844, Thackeray's second American book, but like the first, it added nothing to Thackeray's coffers. The most substantial property to come front Thackeray's pen in the remaining months of 1843 was the serial form of Men's Wives by George Fitzboodle in Fraser's. And in January 1844 the first installment of Barry Lyndon under the same pseudonym appeared in the same magazine. Though Men's Wives seems to have grown in response to favorable reactions to Fitzboodle's Confessions of late 1842, Barry Lyndon was a deliberate attempt to write a novel for eventual book publication. Despite the success of The Irish Sketch-Book, however, Wives and Lyndon both finally became books with no help from, and no immediate benefit to, Thackeray when in 1852 they became parts of a series of small books pirated by Appleton and Company of New York to take advantage of the publicity surrounding the author's first lecture tour of America. In the short term, however, Barry Lyndon gave Thackeray a steadiness of income he was not used to: "it is a comfort to think that there is a decent income arranged for 1844 lease God my health hold good and actually a prospect of saving money at the year's end.... I have begun a story wh. is to last through the year in Fraser, and am to have my own way with the worthy Mr. Punch, whose pay is more than double of that I get anywhere else"

It was with the confidence instilled by this financial prospect, as well as the assurance in his "experience," of which he had written Bedingfield, that one month later he declined to sign a contract for £108 per year with an American periodical publisher a man named Henry Wikoff whose periodical has yet to be identified because it required that Thackeray stay in Paris to write two articles a month on Paris and France. Unwilling to "sacrifice my liberty," Thackeray offered instead that "as I take your word for the payment of the articles you must please to take mine for supplying them."

He outlined a plan for the American to pay a monthly salary and for himself to submit the two monthly articles, concluding: "I am a bad man of business, and only settle with you as I would with any other publisher. If I don't hear from you I shall conclude the negociation at an end". Thackeray's account book for 1844 shows receipts of £4 and £3.10 for "India& American letters" in January and February and 4s. 10d. for an American letter in February; none of these has been identified. We hear no more of the American publisher but need not conclude Thackeray was right to characterize himself as a bad businessman. True, he did not close a deal with Wikoff, but neither did he commit himself to a course he could not or would not follow. Though Thackeray was still in a sense "writing for his life" and still occasionally had to remind friends that he was a "poor day-laborer in the vineyard and must work often when I would like to be taking my diversion", he was not clutching desperately at every chance of work as he had been only a year earlier.

Thackeray's conception of himself as a bad businessman stemmed in large part from his sense of his own lack of steady, disciplined, organized work habits. Capable of enormous work binges, he thought himself lazy for procrastinating. And he could not shake the effects of the unfortunate experiences with the National Standard and the Constitutional. His "failure" to close with Wikoff may have contributed to that sense, as perhaps did also his failure four days later to get the publisher Giraldon to pay for his translation of Eugene Sue's Mystères de Paris, a work he threw over because he was not paid. But the same evidence shows a businessman who knew, perhaps from bitter experience, when to cut his losses and who had a clear sense of himself, his profession, and what he was and was not willing to do.

The letters to Wikoff and Giraldon were not written in financial complacency; in spite of the steady work on Barry Lyndon and the Punch contributions, Thackeray wrote the same month offering Fraser a burlesque originally titled "The Childe of Godesberg"; he proposed substantial reviews for Chapman and Hall's Foreign Quarterly Review only one of which was accepted and asked if they would "send me to any other country to travel"; and he wrote Bradbury and Evans proposing a collection of his shorter pieces. He was prompted to write to Bradbury and Evans under the mistaken notion that Comic Tales had been sold out, though in fact the 1848 reissue of Comic Tales was an attempt to sell off remaining copies of the 1840 impression with a new title page. At the same time he offered to edit a new gentleman's journal with "a decided air of white kid gloves...

I know of no man in Europe who would handle <it better>" The tone of these proposals has changed: the appeals with side references to family obligations and friendship that suggested an undercurrent of desperate need are gone. The letters now have an air of "take it if you will; don't if you won't," suggesting perfect willingness on the author's part to face reality with equanimity. He was grateful, it is true, that Bradbury and Evans approved of his latest Punch contribution, "The History of the Next French Revolution," and he thanked the firm for its remittance, but at the same time his friendly and familiar relations with the publisher are revealed in his mock serious tone when, on reading the first installment in print, he complained: "Having confided to you a few chapters of my forthcoming work on the next French revolution-you are bound in justice to print my words fairly-and I protest in the most solemn manner against several liberties which have been taken with my text. What is a historian without accuracy? A mere romancer and I hold such a creature in the utmost contempt" He pointed out three specific errors, which because "The Next French Revolution" was never reprinted in Thackeray's lifetime have never been corrected.

While Thackeray began as an enthusiastic amateur, a gentleman/author, and had become, because of financial and domestic disasters, a desperate literary hack dependent on the largess of relatively powerful publishers, nevertheless the relations between author and publisher by 1844 had become those between equals, literary tradesmen in the best meaning of the term as Thackeray had redefined it. This relationship did not characterize only Thackeray's dealings with Bradbury and Evans; he wrote in the same tone to Henry Colburn on 15 May, "Here is a very little article but in revenge I think a very good one", and Colburn printed it.

The point is worth emphasizing, for it contradicts another misapprehension that has grown up about Thackeray's relations with publishers. Sir William Fraser, recollecting Thackeray years after the author's death, wrote:

Thackeray's resentment towards the trade of Publishers was deeply rooted. I believe that sixteen publishers refused him the pittance required to print his immortal work, Vanity Fair. Not one of them was capable intellectually of appreciating it. He pours out the vials of his wrath upon them in Pendennis: painting them to the world as the most stupid, the most selfish, and the most vulgar, class of tradesmen.... Calling on a publisher Thackeray waited with a friend, who told me the story: the carpet of the drawing-room was of a gaudy design of red and white: on the host appearing, the author of Vanity Fair said, "We have been admiring your carpet: it is most appropriate! You wade it, the blood and brains of authors," Aside from the exaggeration represented by sixteen publishers without the brains to appreciate Vanity Fair and the distorted overstatement of Warrington's characterization of publishers, both of which reveal more about Sir William than about Thackeray, the final anecdote can be seen as typical of Thackeray's ironic humour rather than as the bitter commentary Fraser obviously took it for.

Other commentators refer to Thackeray's haughty attitude toward publishers and usually point to the portraits of Bacon and Bungay in Pendennis as indications of Thackeray's general attitude. But if one can see Bentley and Colburn in these two portraits, one cannot see Chapman and Hall, Bradbury and Evans, or George Smith in them. I doubt if one can see James Fraser, John Macrone, or Hugh Cunningham there either, though there is precious little factual material with which to build a picture of Thackeray's personal relations with these three publishers.

Thackeray

W. E. Henley

According to Henley's "Prefatory," which self-deprecatingly descibes Views and Reviews as "less a book than a mosaic of scraps and shreds recovered from the shot rubbish of some fourteen years of journalism", this essay was "pieced together" from articles in London, Vanity Fair, The Athenaeum. In editing this text for the Victorian Web, I have retained orginal spelling and punctuation, and I included numbers in brackets to indicate page breaks in the print edition in order to enable users of VW to cite or locate the original page numbers..

His Worshippers

It is odd to note how opinions differ to the greatness of

Thackeray and the value of his books. Some regard him as the greatest novelist of his age and country and as one of the greatest of any country and any age. These hold him to be not less sound a moralist than excellent as a writer, not less magnificently creative than usefully and delightfully cynical, not less powerful and complete a painter of manners than infallible as a social philosopher and incomparable as a lecturer on the human heart. They accept Amelia Sedley for a very woman; they believe in Colonel Newcome — ' by Don Quixote out of Little Nell' — as in something venerable and heroic; they regard William Dobbin and 'Stunning' Warrington as finished and subtle portraitures; they think Becky Sharp an improvement upon Mme.

Marneffe and Wenham better work than Rigby; they are in love with Laura Bell, and refuse to see either or caricature in their poet's presentment of Alcide de Mirobolant. Thackeray's fun, Thackeray's wisdom, Thackeray's knowledgee of men and women, Thackeray's morality, Thackeray's view of life, 'his wit and humour, his pathos, and his umbrella,' are all articles of belief with them. Of Dickens they will not hear; Balzac they incline to despise; if they make any comparison between Thackeray and Fielding, or Thackeray and Richardson, or Thackeray and Sir Walter, or Thackeray and Disraeli, it is to the disadvantage of Disraeli and Scott and Richardson and Fielding.

All these were well enough in their way and day; but they are not to be classed with Thackeray. It is said, no doubt, that Thackeray could neither make stories nor tell them; but he liked stories for all that, and by the hour could babble charmingly of Ivanhoe and the Mousequetaires It is possible that he was afraid of passion, and had no manner of interest in crime. But then, how hard he bore upon snobs, and how vigorously he lashed the smaller vices and the meaner faults! It may be beyond dispute that he was seldom good at romance, and saw most things—art and nature included—rather prosaically and ill-naturedly, as he might see them who has been for many years a failure, and is naturally a little resentful of other men's successes; but then, how brilliant are his studies of club humanity and club manners! how thoroughly he understands the feelings of them that go down into the west in broughams! If he writes by preference for people with a thousand a year, is it not the duty of everybody with a particle of self-respect to have that income?

Is it possible that any one who has it not can have either wit or sentiment, humour or understanding? Thackeray writes of gentlemen for gentlemen; therefore he is alone among artists; therefore he is 'the greatest novelist of his age.' That is the faith of the true believer: that the state of mind of him that reveres less wisely than thoroughly, and would rather be damned with Thackeray than saved with any one else.

His Critics

The position of them that wear their rue with a difference, and do not agree that all literature is contained in The Book of Snobs and Vanity Fair, is more easily defended. They like and admire their Thackeray in many ways, but they think him rather a writer of genius who was innately and irredeemably a Philistine than a supreme artist or a great man. To them there is something artificial in the man and something insincere in the artist: something which makes it seem natural that his best work should smack of the literary tour de force, and that he should never have appeared to such advantage as when, in Esmond and in Barry Lyndon he was writing up to a standard and upon a model not wholly of his own contrivance.

They admit his claim to eminence as an adventurer in 'the discovery of the Ugly'; but they contend that even there he did his work more shrewishly and more pettily than he might; and in this connection they go so far as to reflect that a snob is not only 'one who meanly admires mean things,' as his own definition declares, but one who meanly detests mean things as well. They agree with Walter Bagehot that to be perpetually haunted by the plush behind your chair is hardly a sign of lofty literary and moral genius; and they consider him narrow and vulgar in his view of humanity, limited in his outlook upon life, inclined to be envious, inclined to be tedious and pedantic, prone to repetitions, and apt in bidding for applause to appeal to the baser qualities of his readers and to catch their sympathy by making them feel themselves spitefully superior to their fellow-men. They look at his favourite heroines — at Laura and Ethel and Amelia; and they can but think him stupid who could ever have believed them interesting or admirable or attractive or true. They listen while he regrets it is impossible for him to attempt the picture of a man; and, with Barry Lyndon in their mind's eye and the knowledge that Casanova and Andrew Bowes suggested no more than that, they wonder if the impossibility was not a piece of luck for him.

They hear him heaping contumely upon the murders and adulteries, the excesses in emotion, that pleased the men of 182O as they had pleased the Elizabethans before them, and they see him turning with terror and loathing from these — which after all are effects of vigorous passion‹to busy himself with the elaborate and careful narrative of how Barnes Newcome beat his wife, and Mrs. Mackenzie scolded Colonel Newcome to death, and old Twysden bragged and cringed himself into good society and an interest in the life and well-being of a little cad like Captain Woolcomb; and it is not amazing if they think his morality more dubious in some ways than the morality he is so firmly fixed to ridicule and to condemn.

They reflect that he sees in Beatris no more than the makings of a Bernstein; and they are puzzled, when they come to mark the contrast between the two portraitures and the difference between the part assigned to Mrs. Esmond and the part assigned to the Baroness, to decide if he were shortsighted or ungenerous, if he were inapprehensive or only cruel. They weary easily of his dogged and unremitting pursuit of the merely conventional man and the merely conventional woman; they cannot always bring themselves to be interested in the cupboard drama, the tea-cup tragedies and cheque-book and bandbox comedies, which he regards as the stuff of human action and the web of human life; and from their theory of existence they positively refuse to eliminate the heroic qualities of romance and mystery and passion, which are — as they have only to open their newspapers to see — essentials of human achievement and integral elements of human character. They hold that his book contain some of the finest stuff in fiction: as for instance, Rawdon Crawley's discovery of his wife and Lord Steyne, and Henry Esmond's return from the wars, and those immortal chapters in which the Colonel and Frank Castlewood pursue and run down their kinswoman and the Prince But they hold, too, that their influence is dubious and that few have risen from them one bit the better or one jot the happier.

Which is Right?

Genius apart, Thackeray's morality is that of a highly respectable British cynic; his intelligence is largely one of trifles; he is wise over trivial and trumpery things. He delights in reminding us — with an air! — that everybody is a humbug; that we are all rank snobs; that to misuse your aspirates is to be ridiculous and incapable of real merit; that Miss Blank has just slipped out to post a letter to Captain Jones; that Miss Dash wears false teeth and a wig that General Tufto is almost as tightly laced as the beautiful Miss Hopper; that there's a bum bailiff in the kitchen at Number Thirteen; that the dinner we ate t'other day at Timmins's is still to pay; that all is vanity; that there's a skeleton in every house; that passion, enthusiasm, excess of any sort, is unwise, abominable, a little absurd; and so forth. And side by side with these assurances are admirable sketches of character and still more admirable sketches of habit and of manners — are the Pontos and Costigan, Gandish and Talbot Twysden and the unsurpassable Major, Sir Pitt and Brand Firmin, the heroic De la Plache and the engaging Farintosh and the versatile Honeyman, a crowd of vivid and diverting portraitures besides; but they are not different — in kind at least — from the reflections suggested by the story of their several careers and the development of their several individualities.

Esmond apart, there is scarce a man or a woman in Thackeray whom it is possible to love unreservedly or thoroughly respect. That gives the measure of the man, and determines the quality of his influence. He was the average clubman plus genius and a style. And, if there is any truth in the theory that it is the function of art not to degrade but to ennoble — not to dishearten but to encourage — not to deal with things ugly and paltry and mean but with great things and beautiful and lofty — then, it is argued, his example is one to depreciate and to condemn.

His Style

Thus the two sects: the sect of them that are with Thackeray and the sect of them that are against him. Where both agree is in the fact of Thackeray's pre-eminence as a writer of English and the master of one of the finest prose styles in literature. His manner is the perfection of conversational writing. Graceful yet vigorous; adorably artificial yet incomparably sound; touched with modishness yet informed with distinction; easily and happily rhythmical yet full of colour and quick with malice and with meaning; instinct with urbanity and instinct with charm — it is a type of high-bred English, a climax of literary art.

He may not have been a great man but assuredly he was a great writer; he may have been a faulty novelist but assuredly he was a rare artist in words. Setting aside Cardinal Newman's, the style he wrote is certainly less open to criticism than that of any other modern Englishman. He was neither super-eloquent like Mr. Ruskin nor a Germanised Jeremy like Carlyle; he was not marmoreally emphatic as Landor was, nor was he slovenly and inexpressive as was the great Sir Walter; he neither dallied with antithesis like Macaulay nor rioted in verbal vulgarisms with Dickens; he abstained from technology and what may be called Lord Burleighism as carefully as George Eliot indulged in them, and he avoided conceits as sedulously as Mr. George Meredith goes out of his way to hunt for them. He is a better writer than any one of these, in that he is always a master of speech and of himself, and that he is always careful yet natural and choice yet seemingly spontaneous. He wrote as a very prince among talkers, and he interfused and interpenetrated English with the elegant and cultured fashion of the men of Queen Anne and with something of the warmth, the glow, the personal and romantic ambition, peculiar to the century of Byron and Keats, of Landor and Dickens, of Ruskin and Tennyson and Carlyle. Unlike his only rival, he had learnt his art before he began to practise it. Of the early work of the greater artist a good half is that of a man in the throes of education: the ideas, the thoughts, the passion, the poetry, the humour, are of the best, but expression is self-conscious, strained, ignorant.

Thackeray had no such blemish. He wrote dispassionately, and he was a born writer. In him there is no hesitation, no fumbling, no uncertainty. The style of Barry Lyndon is better and stronger and more virile than the style of Philip; and unlike the other man's, whose latest writing is his best, their author's evolution was towards decay.

His Mission

He is so superior a person that to catch him tripping is a peculiar pleasure. It is a satisfaction apart, for instance, to reflect that he has it must be owned a certain gentility of mind. Like the M.P. in Martin Chuzzlewit, he represents the Gentlemanly Interest. That is his mission in literature, and he fulfils it thoroughly. He appears sometimes as Mr. Yellowplush, sometimes as Mr. Fitzboodle, sometimes as Michael Angelo Titmarsh, but always in the Gentlemanly Interest. In his youth he is found applauding the well-bred Charles de Bernard, and remarking of Balzac and Dumas that the one is 'not fit for the salon,' and the other 'about as genteel as a courier.' Balzac and Dumas are only men of genius and great artists: the real thing is to be 'genteel' and write — as Gerfeuil is written — 'in a gentleman-like style.'

A few pages further on in the same pronouncement a review of Jérome Paturot, I find him quoting with entire approval Reybaud's sketch of 'a great character, in whom the habitué of Paris will perhaps recognise a certain likeness to a certain celebrity of the present day, by name Monsieur Hector Berlioz, the musician and critic.' The description is too long to quote. It sparkles with all the fadaises of anti-Berliozian criticism, and the point is that the hero, after conducting at a private party which Berlioz never did his own 'hymn of the creation that has been lost since the days of the deluge,' 'called for his cloak and his clogs, and walked home, where he wrote a critique for the newspapers of the music which he had composed and directed.' In the Gentlemanly Interest Mr. Titmarsh translates this sorry little libel with the utmost innocence of approval. It is The Paris Sketch-Book over again. That Monsieur Hector Berlioz may possibly have known something of his trade and been withal as honest a man and artist as himself seems never to have occurred to him.

He knows nothing o£ Mousieur Hector except that he is a 'hairy romantic,' and that whatever he wrote it was not Batti, batti; but that nothing is enough. 'Whether this little picture 'is a likeness or not' he is ingenuous enough to add, 'who shall say?' But, — and here speaks the bold but superior Briton — 'it is a good caricature of a race in France, where geniuses poussent as they do nowhere else; where poets are prophets, where romances have revelations.'

As he goes on to qualify Jérome Paturot as a 'masterpiece,' and as 'three volumes of satire in which there is not a particle of bad blood,' it seems fair to conclude that in the Gentlemanly Interest all is considered fair, and that to accuse a man of writing criticisms on his own works is to be 'witty and entertaining,' and likewise 'careless, familiar, and 'sparkling' to the genteelest purpose possible in this genteelest of all possible worlds.

The Influence of Vanity fair upon Thackeray's Reputation and Prosperity.

It is inaccurate to speak of Thackeray's American publishers as though there was a formal relationship, for every American edition was a reprint of material originally published in England, and until 1852 every American edition was unauthorized. Conventional analysis of American literary piracy notes that there was no international copyright law until 1891, that cross-Atlantic literary piracy was not a legal crime, and that American protectionism and isolation stood in the way of international legislation for literary rights. Cynics are fond of noting in addition that whatever effect it had on authors, the absence of the law did not hurt American publishers until such a time as there was an American literature they might be able to sell to an international market. The absence of an international law was not so much a cause as it was a symptom of conditions in the publishing world that prevailed on both sides of the Atlantic, but which publishers on the American side managed to enjoy for a longer time and with fewer inhibitions than did those on the English side.

The first surprising fact is that Thackeray himself found those early unauthorized American appearances of his work interesting and important. The wisdom of his way of looking at the situation is supported by the fact that he eventually came to benefit financially from an American market in spite of the absence throughout his lifetime of any copyright protection for his works in America.

Aside from the author-subsidized publication of Flore et Zéphyr, a book of twelve lithographs with captions produced in London in 1836, American publishers were the first to recognize in the magazinery of the struggling journalist the stuff for book work. The Yellowplush Correspondence, which Thackeray had written as a loosely connected series for Fraser's Magazine in 1837, became, early the next year, in the hands of Cary and Hart of Philadelphia, his first book. The company's "Cost Books" indicate the production of 1,000 copies at a cost of twenty-four cents per copy. That cost, of course, included no payment to the author. I have not found what the books were sold for or how many were actually sold, but there was apparently no demand for a reprint, for none is recorded.

English authors and publishers might rant and rave about American literary piracy, but Americans had, at least in the 1830s and 40s, nothing to fear and no incentive to care what the English establishment thought see Pollard's account of English and American copyright relations for the period. For his part, Thackeray began by looking with sardonic curiosity and a philosophical attitude at his American successes. He may have rued the failure to get any payment for Yellowplush or for the putative reprinting of The Historical Reminiscences of Major Gahagan a work as yet unseen by any bibliographer, but he benefited, nonetheless, by these piracies, for he used their existence to convince his first English book publishers, John Macrone and his successor Hugh Cunningham, to publish Yellowplush and Gahagan along with a few other items in a two-volume collection called Comic Tales.

In the preface to the collection he remarked on the popularity of The Yellowplush Papers in America "where they have been reprinted more than once," adding that Gahagan was "received by our American brethren with similar piratical honours; and the editor has had the pleasure of perusing them likewise." Though Thackeray's journalism continued to be reprinted in American magazines, a lull in book publication set in and lasted until 1844, a condition no doubt irritating to Thackeray who was having a hard time getting anything into book form anywhere.

It is possible that in 1844 J. Winchester, a New York publisher, reprinted The Irish Sketch-Book, without formal arrangements with its author, of course. The Winchester edition is undated, and bibliographers have failed to find or report external evidence of the date of appearance. In the next few years before Vanity Fair, American publishers in New York, Baltimore, and Philadelphia reprinted Notes on a Journey from Cornhill to Grand Cairo and Jeame's Diary with impunity. Throughout his career, in fact, Thackeray expressed willingness to take half a loaf when there was no whole loaf to be had or to dine on mutton when there was no venison. But with the publication of Vanity Fair, January 1847-July 1848, Thackeray's attitude changed along with the shift in his economic situation.

In the early days of Vanity Fair, he wrote that the book "did everything but sell, and appears really immensely to increase my reputation if not my income" Letters 2: 318, But when, in August 1848, he could write that "Vanity Fair is doing very well commercially I'm happy to say at last" Letters 2: 420, he knew he had gained bargaining power, and he quickly developed the ability and habit of persuading publishers to raise his fees.

At first this power did not extend over American publishers. Harper and Brothers was the first to cash in freely on the economic strength of the new superstar, but that firm was in no hurry. Its two-volume paperbound edition of Vanity Fair was published in July and August 1848, after the entire serial had run its course in England Harper MS, Butler. In December, Harper coolly added The Great Hoggarty Diamond to its list by lifting it from Fraser's Magazine, thereby, apparently by coincidence rather than malice aforethought, predating the authorized English reprinting by three months.

With Pendennis, as with Vanity Fair, there was no rush of competition among the American pirates. The first of Harper's eight-part reprint appeared on 14 August 1849, ten and a half months after the London publication of the first serial part. Surviving Harper and Brothers records show no payments to English author or publishers for these three works, though the company's record of reprints over the next twenty-five years indicates how lucrative the piracy of superstars could be.

While lack of competition for Vanity Fair might be attributed to the fact that Thackeray was not yet a popular author, that for Pendennis might have resulted, instead, from the operation of a self-imposed but not very binding "courtesy of the trade" practiced among the more established American publishers. These large publishing houses knew that competition for marginal books was detrimental to profits. In fact, the only book by Thackeray that was published simultaneously by two American publishers was The Virginians. Thackeray attributed the reluctance of American pirates to publish his works to the fact that Harper and Brothers was too difficult to compete with. Probably, however, The Virginians was the first of Thackeray's works thought to be worth fighting over.

When, in October 1852, Thackeray met the Harper brothers in New York at their homes, he reportedly greeted James Harper's daughter with the words, "So this is a 'pirate's' daughter, is it?" Crowe, p. 66 But on 26 November, Thackeray could write to his English publisher George Smith that "Messrs. Harper through your friend Mr. Low have communicated with me & to-night after the Lecture made me an offer of 1,000$ for the publication of my Lectures, simultaneously with the re-issue in England-I shall thankfully accept the same and keep this little sum for myself this time". He went on to describe New York as "the only city in wh. piracy is, I think, most to be feared".

And early in January he eased Smith's anxiety about getting the English edition of the lectures in print, saying, "I should not like the Lectures to go to press without reviewing, & here & there altering them; there's no danger now of their being pirated in this Country, the Harper's being the chief buccaneers, & the perfect terror of all their brethren in these seas". Thackeray's confidence in the horror of American publishing pirates is evident in the tone with which he declined a rival offer for the lectures from George P. Putnam of Philadelphia: "All things considered, I think it best that I should accept their Harper's liberal proposal.

I thank you very much for your generous offer; and for my own sake, as well as that of my literary brethren in England, I am sincerely rejoiced to find how very kindly the American publishers are disposed towards us" Letters 3: 131. Of course, kindness may have had nothing to do with it. There were, for one thing, no printed copies of the lectures available for pirating, so any publisher in this case would have to deal directly with the author or work from transcripts made at the lectures. And in the second place, it might have been the opinion of the American publishers that while one edition of the lectures could be produced profitably, the market would not bear two. Such a judgment, combined perhaps with the workings of trade courtesy, probably kept Putnam from issuing a pirated edition. The Harper records do show payments for all of Thackeray's books beginning with Henry Esmond, but, curiously, they also show a December 1848 payment of £3.3 for Dr. Birch, a Christmas book published in England by Chapman and Hall, which Harper never published. The second American publisher to cash in on Thackeray's growing reputation was William Appleton. In 1852, under the direction of Evert Duyckinck, Appleton launched its Popular Library. Thackeray's name topped the list of proposed authors in the prospectus, and Yellowplush was the first of his works in the series. It is probable that the people at Appleton knew or hoped at the outset of this project that Thackeray would be coming to America in October of that year. Thackeray's first mention of a possible lecture trip to America appeared in a letter written to his mother on 3 January 1851, though one thing after another intervened to postpone the trip until the end of October 1852.

The lecture series in London began in May 1851, and in June he signed the contract with George Smith for Henry Esmond, which was not completed until the end of May 1852. However, in May 1852 Thackeray responded to the New York Mercantile Library Association's invitation to lecture there; so, no doubt, word had by then gotten around that Thackeray was planning to come to America. The trip was actually worked out for Thackeray by James T. Fields, of Ticknor and Fields in Boston, a publishing house which failed to cash in on Thackeray until 1855 when it reprinted a small book of ballads. It seems likely then that the trip was well known far in advance and that Duyckinck planned Appleton's Popular Library with the impending trip in mind.

When Thackeray arrived in Boston on 13 November, the fledgling Appleton Popular Library already contained The Yellowplush Papers, The Paris Sketch Book in two volumes, The Book of Snobs, Men's Wives, and A Shabby Genteel Story. Four more volumes were announced as "nearly ready" in the week Thackeray arrived in New York, though only three of them were published The Luck of Barry Lyndon, in two volumes, and The Confessions of Fitz-Boodle and Some Passages in the Life of Major Gahagan.

In all, nine volumes were produced in the series without a by-your-leave or any planned financial arrangement with the author. Appleton, to its credit, was quick to redress the moral wrong, though there had been no legal wrong committed. Of course, the redress of moral wrongs is never as expensive as that for legal ones; Appleton approached Thackeray with £100 "to edit a couple of volumes out of Punch" Letters 3: 121.

Thackeray recounted that while on board ship just out from Liverpool en route to Boston and before the passengers had acquired sea legs, a young man representing the firm of Appleton approached him with a publishing proposal. What the proposal was or what the outcome, Thackeray did not disclose, for at that moment the ship gave an unusually large heave and the two gentlemen were obliged to approach the rail and bring up accounts of a different nature. There can be little doubt, however, that the proposal was to make up two or three volumes from his contributions to Punch for the Popular Library and to write a preface. Thackeray's response as reported to his daughters in a letter home was, "So you see here is the harvest and let us reap it against the winter comes" Letters 3: 121. In 1853 Appleton published four new volumes of Thackeray's miscellaneous works and produced a second edition of A Shabby Genteel Story.

Thackeray's preface to the first Punch volume in the Appleton series remarks on the authority of the texts and reveals fairly honestly his attitude toward the American appropriation of his work.

On coming into this country I found that the projectors of this series of little books had preceded my arrival by publishing a number of early works, which have appeared under various pseudonyms during the last fifteen years. I was not the master to choose what stories of mine should appear or not: these miscellanies were all advertised, or in course of publication; nor have I had the good fortune to be able to draw a pen, or alter a blunder of author or printer, except in the case of the accompanying volumes, which contain contributions to Punch, whence I have been enabled to make something like a selection. Later in the preface he adds:

That extreme liberality with which American publishers have printed the works of English authors, has had at least this beneficial result for us, that our names and writings are known by multitudes using our common mother tongue, who never had heard of us or our books but for the speculators who have sent them all over this continent. It is, of course, not unnatural for the English writer to hope, that someday he may share a portion of the profits which his works bring at present to the persons who vend them in this country; and I am bound gratefully to say myself, that since my arrival here I have met with several publishing houses who are willing to acknowledge our little claim to participate in the advantages arising out of our books; and the present writer having long since ascertained that a portion of a loaf is more satisfactory than no bread at all, gratefully accepts and acknowledges several slices which the book purveyors in this city have proffered to him of their free will.

If we are not paid in full and in specie as yet, English writers surely ought to be thankful for the very great kindness and friendliness with which the American public receives them; and if he hopes some day that measures may pass here to legalize our right to profit a little by the commodities which we invent and in which we deal, I for one can cheerfully say, that the good will towards us from publishers and public is undoubted, and wait for still better times with perfect confidence and humour.

If I have to complain of any special hardship, it is, not that our favourite works are reproduced,... but that ancient magazines are ransacked, and shabby old articles dragged out, which we had gladly left in the wardrobes where they have lain hidden many years. There is no control, however, over a man's thought-once uttered and printed, back they may come upon its on any sudden day.

The Appleton preface shows Thackeray as a deft diplomatist, expressing his pleasure in the evident pleasure of American publishers and public alike. Thackeray's sincerity in this regard can be measured by remarks he made at about the same time in letters to England- "Even the publishers are liberal one gives me a thousand dollars and another 500 or perhaps 1000 more for books to be republished" Letters 3:132. "I have made 1200£ by coming here already-800 by the lectures and 4 by my books, money wh. I shouldn't have had had I staid home" Letters 3: 149 "It would have been worth my while even for my books to come out here: the publishers are liberal enough and will be still more so with any future thing I may do" Letters 2: 154 "Appleton Harper & others all give or offer me money. I shall be able to add something like 40 per Cent to the value of my future books" Letters 3:158. To the Boston publisher Fields, Thackeray wrote from New York: "The publishers here are acting most generously with regard to my works, past, present, & to come; in fact it was a lucky Friday when I set foot in the country".

However, the possibility of a whole loaf remained very attractive, too. While lecturing in Washington, he dined and talked with a great many persons in government, including the incumbent president, Millard Fillmore, and incoming president, Franklin Pierce. From the American capital he wrote, "I hear the most cheering accounts but this is a secret I believe of the International Copyright bill, wh. upon my conscience will make me 5000 dollars a year the richer" Letters 3:204. The attempt Thackeray referred to as "a secret I believe" was surely something he learned upon his arrival in Washington. The first strategy in the movement to promote an international agreement about copyright had been to jockey a copyright bill through the House of Representatives The following account is derived form Barnes, pp. 177-262, a fascinating and detailed exploration of various attempts to establish an international agreement in America.

It was being promoted by John F. Crampton, British foreign minister to Washington, who had recently taken over that position and project from Edward Bulwer Lytton's brother, Henry. It was a secret because the attempts to orchestrate the necessary support just to get the bill introduced and approved at committee level were complicated, expensive, and drawn out. Its supporters did not want American book publishers, book manufacturers, and that part of the American book-buying population that thrived on low-priced, unauthorized reprintings of British writings to mount a lobby against the bill until it had gotten a head of steam. Thackeray may have known about it before, for an appeal had been made early in 1852 to English authors and publishers for financial support for the effort. Smith, Elder and Chapman and Hall had contributed £50 each; Bradbury and Evans and Charles

Dickens gave £100 each. In all, a variety of authors, publishers, and booksellers contributed £1,000 finance the legislation. Thackeray, however, is not among those recorded as contributors.

In addition to his secret efforts to promote a copyright bill in the House, Crampton was secretly negotiating an Anglo-American copyright treaty with the secretary of state, Daniel Webster. Crampton had to keep information about the proposed treaty from those involved with the House bill because a treaty, since it did not require House action, might be seen in the House as an attempt to circumvent its authority. And then, apparently to Crampton's surprise, a separate petition for a copyright bill was introduced in the Senate by Senator Charles Sumner, with the support of senators Andrew Butler of South Carolina and M. T Hunter and James M. Mason of Virginia. The fact was that there was considerable support in America, particularly among its writers, for a fair copyright agreement. The opposition came primarily from publishers and even more from book manufacturers-typesetters, type foundries, stereotypers, and bookbinders.

By the time Thackeray reached Washington in February 1853, Daniel Webster had died; his successor Edward Everett seemed less keen on dealing with Crampton, whom he apparently did not like; and the publishers had gotten wind of the proposed agreement and had submitted a list of objections to the copyright treaty. Thackeray met Crampton, and together they drafted a response to those objections. The effect must have been good, for on 17 February 1853 Everett signed the treaty, which then had to be delivered to the Senate for ratification. Delay followed delay; the Senate adjourned for the summer; other Anglo-American treaties and crises intervened; proposed amendments were negotiated by the Americans and objected to by the British; and worse, the American opposition lobby gained momentum.

In August 1852 President Fillmore had written to Harper and Brothers asking for its opinion regarding an international copyright treaty. The response was ambiguous and evasive, declining to try to influence the government on a matter affecting so many different kinds of people. In May 1853 a similarly oracular statement was published in the editor's "Easy Chair" of Harper's Magazine: "We may not pass by silently the new stir in relation to an international copyright. And however the question may finally be settled, we welcome the discussion, and the interest in the discussion, as so many tokens of the increased consideration which is given, both by people and by government, to the making and printing of books. Twenty odd millions of people in our commonwealth are furnishing a host of readers; and it behooves government and people to consider wisely what sort of reading is to be furnished, and what sort of pay the furnishers are to receive.". Having lobbed this bit of wisdom from a firm position on the fence, the editor went on to cloud the issue with irrelevant arguments about whether authors could or could not make a decent living and to poke fun at Edward Bulwer Lytton for guessing at the amount of money he could have made had there been an international law.

The fact is that Harper and Brothers, whose history of piracy and whose system of small payments for advance sheets from English authors must have overcome their sense of the fairness of paying full rates in a regulated trade, stood to gain nothing by a copyright treaty. The treaty failed in 1854. There would be no international copyright law until 1891.

Nevertheless, by 1853 Thackeray's power and confidence as a major economic commodity made it possible for him practically to write his own ticket with the publishers in ways unavailable to many of his contemporaries, yet that power did not mean that his relations with publishers went smoothly.

In 1851 the author of Vanity Fair and Pendennis discovered with some astonishment that the lecture circuit was more lucrative in the short run than book publication. The contract for Esmond had stipulated that Thackeray would not publish anything anywhere within six months of the publication of that book, but he did not publish anything except Esmond in the whole of 1852. Yet his income from lecturing and the sale of "moral rights" to his books in America made it the most financially satisfying year he had ever had since 1832 when he came into his patrimony. It should not escape notice that the unauthorized Appleton editions were dragged into the mainstream of textual history when Thackeray used them as the basis for the authorized Miscellanies produced by Bradbury and Evans in London. And it is questionable whether Thackeray actually took the opportunity to select and correct the texts of the three volumes of Punch material; one can only assume that he selected or at least reviewed the selection of items for those three Appleton volumes.

Two of the volumes Appleton had announced as nearly ready in November 1852 did not appear as advertised; their alterations may well have been influenced by Thackeray. Furthermore, the parody of James Fenimore Cooper in Punch's Prize Novelists was emitted either by Thackeray who was already embarrassed by the Bulwer satire or by Evert Duyckinck who may have been more sensitive on behalf of American than British writers. But it is known that Thackeray did little if any correcting, and he did no revising for Appleton. The text of Mr. Brown's Letters to a Young Man about Town, for example, differs from the Punch text only in spelling and punctuation. Some Punch errors were corrected, but a number of new errors were introduced.

No change bears the unmistakable stamp of authority. Most of the alterations are neither errors nor corrections, though unlike Harper and Brothers, which systematically house-styled Thackeray's spelling and punctuation for its reprints, Appleton did not. The effect, therefore, on the authority of the Bradbury and Evans reprints of the mid-1850s, even though Thackeray did revise slightly at that time, is that of progressive minor deterioration of textual authority.

In April 1853 Thackeray returned to England and soon agreed with Bradbury and Evans, the publishers of Vanity Fair and Pendennis, to write The Newcomes in twenty-four monthly parts. In June he wrote to Harper that "it will appear as soon as possible after the termination of Mr. Dickens' serial, and I hope you will be inclined to treat with me for the republication of my story in America, upon the same terms wh. you give Mr. Dickens and Sir Bulwer Lytton. I do not intend to begin to publish until several numbers are completed, and propose to devote the whole of the next 12 months to this story... please to tell me that you have paid to my account... the $1000 I am to receive from you for the publication of my lectures. I hope they have been as successful with you as in London, where we sold the whole of the first edition of 2500 in a week."Robert F.

Batchelder Catalogue no.60, item 95. During the next few months Thackeray visited with his family, toured the Continent, and wrote four numbers of The Newcomes with which he returned to London on the first of September where he discovered that in his absence Harper and Brothers had offered him £10 per number. Thackeray immediately wrote to Bradbury and Evans noting Harper's condition that "they could get my numbers 6 weeks before it was printed here-so unless we put off till Nov. I lose £240" Letters 3: 300. Bradbury and Evans did not put off the projected publication, the first number appearing in London on 1 October.

Later that month Thackeray wrote Bradbury and Evans again: "I just find a letter from Mr. Low... proposing still to treat with me on behalf of Messrs. Harper, and to secure you." By this time his tone is plaintive, perhaps on the edge of irritation: "Could one of you see Mr. Low without delay to day if possible as a Steamer starts tomorrow wh. might take out no 3 if you so chose. They did not publish no 1. No Briton has pirated it-it is impossible that it should now be touched and I have the consolation of thinking that my £300 have been lost from a panic where there was no danger.

Some of it however may be recovered if you'll have the goodness to go to Lowe. Do try to day". The Harper "Priority List" of payments made to English publishers for advance sheets indicates that Harper paid only it £150 for The Newcomes Harper MS, Butler, which appeared in Harper's Magazine from November 1853 through October 1855.

Whether or not a lesson in international relations had been learned from the experience with The Newcomes is impossible to know, but the arrangements for The Virginians, which began publication in London on 1 November 1857, seem to have worked out a little better from Thackeray's point of view and worse from Harper's. As before, the negotiations with Harper's agent, Sampson Low, were carried out by Thackeray, but the business of collecting the money and sending the advance proofs was left to the publisher. When in early October 1857 news of bank failures in America reached England, Thackeray wrote to his American friends the Baxters fearful "that all the American savings were gone to smash, including the 500£ from Harper Brothers for the Virginians". It was with some relief that he wrote a note to Bradbury and Evans on 3 December saying: "I hear that Messrs. Harper of New York have forwarded funds to meet their engagements in this country, and shall be glad to have payment for my 2 numbers of the Virginians. Will you or Mr. Joyce call on Messrs. Low and receive the monthly money on behalf of Yours very Faithfully W M Thackeray".

Meanwhile, a sticky situation was developing for the chief of American literary buccaneers. Serialization in Harper's Magazine began in the issue dated December, which appeared in the middle of November. A few days later The Virginians reappeared in the New York Semi-Weekly Tribune. Harper immediately appealed to Thackeray through Sampson Low to do something; on 11 December he replied:

I am sorry to hear from you that the N Y. Tribune is reprinting the Virginians, and no doubt hurting the Messrs, Harpers' Issue of the story, who pay me 100$ per month for early impression. But I do not see what good any remonstrances of mine can effect. If American houses choose to reprint our books we can't prevent them, and the Tribune will doubtless take it's own course, in spite of any objections of mine or Messrs. Harper. Could English writers have remonstrated with any effect we should have done so years ago: but I am sure an outcry at present would neither be useful nor dignified; and can only express my regret that I dont see how, in the present instance, I can be of any service to a House wh. shows itself inclined to act in a kind and friendly manner to English literary men. A postscript in a scribal copy of this letter notes, "I am just advised of your payment for No I & II & hope to send you no III next week". This letter is barbed which may account for why the postscript was deleted from the letter actually sent: the reference to English authors being unable to prevent American houses from printing their works and the explanation that the unhappiness of the situation was one which English writers had been frustrated about for years are pointed reminders that there was no international copyright agreement.

Thackeray must have known of the Harper firm's failure to take any active role in support of the copyright initiatives in 1853-54, though the firm had assured President Fillmore in 1853 that an international copyright arrangement "becomes more and more manifest."Harper, p. 107 Thackeray probably could not help hinting to the company that it was merely suffering the consequences of its own complacency and receiving, besides, only what it had dished out so generously over the years in which it had gained the reputation of a pirate. On the other hand, Thackeray's letter shows his deft diplomacy in the reference to Harper's freely chosen attempts to be kind and friendly to English literary men.

Harper and Brothers continued to chaff ineffectually at the Tribune, accusing the newspaper of lifting the story from Harper's and remarking sarcastically that the Tribune "had been leading advocates of an International Copyright Law," The Tribune claimed on 26 November that the novel was "carefully reprinted from a London copy" and that readers could expect it "in the Weekly and Semi-Weekly Tribune, usually a few days in advance of its appearance in any other American publication."

Harper's printed response was: "This is simply untrue-HARPER'S MAGAZINE for January was published on the 17th of December; it contained Part II of Mr. Thackeray's Novel, in which three slight corrections were made from the London copy. The Virginians was 'carefully reprinted,' with these alterations in the Semi-Weekly Tribune the next day. When the Editor of the Tribune receives a London copy, he will be able to ascertain what these alterations are." Confronted with this damning evidence, the Tribune countered that the Harper's was contaminating the text and thus breaking faith with the public. The legalities were a moot point, a fact not lost on the newspaper, which had nothing to fear but a little bad publicity.

Once George Smith had fished for and netted Thackeray, a series of complicated and restrictive contracts organized his financial fortunes from 1860 until his death in 1863. In these contracts Smith specified that the income from foreign editions would go to the publisher, and Thackeray no longer concerned himself with the proper fulfillment of these foreign agreements. But until then the frequently frantic negotiations on his own behalf which characterized Thackeray's dealings with his publishers on both sides of the Atlantic may be an indication that the absence of all international copyright law was merely a symptom, not a cause, of the turmoil and uncertainty in the transatlantic profession of authorship in the 1840s and 1850s. The cause seems to have been the laissez-faire economics that made a free-for-all in which the devil might take the hindmost on both sides of the Atlantic even in the case of popular authors. In such conditions the publishers had the upper hand; the history of copyright legislation from that time forward was the history of increased protection of authors' rights, not publishers' rights.

Bibliography

The American Home. Vol. 7 Number 3 (December, 1931).

Amory, Cleveland and Frederic Bradlee eds. Vanity Fair: A Cavalcade of the 1920s and 1930s. New York: The Viking Press, 1960.

Barthes, Roland. Mythologies. Trans. And Ed. Annette Lavers. New York: Hill and Wang, 1972.

Berger, John. Ways of Seeing. London: Penguin Books, 1972.

Cooney, Terry A. Balancing Acts: American Thought and Culture in the 1930s. New York: Twane Publishers, 1995.

Eliot, T. S. Selected Prose of T.S. Eliot. Frank Kermode, ed. New York: Harvest Books, 1988.

Emerson, Ralph Waldo. Selections From Ralph Waldo Emerson. Stephen E. Whicher, Ed. Boston: Houghton Mifflen, 1960.

Harpers Magazine. Number 962 (July 1927).

Hoffman, Kitty. "*A History of Vanity Fair; A Modernist Journal in America.*" Diss. U of Toronto, 1980.

Lears, Jackson, "*The Ad Man and the Grand Inquisitor Intimacy Publicity Managed Self in America 1880-1940.*" Constructions of the Self. Ed. George Levine. New Brunswick: Rutgers UP, 1992. 107-141.

Fables of Abundance: A Cultural History of Advertising in America. New York: Basic Books, 1994.

Nye, Russel. The Unembarrassed Muse: The Popular Arts in America. New York: Dial Press, 1970.

Ohmann, Richard. Selling Culture: Magazines, Markets, and Class at the Turn of the Century. New York: Verso, 1996.

Staley, Eric. "*Influence, Commerce, and the Literary Magazine.*" Missouri Review 7 (1983): 177-193.

Sunset Magazine. Vol. 62. Issues 1, 4, 5, 6. (January through June, 1929).

Tucker, Robert C. Ed. The Marx-Engles Reader. New York: W.W. Norton, 1978.

Vanity Fair. 1913-1936.

What Is Best Society? New York: Social Culture Publications, 1923.

Wilson, Richard Guy, Dianne H. Pilgrim and Dickran Tashhian. The Machine Age. New York: Brooklyn Museum, 1986.